THE BEST OF
BIRDS & BLOOMS
2006

THE BEST OF BIRDS & BLOOMS 2006

Editor: Heather Lamb
Art Director: Kim Sumrall
Copy Editor: Susan Uphill
Associate Editors: Stacy Tornio, Deb Mulvey
Graphic Art Associates: Ellen Lloyd, Catherine Fletcher
Art Associate: Monica Bergwall
Photo Coordinator: Trudi Bellin
Assistant Photo Coordinator: Mary Ann Koebernik
Executive Editor, *Birds & Blooms*: Jeff Nowak
Associate Editor, *Birds & Blooms*: Rachael Liska
Editorial Assistant: Marie Brannon

Creative Director: Ardyth Cope
Senior Vice President, Editor in Chief: Catherine Cassidy
President: Barbara Newton
Chairman and Founder: Roy Reiman

Birds & Blooms Books
©2005 Reiman Media Group, Inc.
5400 S. 60th St. Greendale WI 53129
International Standard Book Number: 0-89821-475-0
Serial Number: 1553-8400
Printed in U.S.A.

To order additional copies of this book,
visit *www.countrystorecatalog.com* or call 1-800-344-6913.
Learn more about *Birds & Blooms* at *www.birdsandblooms.com*.

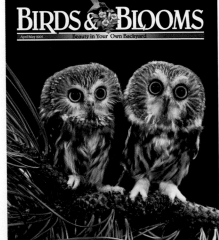

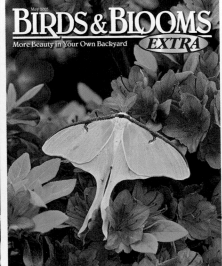

WELCOME

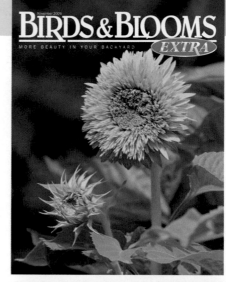

WE THINK you'll find that we've outdone ourselves with *The Best of Birds & Blooms 2006*.

Not only does it contain the top stories, tips and ideas from the past year of *Birds & Blooms*, we've also gathered the best material from our newest publication, *Birds & Blooms EXTRA*.

That means you get more bird profiles, more garden features and more gorgeous butterflies than ever before! Plus, we've added a new chapter, "All About Hummingbirds," in recognition of the wonderful stories readers send us about these amazing flying jewels.

Your favorite features and useful hints are still here at your fingertips, organized into chapters and referenced in a complete index, so you can easily find what you're looking for. No more paging through stacks of magazines! And we've once again included a "Back of the Book Bonus," as well as other bonus features not found in the magazines this year.

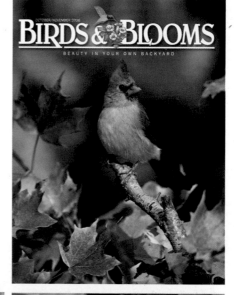

Everything you've come to expect from *Birds & Blooms* is right here—birds, flowers, butterflies, expert advice, reader ideas, beautiful photos and, most of all, fun. And now it's in one big, colorful and easy-to-use book! We hope you enjoy it!

Heather

Heather Lamb
Editor, *Birds & Blooms*

CONTENTS

16 96 138

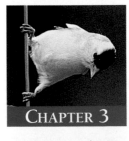

16

24

36

TOP BILLING

18

AMERICAN ROBIN

This early bird will sing its way into your heart.

By George Harrison, Contributing Editor

ALIVE WITH ACTIVITY. Robins are often bustling about the backyard. And contrary to common belief, they will stick around in winter in areas with an abundant food supply.

Come springtime, my wife, Kit, often gets a predawn wake-up call.

"How did you sleep?" I'll ask her.

"Fine. Until 4:30, when the robin started to sing," she'll answer.

Spring in our southeastern Wisconsin yard means the morning chorus of birds is at full volume, led by a male American robin that sings just outside our bedroom window.

Kit loves the robin's song, but it does awaken her early, almost every spring morning. I sleep through the serenade, since I wear hearing aids that spend the night on a side table.

American robins have been part of my love of nature nearly all my life. I was 6 years old when I had my first close-up experience with the bird. Neighbors in my boyhood town in Pennsylvania invited me across the street to see their nesting robin. When I gazed through their kitchen window at the female sitting on her nest on the sill, 3 inches from my nose, I was truly amazed.

Though I was only a little boy, my fascination with that robin was one of the building blocks of my career as a nature journalist. It was a classic example of experiencing the wonders of nature through the eyes of a child.

Clearing Up Myths

Though it is true that the American robin is the best known of all song birds in North America, this familiarity has led to some widespread myths about the backyard favorite.

For example, the American robin is not a true "robin" at all. It is a thrush, misnamed by our founding fathers. Its red breast reminded them of the European robin, a smaller dainty bird with a red breast that is not found in North America. Like all other thrush babies, young robins have spotted breasts, which they lose when they get their adult plumage.

Another legend about the robin is how it finds earthworms as it hops across our lawns. The bird doesn't listen for earthworms as it cocks its head. It sees them. Because a robin's eyes are located on the sides of its head, it has to turn toward the ground to see its prey.

Then there is the mystery about why robins (and northern cardinals, too) fly themselves into windows. This strange behavior is caused when a robin sees its own reflection in the glass and tries to chase the "other" robin away from its territory.

"Robins have been part of my love of nature nearly all my life..."

Maslowski Productions

A BIT OF SUNSHINE. It's hard not to smile when a robin hops across your lawn. But did you know that it cocks its head (left) to look for earthworms, not listen for them? The juveniles (above) have spotted breasts.

Snow Birds?

Finally, it used to be said that seeing the first robin in February or March in northern states meant spring had arrived. Although that was once generally true, warmer winters and abundant food mean the robin—and that other sentinel of spring, the bluebird—now spends winter almost anywhere on the continent, even the North.

Yet, competition to see the "first robin" of the year continues. Every spring, Rhonda Norris of Elkton, Maryland and her aunt compete for the first sighting. It was her aunt who got Rhonda excited about nature when she was a little girl.

"Now I relish and anticipate each year's competition more and more," Rhonda writes. "It doesn't matter if I win or lose. Every time I see a robin in my yard, I'm reminded of my aunt's spirit, strength and unselfishness for passing on her love and knowledge of nature."

One Nest, Then Another

The home life of the American robin starts with the selection of a nesting site, but this usually isn't a snap decision. Female robins often are indecisive.

I found this to be true when I watched a female robin build

a nest on the ledge of a backyard shed in Pennsylvania. Then she built another nest and another, until she built 13 nests side by side before selecting where to lay her eggs.

Another female robin, and her generations of offspring, has nested on a coach lamp at the side of my house almost every year for 3 decades. She usually builds a second nest on a similar coach lamp at my neighbor's house before deciding which to use.

Sometimes a robin's confusion over her nests becomes unbelievable. Near Cincinnati, Ohio, photographer Steve Maslowski took pictures of an American robin nest shared with a northern cardinal.

"Three young cardinals and four robins were all reared together," Maslowski says. "The four adults shared parental duties, though each species was apparently more inclined to take care of its own brood."

Lost and Found

The female builds a nest by first gathering mud in her bill and carrying it to the nesting site. Then she adds grasses and other items, such as string—or whatever else she can find.

A robin building a nest in Mt. Vernon, Illinois collected strings from the price tags at a lawn ornament shop owned by Marvin and Joyce Eller. Joyce assumed the wind had blown the tags away, until Marvin noticed a robin's nest above the shop's window with small white tags dangling from it. Mystery solved!

In autumn, when all the babies have grown, American robins gather into large flocks that may or may not move south. They sustain themselves by searching out berries and other fruits during winter.

If you want to give them a helping hand, offer fruit or mealworms on a tray feeder. You may discover that a midwinter robin is the perfect reminder of your favorite springtime sights—and sounds. 🕊

Backyard Birding Bio

Common Name: American robin.
Scientific Name: *Turdus migratorius*.
Length: 10 inches.
Wingspan: 17 inches.
Distinctive Markings: Adult has a slate-gray back, brick-red breast and belly, and a white line above and below the eye. Juvenile is speckled gray above and spotted orange below. Males and females look alike, although the female is duller overall.
Distinctive Behavior: Hops around lawns in search of earthworms, often cocking its head to one side to look for them.
Habitat: Grassy yards with plentiful shrubs and trees, farmland and open woods.
Song: Male performs a caroling, liquid and thrushlike song that is delivered in two or three phases, often repeated. Alarm call is a low mellow "putt" or a sharp cluck.
Nesting: Female builds a nest of mud in a shrub or tree fork, along a horizontal branch or on a ledge. It contains grasses, strips of cloth and string worked into the soft mud; the contours of the female's body mold the nest into a deep cup. The female incubates three or four blue eggs for 12 to 14 days; young fledge 14 to 16 days after hatching. Pairs often raise two broods a year.
Diet: Mostly earthworms, but also cutworms, caterpillars, spiders, grasshoppers, fruit, berries and occasionally cracked sunflower seeds.
Backyard Favorite: Both adults and youngsters often use birdbaths. May use a nesting shelter with two sides, a roof and a floor (6 inches square and 8 inches tall), placed on the side of a building or fence.

Summer
Year-Round
Winter

Roland Jordahl

Richard Day/Daybreak Imagery

ALIVE WITH ACTIVITY. Robins are often bustling about their nests, whether it's tending young (above left) or watching a cozy clutch of "robin's-egg blue" eggs (left).

PILEATED WOODPECKER

This red-crested wonder is the head of its class.

By George Harrison, Contributing Editor

Anyone who has spotted a spectacular pileated woodpecker will tell you the sight of this large dramatic bird is second to none.

Although bird enthusiasts around the world are focusing on the rediscovery of another member of the woodpecker family—the larger and once believed extinct ivory-billed—the pileated is remarkable in its own right.

Not only is it a breathtaking creature to watch, but unlike the ivory-billed, both males and females sport red crests, making them a handsome couple.

A Sight to See

A pileated woodpecker in flight is something you won't soon forget. About the size of crow, the pileated soars powerfully with rowing-like wing beats, often through lush dark forests. Its black wings flash white patches underneath, and its red crest and long neck and tail make for an eye-catching sight.

When Mark Catesby first discovered the pileated woodpecker in 1731, he gave it the name "log-cock." Ornithologists later renamed it "pileated," from the Latin word *pileatus*, which means capped.

It is a reclusive woodland bird, but is more common than it might appear. This red-crested wonder breeds on both coasts, southern Canada and the eastern half of the U.S.

Defending the Nest

The bird's prominent markings make it hard to miss when it's flying through the air or hammering on a tree, but the nests can be difficult to detect.

Despite a lifetime of bird-watching, I've seen only one pileated woodpecker nesting cavity. It was in mature woodland at Cook's Forest State Park in Pennsylvania, 35 feet above the ground in a dead white oak.

It was early May as I approached the nesting cavity, and the female inside was either incubating eggs or brooding young. She left the nesting hole and noisily flew to a tree trunk about 100 hundred yards away, then began expressing her discontent. The beating of her great wings was surprisingly loud, and a little intimidating. The bird made a terrific clucking racket, causing the woods to ring with her cries. Instantly, a male appeared, but remained silent.

Confronted with this protective display, I retreated some distance away and watched as the female flew back to the nesting hole and disappeared inside.

Pileateds create a new cavity for each brood they raise, and add no nesting material to the 2-foot-deep tunnel they chisel out with their bills.

The entrance to a nesting cavity is usually round. If you spot a pileated near an oblong or triangular hole—their trademark—these are used for roosting or created as the woodpecker searches for food in the wood. At the bottom of the cavity, the female lays three to five pure-white eggs, which both parents incubate for 18 days until they hatch.

Youngsters' Fare

A few weeks later, when I returned to that nesting tree I had found in Pennsylvania, two young pileated woodpeckers were hanging out of the cavity, stretching their necks and calling for food in rasping voices.

Staying out of sight, I watched the parent birds feed the youngsters several times, depositing partially digested food into their mouths.

Though I can only guess what the parents were feeding their young, I do know that the pileated's preferred food is carpenter ants, which they gather by ripping the bark off dead trees with their hammerlike bills. I've also seen a female gather food by pushing her bill into the soft wood of a stump and stretching out her long sticky tongue to collect ants.

HOLE IN ONE. Pileated woodpeckers are known for the holes they create. They chisel out round ones for nesting, but use triangular or oblong entrances (left) to roost or search for food.

Bill Leaman/Dembinsky Photo Assoc.

FEEDING TIME. You can distinguish the males from the females by looking for the red "mustache" of the male. These birds might eat suet (below) or forage for insects (at right).

Patricia Jurgonis

Pileateds in the Backyard

In winter, pileated woodpeckers remain in the general area where they nested, and will use the round nesting cavity or drill a new oblong cavity for roosting. The pair bonds are quite strong among pileateds, and they will remain together throughout the year.

I have never been lucky enough to attract pileated woodpeckers to my own backyard feeders, but I know several people who have. Among them are friends in Rhinelander, Wisconsin and in rural Pittsburgh, Pennsylvania. They reported that the big red-crested birds regularly came to eat suet in the feeders hanging from mature trees in their forested backyards.

Both friends were ecstatic about attracting pileated woodpeckers, as they should be. These birds are very wary and often elude would-be observers with their great alertness.

Though they may be vocal during their breeding season, drumming on trees and other surfaces, or loudly protecting their nest, pileateds are silent for much of the year. That makes the challenge of finding one—and the reward of a sighting—even greater.

READER TIP

If you spot a pileated near an oblong or triangular hole—their trademark—these are for roosting or created as the woodpecker searches for food in the wood. The entrance to a nesting cavity is usually round.

Ron Holt/Unicorn Stock Photos

Backyard Birding Bio

Common Name: Pileated woodpecker.
Scientific Name: *Dryocopus pileatus.*
Length: 16-1/2 inches.
Wingspan: 29 inches.
Distinctive Markings: Prominent red crest, black wings and tail, and a white stripe on its long neck. Males and females look alike, except the male has full red crest that extends to the top of his bill, and a red "mustache" (like the one at left). The female has a red crest on the back of her head and a black mustache (see photo above).
Distinctive Behavior: Searches for carpenter ants by ripping large oblong or triangular holes in the trunks of standing or fallen timber.
Habitat: Mature conifer and deciduous forests and large tracts of mixed woodlands.
Voice: Contact call is a deep and loud "wek" or "kuk." Its territorial call is a higher-pitched cackle that sounds like "flick-a, flick-a, flick-a."

Year-Round

Nest: Pairs excavate a new nesting cavity each year in generally the same area. It's located in a tree 15 to 70 feet high, typically faces south and has a round entrance hole. The pair spends about a month creating the cavity, which is up to 24 inches deep.

Using no nesting material, the female lays 3 to 5 white eggs, which both parents incubate for 18 days. They raise one brood per year.
Diet: Mostly carpenter ants, as well as beetles, insect larvae, wild berries and acorns.
Backyard Favorite: Suet in feeders, located at least 10 feet above the ground on the trunk of a mature tree in wooded habitat.

BREAKFAST
WITH THE
EAGLES

In winter, majestic birds savor "Eagle Lady's" morning buffet.

By Cary Anderson, Anchorage, Alaska

FLY-IN RESTAURANT. For almost 30 years, Jean Keene, the "Eagle Lady" (above), has fed fish to hungry bald eagles each winter near her Alaska home.

Chapter 1

A long finger of land, known as the Homer Spit, juts out into Alaska's Kachemak Bay. From here, you can marvel at a jagged horizon of snow-capped mountains, inhale an ocean breeze and watch waves lap the beach.

You may witness a passing whale or a flock of seabirds. And if you're lucky, you may glimpse the "Eagle Lady."

Eighty-one-year-old Jean Keene is the Eagle Lady. Better known by her nickname than her real name, Jean and her eagles are legendary. But unlike many legends, the Eagle Lady's story is unembellished.

A Modest Start

Jean lives in a small mobile home at the Homer Spit Campground, surrounded by a driftwood-ornamented fence. Fishing floats, whale bones and snowshoes decorate her small yard.

The seeds of Jean's notoriety were planted on a gusty winter day nearly 30 years ago, when she spotted a pair of bald eagles standing on the gravel beach near her home. Jean had long maintained a feeder stocked with sunflower seeds for finches and other small birds, but eagles seldom came near.

Perhaps, Jean thought, the eagles might like something to eat. Jean worked at the nearby fish processing facility, where salmon and cod scraps were plentiful, so she had a steady supply of eagle food. She took home some leftover fish heads and tossed them over the short fence to the eagles. They eagerly devoured them.

"It all started with a few fish heads in a bucket and two eagles," Jean recalls. "It grew from there."

The following day, she offered them more. Jean continued to feed the birds daily. Tossing fish to the pair of eagles soon evolved into a morning ritual during that winter in the late 1970s. By the end of winter, four or five eagles were showing up at Jean's place for breakfast.

When spring arrived, the handful of eagles disappeared as their breeding season began. But once winter returned, and the birds had finished nesting, the eagles came back. Jean began feeding again. In a matter of weeks, more than a dozen eagles were showing up. Jean fed them throughout winter. As before, the eagles left in spring.

Growing Clientele

The pattern continued. Eagles arrived in winter and departed in spring. Each year, the number of eagles increased. Within 7 years, more than 100 eagles were homing in on the Eagle Lady's generosity.

Like squadrons of warplanes, eagles flew in from the distant shores of Kachemak Bay. They came from miles around. Other fish-eating birds, including ravens and gulls, also gathered for the feast.

After 10 years, more than 200 eagles were stopping by for fish handouts. The morning arrival of so many eagles at the Homer Spit Campground became an astounding phenomenon that must be seen to be believed.

To keep pace with the rising demand for eagle food, Jean brought home more and more surplus fish from the seafood plant.

"I hate to see anything go to waste," Jean says. "Not when

WINGED RESIDENTS. In winter, it's common to see eagles soaring over nearby resorts or perched on buildings.

someone can make good use of it."

Jean's morning routine steadily evolved from a minor chore into a strenuous job. Few people realize the depth of her dedication or how much work is involved. By the mid-1980s, Jean was no longer doling out mere buckets of fish. She was serving up scraps of salmon, herring, cod and halibut by the barrel.

On average, Jean distributes more than 50,000 pounds (that's 25 tons) of fish to the eagles from late December through mid-April. That works out to an average of 500 pounds per day.

Some people have criticized Jean over the years for feeding the eagles, even though it is not against the law in Alaska. And wildlife authorities concede that offering fish to eagles is not much different than dispensing seed to songbirds at a backyard feeder.

None question her dedication.

Jean and her eagles are legendary.

Always There with a Meal

From January through mid-April, day after day, Jean persists. Eagle attendance at Jean's place has fluctuated, but typically 200 to 300 eagles fly in for her fish breakfast.

Through wind-driven rain, blizzards and sub-zero weather, Jean dutifully feeds them. When frostbite injured one of her toes during a sub-zero cold snap, she carried on with little complaint. There'd be time to rest later.

"I'm a tough old bird," she once told CBS TV news correspondent Jerry Bowen.

In his coverage of the Eagle Lady, the journalist agreed. He concluded his story by saying that Jean was, perhaps, "the toughest bird of them all."

Editor's Note: Read more about Jean in Cary Anderson's new book, *The Eagle Lady*. It contains nearly 100 fascinating photos and is available on-line at *www.eaglelady.com*.

NEITHER SLEET NOR SNOW STOPS THE
COMMON REDPOLL

By Rachael Liska, Associate Editor

Don't feel sorry for the common redpoll. If you spot a group of these tiny brown-streaked birds burrowed in a snowdrift, they're far from cold and miserable. More likely, they're just fine.

Weighing only half an ounce each, these diminutive finches are some of the toughest songbirds around. That stint in the snowdrift? Burrowing in wet snow is one way common redpolls bathe themselves in the winter.

A familiar sight in Alaska and the upper regions of the Canadian territories, common redpolls are right at home in scrub forests, tundra, brushy pastures, and open thickets of willow and birch.

Food Followers

During the winter months, when food is scarce in the North, foraging flocks numbering a few million may leave their breeding grounds and travel south, even as far as California, Oklahoma and the Carolinas, in search of a meal.

These sporadic invasions are greeted with enthusiasm by bird-watchers, who sometimes see dozens of these gregarious visitors squabbling for a turn at their winter feeders.

At the backyard feeder, nyjer, millet and sunflower seeds are satisfying substitutes for the common redpoll's natural winter diet of birch, willow, grass, weed and alder seeds. It's not uncommon to spy these hungry vagabonds feverishly tearing apart dried flower stalks and then rushing to the ground to pick up the seeds that have fallen.

These high-calorie food sources are essential to provide the oils common redpolls need to keep their bodies warm when temperatures plummet.

Just before darkness, redpolls fill a special storage pouch in their esophagus, called a crop, with food. As the birds roost overnight, the seeds are digested and converted into energy, warming their bodies.

What's in a Name?

Look up "poll" in the dictionary, and you'll find it means "head." So, it's not surprising that the common redpoll gets its name from the bright-red or orange spot that marks its forehead.

Both males and females sport this conspicuous cap, as

Backyard Birding Bio

Common Name: Common redpoll.
Scientific Name: *Carduelis flammea*.
Length: 5-1/4 inches.
Wingspan: 9 inches.
Distinctive Markings: Brown-streaked finches with red foreheads and black throats. Adult males have rosy feathers on their upper breast.
Distinctive Behavior: Large flocks often wander south in search of food. They can survive extremely cold temperatures and are almost fearless around people.
Habitat: Scrub forests, tundra, brushy pastures, as well as open willow and birch thickets.
Song: A series of short, repeated notes; mainly call notes and short trills.
Nesting: Raises one to two broods a year; females choose a nesting site 3 to 6 feet off the ground. Low shrubs, rocky outcroppings and the crotch of alders or willows are common choices. Nests are constructed first with twigs, then loosely lined with grass, moss, feathers, rootlets and animal fur. Females lay four to five greenish eggs marked with spots.
Diet: Seeds of birch, alder, willow, pine, elm and basswood; seeds of grasses and weeds; insects in summer.
Backyard Favorites: Nyjer, millet and sunflower seeds.

Summer
Year-Round
Winter

Marie Read

HUNGRY VISITORS. The rosy breast of the male common redpoll brightens up the bleak winter landscape (far left). Always on the lookout for food, it's not unusual to see dozens of these friendly birds at the feeder (above), especially tube feeders.

---

well as a tiny yellow bill, white wing bars, a black throat, a blackish-brown notched tail and dark gray-brown streaks on their backs and sides.

It's the males, however, that really stand out in the snow-covered landscape. By their second year, their white upper breast becomes a brilliant rose hue.

But you don't have to see a common redpoll to know one is in your backyard. Just listen for their bubbly song. It's a series of short trills and repeated notes that sound like "chit chit chit twirrrrrr toweeoweeowee chrr chit chit chit tiree tiree."

Back Home They Go

Mid-March marks the start of the breeding season and the common redpoll's journey home. Once back in the northern wilderness, they begin courting. The female crouches with drooped wings and twitters, while the male stands rigidly in front of her and bows. If the courtship dance is successful, the pair may raise one to two broods that year.

Believed to be monogamous and nonterritorial, common redpoll pairs often nest close to one another. Between April and August, females choose a site for their nest, generally hiding them in dense low shrubs. The birds line their twig nests

with grass, moss, feathers, rootlets and animal fur, creating cozy shelters for the eggs in their often unforgiving northern surroundings.

The female lays four to five pale green to blue-green eggs with purple to reddish-brown spots. She incubates them for 10 to 11 days until they're ready to hatch. The male usually pitches in by feeding his partner during this time.

After hatching, the new brood is well-cared for, as both parents gather insects for their young ones to eat. Twelve days later, the fledglings leave the nest, and another generation of these remarkable and resilient birds takes to the sky.

So why not set out some of their favorite seed this winter? Perhaps this will be the year the common redpolls wander into your backyard.

READER TIP

Common redpolls will visit backyard feeders to eat nyjer, millet and sunflower seeds. They'll also tear apart dried flower stalks, then eat the fallen seeds from the ground.

BLUEBIRDS

*They give cheerful meaning
to having the "blues."*

By George Harrison, Contributing Editor

When I was a boy, I remember that the appearance of the first bluebird meant spring was close behind. Numerous poets and songwriters latched on to this connection over the years, and penned verse that further intertwined bluebirds with springtime.

But that notion is no longer true.

Fifty years ago, bluebirds, especially eastern bluebirds, were true signs of warmer weather when they returned to northern states in March. But with mild winters during the past couple of decades, many bluebirds now spend winters in their nesting areas all across the North.

Spring Song

Still, for me, the soft notes of the first bluebird warble "tru-al-ly, tru-al-ly," are among the most welcome sounds of spring.

There sits the male eastern bluebird on a fence post along the country road where I live in Wisconsin, and I watch with thankful eyes. He appears to wear the velvet-blue sky on his back and shoulders, and his breast reflects the reddish-brown earth.

The activity will pick up a week or two later, when the female appears. Then, to the accompaniment of his own warbling, the male will pursue his chosen mate from one perch to another, often showing her areas available for nesting.

That's a signal for me to set up a tray feeder and fill it with the live mealworms I buy at a local pet store. In my experience, placing the feeder in the vicinity of the birdhouses encourages bluebirds to nest there.

Making a Comeback

There was a time, in the early to mid-1900s, when bluebirds were in trouble. Due to loss of habitat and competition for nesting sites, people thought the birds would disappear.

But through the great efforts of many people who love bluebirds, trails of birdhouses made just for them have popped up throughout North America, especially in the East.

The millions of bluebird houses nailed to fence posts along rural roads and highways, 100 yards or so apart, produced a recruitment of bluebirds beyond anyone's dreams.

Today, all three species of bluebirds—eastern, mountain and western—are at healthy population levels, and the future looks bright.

That doesn't mean that bluebirds are without challenges.

He appears to wear the velvet-blue sky on his back and shoulders.

Bill Leaman/The Image Finders; opposite page, Maslowski Productions

Hal Harrison

Indeed, competition for nesting sites from house sparrows, house wrens, European starlings and tree swallows is a major problem that both bluebirds and their fans face every spring.

Just about the time a pair of bluebirds settles into a birdhouse and begins to nest, one of the four enemy birds takes over the house and keeps the bluebirds from claiming it for themselves.

House wrens will even poke holes in the bluebirds' eggs. The frustrating part of this aggressive behavior is that once they win the battle, these other bird species often vacate the house.

Invite Bluebirds to Nest

Nesting starts early among bluebirds, so they can raise at least two broods each year. Tree cavities are natural nesting places, but they readily accept man-made nest boxes.

There is a great variety of bluebird houses, but most are as good as any other. The house should be made of untreated wood, 4 by 4 inches to 5 by 5 inches square and 7 inches high, with a 1-1/2-inch entrance hole about 6 inches above the floor.

A removable overhanging lid makes for easy observation and cleaning, and it should be ventilated at the top with drainage holes in the floor. Paint or stain it a natural color, then place it on a post 5 to 10 feet above the ground at the edge of an open grassy field, facing away from the wind and sun.

The North American Bluebird Society (NABS) is one of the organizations that formed to help save the bluebird. This group recommends that bluebird houses be spaced at intervals of 100 to 150 yards (300 yards for mountain bluebirds). If house

---

BLUEPRINT FOR SUCCESS. Want to attract bluebirds? Place a house for them in an open area, and these spirited songsters might start a nest, like this eastern bluebird pair (left). The female bluebirds of all three species—eastern, western and mountain (at top)—lay four to six pale-blue eggs (inset).

Western bluebird   Mountain bluebird

Rob Curtis/The Image Finders   Roland Jordahl

wrens are in the area, be sure the box is mounted at least 200 feet away from a wooded or brushy area.

If tree swallows or violet-green swallows are likely to use the box, try setting out two boxes about 10 feet apart. That way, bluebirds can use one and swallows the other.

Most bluebird box landlords have found this practice allows both species to nest side by side in relative peace, according to NABS.

To keep house sparrows away from bluebird houses, NABS emphasizes the importance of box location.

Avoid placing boxes near farmsteads, feedlots, barns or old outbuildings. Boxes placed in or around towns and cities will likely be claimed by house sparrows. If sparrows do take up residence, one option is to relocate the box to a site farther away from people.

Watching in Awe

If the bluebirds are successful, and you're able to watch the whole process, from nest building to the young birds fledging, it is one of the most rewarding experiences in nature.

I remember the pair of bluebirds that set up housekeeping in a nesting box attached to an apple tree in our backyard a few years ago. I set out a feeder tray with mealworms about 10 feet away. I watched the pair carry grasses into the house for a few days, and then the female laid one egg a day for 5 days.

The female began incubating on the fifth day, and she sat on them for 14 days, while the male brought her food—often a mealworm from the tray feeder. During one of the rare times when she left the house, I peeked inside to admire the pale-blue, almost white, eggs she had been incubating.

READER TIP

In my experience, placing a mealworm feeder in the vicinity of my bluebird houses encourages bluebirds to nest there. —**George Harrison, Contributing Editor**

OPEN WIDE. Even after the juvenile bluebirds take flight from the nest box, the adults continue to feed them, like the male eastern bluebird offering mealworms to a fledgling (above right). Residents of the West have two bluebirds that could frequent yards—the mountain (above) and the western (above left).

When the young hatched on the 15th day, both parents began feeding them. The morsels of insects they delivered were tiny at first, but as the days passed, the offerings increased in both size and frequency.

By the time they were 18 days old, the youngsters were ready to leave the house. One at a time, they sat at the entrance and then popped out of the house and proceeded to fly erratically to the safety of a nearby tree or bush.

Nothing is cuter than a pudgy bluebird fledgling awaiting a meal.

Bluebird fledglings (like the one above right) have spotted breasts, similar to other members of the thrush family, including the American robin. Nothing is cuter than a pudgy bluebird fledgling waiting for a meal, as it hunkers down on a tree branch.

New Beginnings

Far from slowing down, the bird activity once the young left the box was feverish. While the male was running a "meals on wings" service to the young, the female was preparing for the second brood.

She built another nest on top of the first, in the same house, rather than selecting another house nearby.

Before I knew it, the first youngsters were on their own, and the male was attending to his mate, who had started laying eggs.

Later, after the eggs hatched, I saw the young of the first brood helping their parents feed the second brood. This practice, called "cooperative breeding," is common among bluebirds.

Bluebirds are one of the most beautiful avian species around. The sight of them often elicits gasps of amazement, and I feel lucky to have witnessed their complete nesting routine many times.

As the song goes, they truly are the "bluebird of happiness," bringing excitement, color and adventure to any yard.

Eastern bluebird

Backyard Birding Bio

Common Name: Eastern bluebird.
Scientific Name: *Sialia sialis*.
Length: 7 inches.
Wingspan: 13 inches.
Distinctive Markings: Males have a blue back, wings and head, with a white belly (above). Orange on breast extends onto throat. Females have the same markings, but duller.
Habitat: Open backyards and farmland.
Song: Soft warble, "tru-al-ly, tru-al-ly."
Nesting: Built mostly by the female, the nest is made of dried grasses and lined with finer grasses, hair and feathers. She lays four to six pale-blue, sometimes white, eggs between March and July, then incubates them for 12 to 14 days until they hatch. Both parents feed the nestlings.
Diet: Insects and berries.
Backyard Favorite: Live mealworms.

Common Name: Western bluebird.
Scientific Name: *Sialia mexicana*.
Length: 7 inches.
Wingspan: 13-1/2 inches.
Distinctive Markings: Males have a blue back, wings, head and throat, plus a bluish tinge on belly (see photo above far left). Orange on breast extends onto back. Females have the same markings, but are much duller and have a grayish cast.
Habitat: Open woodlands with scattered old trees, plus farmland and orchards.
Song: A subdued "f-few, f-few, f-few."
Nesting: Pair builds a nest of grasses, then lines it with finer grasses. The female lays four to six pale-blue eggs in April and May, then incubates them for 13 to 14 days until they hatch. Both parents feed the nestlings.
Diet: Insects and berries.
Backyard Favorite: Live mealworms.

Common Name: Mountain bluebird.
Scientific Name: *Sialia currucoides*.
Length: 7-1/4 inches.
Wingspan: 14 inches.
Distinctive Markings: Males are brilliant blue all over (see photo above near left). Females are gray overall with pale-blue feathers on their tail and wings.
Habitat: Meadows, clearings and open forests up to elevations of 10,000 to 12,000 feet.
Song: Similar to the eastern bluebird's song, but slightly higher pitched.
Nesting: Pair builds a grass nest often lined with finer material. The female lays four to six pale-blue eggs between April and July, then incubates them for 13 to 14 days until they hatch. Both parents feed the nestlings.
Diet: Insects and berries.
Backyard Favorite: Live mealworms.

■ Summer
■ Year-Round
■ Migration
■ Winter

WHIP-POOR-WILL

Listen up, or you may not spot this hidden songster.

By George Harrison, Contributing Editor

Harrison Productions

The whip-poor-will has been a special bird for me ever since I was a little boy. One of these talented vocalists would sing me to sleep every night at my family's cottage, which was along the Allegheny River in western Pennsylvania.

I remember its haunting call, "whip-poor-will, whip-poor-will, whip-poor-will," continuing on and on until I fell asleep. It often called from the top of a 50-gallon oil drum outside my bedroom window, a fact I confirmed one night by using my dad's big flashlight to find the bird's reflective red-orb eyes in the dark. Those eyes made the bird seem even more mysterious to me.

I have heard its nighttime call on many occasions since then and in various locales. One time while visiting friends in the Blue Ridge Mountains of Virginia, I lay in bed wondering how many times the bird would call without stopping. So, I started to count them like sheep. I got well into the hundreds before sleep overtook me. John Burroughs, one of the nation's greatest ornithologists, once recorded 1,088 repetitions without a pause.

Like most people, I used to think that whip-poor-wills sounded their name exactly. But one night, when I was very close to a singing bird, I could hear an additional "chuck" sound between the "whip-poor-will" calls.

Hearing this member of the nightjar family is far easier than spotting the highly camouflaged bird. Its brown mottled feathers and squat shape don't make it the most attractive bird around, but they're the perfect characteristics for hiding among leaves on the ground or along tree branches.

Maslowski Productions

MASTER OF DISGUISE. The whip-poor-will's mottled feathers and squat shape are excellent camouflage. This allows the females to blend in while incubating eggs among dried leaves (like the bird at left), and helps the birds keep a low profile on daytime roosts (far left). The dappled markings on the young birds (below) and eggs mimic the sunlight and shadow pattern of the bird's leafy forest habitat.

Todd Fink/Daybreak Imagery

Perfect Camouflage

One day, I accidentally scared a female whip-poor-will off her eggs. I was surprised that she made no noise when she flew. She fluttered about 20 yards away, as silent as a moth, and began feigning a broken wing to draw me away from the eggs.

A few days later, I returned with a camera to photograph the bird and could not find her, even though I had memorized the nest's location. After 15 minutes of looking, I finally saw her in the exact spot I had been staring the whole time. It was as if I'd put on 3-D glasses that brought the forest floor to life. She blended in almost perfectly.

In late April or early May, whip-poor-wills arrive in their northern nesting grounds in mature hardwood forests. The boisterous males immediately make their presence known, using their distinctive call in hopes of attracting a mate and to defend their territory. They'll continue to sing until the nesting season ends in late July or early August.

Once coupled, the female lays two gray-spotted eggs on the dry and dead leaves of the forest floor. Although there is no nest, as the female incubates the eggs, the depression in the leaves becomes deeper. She keeps the eggs warm until they hatch 19 days later. The pair may raise a second brood in warmer regions.

In-Flight Meals

The way a whip-poor-will gathers food is unique—even among some birds in the same family. Unlike close relative the common nighthawk, which darts around the sky to gather insects, the whip-poor-will flies close to the ground in smooth silent motions.

With its mouth agape, it funnels mosquitoes, moths and other nocturnal flying insects into its wide mouth. The hair-like feathers around its bill help direct the insects into its mouth.

Unfortunately, whip-poor-will numbers have declined in recent decades due to several factors, including the loss of habitat in both summer and winter ranges; pesticides that reduce the number of insects for food; and losses to nocturnal predators, such as great horned owls.

Though these birds have never been a common backyard species, any bird enthusiast who can hear a whip-poor-will through the bedroom window is in for a nightly treat. ✦

Backyard Birding Bio

Common Name: Whip-poor-will.
Scientific Name: *Caprimulgus vociferus*.
Length: 9 inches.
Wingspan: 19 inches.
Distinctive Markings: Heavily mottled with gray, black and brown above and paler gray and black mottling below. The male has white patch borders below its black throat and the tips of its outer tail feathers. Females are buff-colored in those areas.
Distinctive Behavior: Nests, almost unseen, among dried leaves on the ground.
Habitat: Open deciduous woodlands, where dead leaves carpet the forest floor.

☐ Summer
▨ Migration
▩ Year-Round

Song: Distinctive nighttime call that resembles its name, "whip-poor-will," repeated over and over again.
Nest: None. The female lays two oval light-brown eggs with gray spots and blotches in dead leaves on ground, typically where light and shadows filter through the trees to help the incubating bird blend in with its surroundings.
Diet: Small flying insects caught in flight.

BLUE JAY

These boldly colored birds are nature's noisemakers.

By George Harrison, Contributing Editor

Photo: Marie Read

*A blue jay's call
may warn other
birds of danger.*

They certainly aren't a secretive species. If you have blue jays in your yard, they're almost impossible to miss. When I'm outside watering the garden, taking out the trash or walking along the road, I can often hear one or more blue jays screaming at me, "jay, jay, jay."

One of the most noticeable characteristics of this bright member of the crow family is the noise it makes. And blue jays have quite a repertoire of calls.

In addition to the alarm call (the "jay, jay, jay" that many of us recognize), there is its charming bell-like "tull-ull" call that it uses to communicate with its mate and other members of its family. There also is the so-called "whisper call" that parent birds use around their nests during a period when they are otherwise very quiet.

Blue-Feathered Bandits

Blue jays also imitate the sounds of winged predators to chase other birds and squirrels from feeders.

Typically, a flock of blue jays will arrive at feeders screaming like hawks to scare away the other birds. Then four or five of these cocky impersonators, showing off their flashy blue and white feathers, sail into the empty feeders and begin to eat whatever and wherever they want.

Sometimes, they are like wolves in blue suits that will raid the nests of other birds, eating eggs and nestlings. This flashy and arrogant behavior is why some people consider blue jays "bully birds" that are unwelcome at their feeders.

Yet, other birds sometimes benefit from the blue jay's boisterous personality. Their calls may warn of danger, like the scene Pattie Glaze witnessed in her Claremore, Oklahoma backyard.

"Early one fall day, my husband, Richard, and I were sitting on our back patio enjoying the small birds at our feeders," Pattie writes. "I looked up and saw a rather large brown bird sitting at the top of our neighbor's tree.

"As I wondered what species it was, a blue jay perched in another tree began making a loud steady noise. The smaller birds quickly disappeared.

"Just then, the larger bird swooped toward us. As it flew

TURN UP THE VOLUME. Blue jays often make quite a racket in the backyard. They may imitate hawks to scare other birds away from a feeder (top photo). However, when they're nesting, they become very quiet. Both the male and female build the nest (above photos) and incubate the eggs until they hatch.

over our heads, we realized it was a Cooper's hawk! The blue jay's screams apparently had warned the smaller birds that danger was near."

In addition to warning of nearby predators, blue jays will often attack hawks and owls by "mobbing" these larger and more dangerous birds of prey. This usually causes such a ruckus that other songbirds heed the warning about the raptors' presence.

Hide and Seek

When I was a boy helping my dad photograph birds, we often had blue jays living in our home. Keeping native wild birds as pets was legal then, and I'm glad I had the experience of having jays inside. I recall that it was not safe to leave anything shiny lying around the house when the birds were loose. Invariably, they would pick up those objects and carry them around or hide them.

I also learned a great deal about their eating habits. I watched a blue jay swallow one whole sunflower seed after another, not eating them, but stashing the seeds in its throat pouch to transport to a more secluded site. The jay later coughed up the seeds and either cracked them open and ate or hid them.

Researchers have found that blue jays do, in fact, remember where they cache some of their food, but much of it is either pirated by other wildlife or forgotten.

Creating a Family

Courtship for blue jays begins in early May, when a troop of seven or eight jays gathers in the top of a large tree to play follow the leader, stopping now and then to bob their heads up and down. Presumably, the leader is a female, and the followers are hopeful male suitors. When the leader flies away,

FLOCKING FOR FOOD. In the winter, blue jays often travel in groups, searching woodland areas for fruit, grains and nuts. They will often visit backyard feeders to eat sunflower seeds and suet.

the group of other jays is always right behind it.

After the female selects a mate, the new couple gathers twigs and carries them around until they locate a suitable nesting site.

Those sticks eventually wind up in a well-hidden bulky nest, usually in the crotch or outer branches of a tree, 10 to 25 feet above the ground. Four or five greenish eggs hatch 17 to 18 days after being incubated by both blue jay parents.

Three weeks later, the blind and naked chicks have transformed into fully feathered miniatures of their parents, and are ready to leave the nest. It's common for pairs in the North to raise one brood a year, while southern parents usually raise two broods.

Watching these young birds interact with the world around them is a thrilling experience, as Lynda Saye discovered while witnessing a fledgling blue jay as it learned to fly in Panama City, Florida.

"I noticed that the bird was not hopping very fast and realized that it was a baby blue jay," Lynda writes. "The parent birds soared back and forth over its head, while the baby flapped its wings as fast as it could, but only seemed to clear a couple of inches above the ground before crash landing.

I was reminded of my grandchildren learning to walk. It was an amazing sight."

By late August or early September, both youngsters and adults join other blue jays in groups of several families. These flocks stay together through the winter, cruising woodland areas in search of food, and pestering owls and hawks at every opportunity.

Some jays migrate farther south, while others remain near their nesting range. Wherever they end up, however, you're sure to hear them.

READER TIP

Attract blue jays by offering sunflower seeds at a tray feeder or supplying suet cakes. They'll also bathe and drink from birdbaths and pools.

Backyard Birding Bio

Winter
Year-Round

Common Name: Blue jay.
Scientific Name: *Cyanocitta cristata*.
Length: 11 inches.
Wingspan: 16 inches.
Distinctive Markings: Males and females are alike. Pale blue above with paler underparts, a blue head crest and a black necklace. Its wings and tail are barred with white.
Distinctive Behavior: Will noisily chase other birds from feeders.
Habitat: Open woods, parks, wooded farmlands and backyards.
Voice: A noisy jay, jay, jay or jeer, jeer, jeer is the blue jay's most familiar call, but

a bell-like double note "tull-ull" is also characteristic. The male's courtship song is a whispering chatter.
Nesting: In a bulky nest 10 to 25 feet above the ground, the female lays four to five spotted olive to buff-colored eggs. Both parents help incubate the eggs for 17 to 18 days until they match.
Diet: Although jays are omnivorous, about 75 percent of a blue jay's diet is fruit, grain and nuts. The remainder consists of insects as well as small animals.
Backyard Favorite: Sunflower seeds and suet cakes. They will also bathe and drink from a birdbath or pool.

YELLOW WARBLER

*This bright songster is
a summertime delight.*

By George Harrison, Contributing Editor

Photo: Marie Read

Even in this family of brightly colored birds, the yellow warbler stands out. Not only do the males display overall golden feathers, but they're also less timid than the 55 other North American birds in the wood warbler family. In fact, it's the only wood warbler that regularly visits backyards.

The first time I witnessed yellow warblers up close was at the Pymatuning State Park headquarters in northwestern Pennsylvania. They were in a multiflora rose hedge that had grown out of control.

> *Their ongoing musical display of "sweet sweet sweet" is one reason its "warbler" name is quite fitting.*

Perfect Habitat

Multiflora rose is one of those shrubs that farmers hate because it takes over land for grazing and crops. It is even outlawed in some states. Yellow warblers, on the other hand, love it because it is dense and prickly. This makes it a good hiding spot that also provides protection for their nests, and its blossoms attract insects they can eat and feed to their young.

This particular rose was so perfect that a whole colony of yellow warblers nested in it. It was an amazing sight, though rare, since warblers generally do not nest in groups.

More recently, my observation of yellow warblers is at the tiered recirculating birdbath on my southeastern Wisconsin patio. There, a pair of yellow warblers frequently bathes and drinks from May through July.

I love to watch one particular male stand on the spillway, face upstream and dip his head into the flow. Even when his bright-yellow feathers are soaking wet, I can plainly see the distinctive reddish-brown streaks on his breast.

Yellow warblers are interesting birds for many reasons. Not only are they one of the most widespread of any native songbird (they breed from Mexico all the way to the Arctic Circle), but they spend less time in their breeding grounds than other songbirds—arriving in May and leaving just a few short months later, by August.

The yellow warbler is also one of the most frequent targets for the brown-headed cowbird, a species which lays its eggs in the nests of other birds, then abandons them.

When this happens, yellow warblers will often build a

LOVELY LADY. You can recognize the female yellow warbler (like the one at left) by the slightly duller—but still eye-catching—feathers. While females incubate eggs, males continue to sing frequently and bring food to her. At right, yellow warblers prefer birdbaths with recirculating water.

Al Cornell

new floor in its nest to cover the cowbird's egg. This defense keeps the eggs from hatching.

Life at the Nest

Though yellow warblers build neat and compact cup-shaped nests of plant fibers and down, they are known to steal some of that material from neighbors' nests, or from a nest they've previously built and deserted.

It takes the female about 4 days to complete construction, while the male sings and supervises. Then he feeds her as she incubates four to five eggs for 11 to 12 days. Once the eggs hatch, the male pitches in to help feed the young, mostly with small caterpillars.

Though he is busy gathering food and feeding young, the male yellow warbler continues to carol his lovely "sweet sweet sweet" song at a rate of about once every minute. The ongoing musical display is one reason its "warbler" name is quite fitting.

Southward Bound

In another 9 to 12 days, the young are ready to leave the nest, though they require feeding and protection for another couple of weeks. As soon as the young are able to take care of themselves, the adults leave the breeding territory and head south. They seem to disappear overnight, which may be exactly what happens, because they migrate after dark.

Though yellow warblers are frequent visitors to backyards, they also inhabit swamps, marshes and bottomlands. I spotted one in a marsh in Cuba, and was surprised to discover it was the very same species that I see bathing in my Wisconsin backyard.

Because it is so widespread, the yellow warbler appears in several different geographic forms. Those in the North and West have slightly drabber yellow plumage; in the Southwest, they're paler. In the Florida Keys, yellow warblers reside year-round and exhibit rich golden feathers.

But no matter where you are, the sight of this bright-yellow bird of summer is an event to cherish. ✦

READER TIP

Yellow warblers are drawn to backyard birdbaths, especially those with moving water. Contributing Editor George Harrison sees a pair of them bathing and drinking from his tiered recirculating birdbath from May through July each year.

Backyard Birding Bio

Common Name: Yellow warbler.
Scientific Name: *Dendroica petechia*.
Family: Wood warbler.
Length: 5 inches.
Wingspan: 8 inches.
Distinctive Markings: Adult male is bright yellow with reddish-brown streaks on its breast; adult female is duller yellow; first-year juveniles may be gray overall.
Distinctive Behavior: Hunts for food in shrubbery and thickets; male hunts higher in vegetation than females.
Habitat: Backyard gardens, along waterways, swamp edges, marshes, brushy bottomlands, orchards, hedgerows and roadside thickets.
Song: "Sweet sweet sweet sweet sweeter sweeter," or "sweet-sweet-sweet-chit-tit-tit-teweet."
Nest: Strong compact cup of firmly interwoven milkweed fibers, hemp, grasses and plant down that's lined with felted plant down, hair and fine grasses. Female places the nest in an upright fork or crotch of a shrub, tree or briars, 3 to 8 feet above the ground. She then incubates the four to five eggs for 11 to 12 days while the male brings food to her.
Diet: Insects, mostly caterpillars, but also the mayflies, moths, treehoppers and other insects, plus spiders.
Backyard Favorite: Birdbaths, especially those with moving water.

Summer
Migration
Winter
Year-Round

TEACHING BIRDS TO FLY

Conservation groups take to the sky to keep whooping cranes from becoming extinct.

By Stacy Tornio, Associate Editor

Photos courtesy of the Whooping Crane Eastern Partnership and Operation Migration

"Eventually, we won't need to use ultralights."

TRAINING CAMP. Operation Migration conditions juvenile whooping cranes to think of the ultralight aircraft (far left) as a parent. To do this, experts wear costumes to disguise themselves (far left inset). They also use puppet-like crane heads for feeding (above), teach the birds their traditional courtship dance (below), and acclimate them to the constant company of the ultralight and its pilot. The reward is a successful migration, like the three soaring juvenile whooping cranes at left.

"Daddy is flying with the birds." According to 5-year-old Alex, this is where her father, Joe Duff, goes each fall. And that description isn't just the result of a child's creative imagination, either.

Every October, Joe climbs into a tiny ultralight aircraft to lead a flock of graceful whooping cranes from Wisconsin to their winter home in Florida. He is the cofounder of Operation Migration, a group chosen by Canadian and U.S. wildlife officials to help keep the whooping crane population from becoming extinct.

To do this, the organization does exactly what Alex says—they fly with the birds.

A Fading Treasure

By the early 1940s, the population of whooping cranes—the largest bird in North America—had fallen as low as 15 birds. The U.S. government took action and created a winter

Top Billing

refuge for this migrating Canadian whooping crane flock at the Aransas National Wildlife Refuge along the Gulf of Mexico in Texas. The location is still used by the wild population today, which has grown to include nearly 200 birds.

But experts knew they couldn't rely on this single flock to avoid extinction, so in the early 1990s, they established a group of nonmigratory whooping cranes at Kissimmee Prairie in Florida.

Meanwhile, the rest of the birding world was starting to hear news of an innovative concept. Humans were teaching birds how to fly...or more specifically, how to migrate.

In 1993, Joe joined pilot Bill Lishman on the first human-led bird migration of a flock of Canada geese. That experience led Joe to help with the 1995 movie about the subject, *Fly Away Home*. He didn't lose sight of his goal, however. He continued studying the concept of using ultralight planes to lead migrating birds.

The more he and his colleagues learned about the process,

the more excited they became. Test trials with Canada geese and sandhill cranes continued to be successful. It didn't take them long to convince officials that a similar plan could work to establish a new migratory flock of whooping cranes. They would simply teach the youngest chicks to follow the aircraft.

Plan Takes Off

It was December 3, 2001, when six whooping cranes made the first airplane-led flight from Necedah, Wisconsin to the Chassahowitzka National Wildlife Refuge in Florida. The 1,250-mile trip had taken nearly 2 months, three ultralights and a 14-member team.

"During that flight, I didn't relax for a minute," remembers Joe, who was the lead pilot. "When we arrived with the first flock, it was a huge relief."

The following years continued to be demanding. Weather conditions have to be perfect for flying, which means the team and cranes often spend hours, or even days, grounded.

"Last year, the migration took 64 days, and we only flew on 23 of those," Joe says. "We do a lot of sitting in a trailer, waiting on the weather so we can take off."

With the amount of time and effort it takes to help the birds migrate, it's no surprise that the project carries a hefty price tag. Joan Garland is the outreach coordinator for the International Crane Foundation, one of the organizations that help support the effort. She said it takes an estimated $1.8 million to complete the migration each year.

Migration Milestone

The fall of 2005 was an important time for Joe and his team. Twenty-one juvenile cranes—the fifth and largest flock—made the trip. Upon their successful arrival, the Wisconsin/Florida migratory group will have more than 60 birds.

Another new development is a change in the training. Unlike previous years, when all newly hatched chicks train with the ultralight aircrafts, in 2005, five chicks did not receive the same preparation.

Joan says they are hoping these five birds will have the natural instinct to follow the other migrating birds.

"Eventually, we won't need to use ultralights," she says. "Once enough birds are making the migration on their own, hopefully those older birds will be able to show the new chicks the proper migration route."

Cranes from previous years already are migrating to and from Florida on their own. The ultralight training will continue until there are enough mature birds to teach the younger ones every year.

Whooping crane supporters want the birds to be able to live like they once did, as wild migratory birds. This is why the handlers at the Necedah National Wildlife Refuge in Wisconsin—

SOUTH FOR THE WINTER. It's hard to imagine that such majestic birds were once on the brink of extinction. The juveniles are just as beautiful as the adults, but display tan markings on their wings and neck (above left). Soon, that coloring will begin to fade until the bird displays the snow-white feathers and red crown of an adult (at right). At left, a whooping crane surveys its surroundings at the Necedah National Wildlife Refuge in Wisconsin. Once the birds are taught the migration route, they can then make the trip on their own.

where the chicks hatch and train—take careful precautions to disguise themselves when working with the birds.

"We have to eliminate everything that is human," says Joe, who is one of the few people who work one-on-one with the birds. "We wear a big costume, we don't talk anywhere near the birds and we carry a recorder that plays crane sounds."

It's important for the birds to avoid any human contact, so they can learn to survive on their own. Imprinting starts when the chicks are only 7 days old. The handlers use puppet-like crane heads to feed the chicks and train them to think of the ultralight aircraft as a parent. That way, when it comes time to migrate, they will follow it.

One unique aspect of the whooping crane effort is the amount of support it receives from people and organizations throughout North America. Chester McConnell lives in Tennessee and is a retired wildlife biologist. He says he's a preservationist at heart, which is why he belongs to the group, Whooping Crane Conservation Association.

"This is my life," he says. "I love it, and I just can't turn it loose."

Chester says it's encouraging to know groups like his are making a difference, as seen in the rising numbers of whooping cranes.

"This is the symbol of conservation in this country," Chester says. "So many people have come together for the same joint effort."

Currently, there are roughly 450 whooping cranes throughout North America. As the number continues to grow, supporters have their eyes on a common goal—improving the cranes' status so they can be removed from the endangered species list. They know it's something that won't happen overnight, but are confident it's attainable.

"So many endangered species programs just focus on why there is a decline, but with this, we get to give back," Joe says. "We get to save the species."

ROAD TRIP. This map shows the migration route of the whooping cranes. Beginning each October, they travel from Wisconsin to their winter home in Florida. The Whooping Crane Eastern Partnership and Operation Migration provide an up-to-date route tracker and information about the cranes. Visit *www.operation migration.org* or *www.bringback thecranes.org*.

Did You Know?

■ As the tallest bird in North America, the whooping crane can reach up to 5-1/2 feet with a wingspan of 7 feet.

■ These cranes got their name from their distinctive whooping call. Sometimes referred to as a duet, this loud mating ritual can be heard from more than a mile away.

■ Whooping cranes select a mate for life between the ages of 2 and 3. The ritual includes a courtship dance known as the unison call.

■ They can live up to 25 years, but whoopers face a lot of dangers along the way, including predators and disease.

■ The birds feed on insects, crabs, crayfish, rodents, roots, seeds and marsh plants.

■ Whooping cranes lay two eggs, which hatch after about 34 days.

NORTHERN SAW-WHET OWL

By George Harrison, Contributing Editor

A trusting little northern saw-whet owl perched and stared at me through round golden eyes, dotted with big black pupils. It was the first saw-whet I'd ever seen. I knew that it was the smallest owl in the East, but I was not prepared for this dainty beautifully marked bird that appeared to have no fear of me.

I was on Mt. Desert Island, Maine, helping my dad search for a nest of these diminutive owls to photograph for his *Peterson Field Guide to Eastern Birds' Nests*. We had put up a half dozen nesting boxes in the hope of attracting these cavity nesters, but the birds had not used them, even though we heard them calling in the area at night.

Northern saw-whet owls have a number of utterances. The one I heard in Maine reminded me of the beep of a truck backing up. It also has a call that early ornithologists thought sounded like a lumberjack sharpening his saw. Thus, the name "saw-whet."

Finally, a friend and resident of Mt. Desert Island, Ralph

Long Jr., found a nest for Dad in an old woodpecker cavity. He noticed a swarm of mosquitoes at the entrance, indicating that a warm-blooded animal was inside.

The little guy I spotted was perched in a hemlock tree, about 10 feet above the ground. Though females are slightly larger, the sexes look alike, so I did not know which I was looking at, even at close range.

Getting to Know "Hoo"

Because saw-whets are totally nocturnal, people rarely see them. But reader Emily Grey of Onancock, Virginia has seen many of them. That's because she assists with the banding of the birds at the tip of the Delmarva Peninsula near her home. The banding effort is part of a much larger program known as Project Owl Net, with banding stations in many eastern states.

Emily says that the average saw-whet she handles weighs about 3 ounces and is covered in down and feathers, even on its legs, almost to the ends of its needle-sharp talons.Except at the banding sites, Emily had never encountered a saw-whet owl in the wild. That is, until one cold March evening, when she spotted a tiny bird no larger than an American robin drinking from a puddle at her mother's house.

"I watched in fascination as the buff-colored adult owl lowered its head, raised up and slightly tilted its crown back, swallowing the cool refreshment," she relates.

Moving South

Despite the fact that the northern saw-whet has been banded more often than any other North American owl (more than 60,000 individuals), relatively little is known about its behavior and movements.

It was once believed to be a strictly northern dweller of coniferous and mountainous forests. But recent banding records have shown that it is more widespread than anyone knew, especially in winter.

A northern saw-whet was found as far south as northern Florida. Like northern finches, some populations of this owl

It is more widespread than anyone knew.

seem to "irrupt" periodically—moving south en masse to search for the small mammals like mice, moles and shrews that comprise most of their diet.

Although most northern saw-whet owls nest in abandoned woodpecker tree cavities, they can be enticed into man-made nesting boxes. If you live in or near northern or mountainous coniferous forests, you might want to build a couple of nesting boxes for your backyard. Visit the Shaw Creek Web site for building plans for a saw-whet owl box *www.shawcreekbirdsupply.com/plans_saw_whet_owl.htm*).

Perhaps one night, you'll find yourself peering into the captivating yellow eyes of a northern saw-whet owl.

NEED A HAND? A northern saw-whet owl (above) perches for a moment on volunteer Kristina Baker after it was banded at the Big Oaks National Wildlife Refuge in Madison, Indiana.

READER TIP

You can find a hidden saw-whet owl nest by looking for signs like a swarm of mosquitoes at the entrance of an old woodpecker hole. That indicates there is a warm-blooded animal inside.

—George Harrison, Contributing Editor

Backyard Birding Bio

Common Name: Northern saw-whet owl.
Scientific Name: *Aegolius acadicus*.
Length: 8 inches.
Wingspan: 17 inches.
Distinctive Markings: Adult is reddish-brown above, white below with reddish streaks. Facial disks are reddish, without dark borders, and its beak is dark. Juveniles are strongly reddish above, tawny-rust below. Males and females look alike.
Distinctive Behavior: Hunts almost entirely at night, using sound and sight to find its prey.
Habitat: Coniferous forests, sometimes oak woodland or streamside groves in arid country.
Call: Repeated low whistled toots. Also has a wheezy, rising, catlike screech or soft nasal barks, or a soft and whining whistle.

Summer
Winter
Year-Round

Nest: In a cavity, usually an abandoned woodpecker hole, that's 14 to 60 feet above the ground. Will use a birdhouse. Uses no nesting material, only breast feathers. Lays five to six pure-white eggs, laid at intervals of 1 to 3 days. The female incubates for 21 to 28 days, beginning with the laying of the first egg. The male helps feed the young.
Diet: Mostly small mammals, but occasionally insects and frogs.
Backyard Favorite: Nesting box, 16 inches tall and 12 inches wide with a 3-inch entrance hole.

Marie Read

Black-Capped Chickadee

These little charmers are true feathered friends.

By George Harrison, Contributing Editor

Of all the common backyard birds, the black-capped chickadee takes the prize as the most entertaining.

The little birds are so delightful that my wife, Kit, often says she'd like to come back as one in another life, if there were such a thing as reincarnation.

Why? "Because chickadees seem to enjoy life," she says.

It's true. These vivacious and carefree birds do exhibit a friendly energy. When two or more of them are together, they are full of conversation, exchanging cheerful remarks.

A Bird in Hand

Another of the black-capped chickadee's many remarkable traits is its tameness. It is so approachable around bird feeders that it may even eat seeds from an outstreched hand.

Hugh Wiberg, the author of several books, including *Hand-Feeding Backyard Birds*, still remembers the first time a black-capped chickadee snapped a seed from his open palm 25 years ago.

"Of the many species that have eaten from my hand since

Chickadees are named after the sound of their alarm call.

then, those fearless black-and-white bundles of energy are without question the easiest birds to charm to your hands," he says.

I, too, was thrilled the first time a black-capped chickadee fed from my hand. I was just a little boy helping my dad maintain a bird-feeding station behind our house in western Pennsylvania.

"If you stand very still with sunflower seeds in your hand, a chickadee may stop for a snack," my dad said.

So I did as he instructed and sure enough, in a few minutes, a tiny chickadee landed on my hand. In a flash, the bird seized a seed in its bill and was gone. The chickadee was so lightweight that I really couldn't feel it, until it pushed off. The most memorable part was seeing all the detail in the bird's feathers, beady black eyes and sharp tiny bill. I was ecstatic.

But don't let a chickadee's petite appearance fool you.

"Chickadees are not the suburban wimps that some people think they are," says wildlife ecologist Margaret Clack Brittingham, who studied the birds at the University of Wisconsin in Madison.

For three winters, she kept track of 576 black-capped chickadees. As the small birds struggled against starvation and stinging cold, they earned her respect, too.

"They are tough survivors that live close to the edge of life," she says.

One notable finding was that chickadees don't depend on bird feeders, even when they're readily available. During normal winter weather, chickadees that had access to feeders survived at the same rate as those chickadees without feeders.

In fact, despite the feeders, the birds still gathered a majority of their food from the wild. This should ease the concerns of people who cannot replenish their bird feeders on winter days when they are away from home.

"The thing that really impressed me about chickadees is

George Harrison

BACKYARD ATTRACTIONS. Black-capped chickadees are common—and welcome—backyard visitors. They'll stop by for a bite of sunflower seeds (far left) or raise their young in a birdhouse (above), preferably one with a 1-1/4-inch entrance.

their metabolism," she says. "We weighed birds early in the morning and found that they had virtually no body fat. Yet, the same birds examined in the afternoon of the same day were bulging with fat."

These fat stores are what allow these tiny imps to make it through a long sub-zero night.

They Will Survive

Chickadees have other winter survival strategies as well. During winter nights, they can reduce their metabolism by

ALWAYS ON THE GO. The endless energy of black-capped chickadees makes them a delight. So it's no surprise that many bird-watchers list this bird as their favorite species. It's common to spot them plucking sunflower seeds or other treats from a feeder (left). But this sight of a chickadee hovering in mid-air as it sips water from a melting icicle (above) is simply amazing.

slowing their heartbeats, breathing and energy consumption.

They also are adept at finding fluids in winter—sometimes from unexpected sources, like the scene Elizabeth Williams witnessed in her West Bloomfield, Michigan yard.

"As I peered out from my sunroom, I noticed the icicles on my pussy willow were beginning to thaw," she says. "The melting ice must have caught the eye of a black-capped chickadee, too, because it flew to a branch directly below one of the dripping icicles. As the drops fell, the chickadee opened its bill and caught each one. What a sight!"

Music with Meaning

Chickadees also are very vocal birds. Named for their alarm notes, "chick-a-dee, dee, dee," they communicate a great deal more with that call than we might realize. New research at the University of Montana has shown that their "dee" calls are filled with information.

Researcher Christopher Templeton discovered that the spacing of the "dees" describes the level of danger from a nearby predator. Large birds of prey, like great horned owls, which don't pose much threat to tiny chickadees, elicited fewer "dees" than did smaller, more maneuverable raptors, like pygmy owls. More "dees" drew a greater group defense of fellow chickadees against the predator.

A totally different black-capped chickadee vocalization is

READER TIP

Another of the black-capped chickadee's many remarkable traits is its tameness. It is so approachable around bird feeders that it may even eat seeds from an outstretched hand.

Alan G. Nelson/Dembinsky Photo Assoc.

Larry Mishkar/Dembinsky Photo Assoc.

HAND IT TO THEM. One of the black-capped chickadee's most remarkable traits is its tameness. These birds are among the easiest species to feed from your hand (left). Summer is a busy time for chickadee parents as they tirelessly work to keep their six to eight hungry young ones fed (above).

the male's courtship song, a sweet and lazy "phee-be" that's used to maintain pair bonds and nesting territories. When I hear the first black-capped chickadee's courtship song in the late winter, I know spring is not far behind.

Pairs of chickadees begin checking out nest sites as early as March, and gather nesting material in April. Barbara Humes of Orcas, Washington inadvertently began providing chickadees with a unique nest material several years ago. It all started when she left an old cotton mop on her porch. Later that day, she noticed a black-capped chickadee inspecting it.

"Glancing around occasionally, the bird removed strings one by one until its bill was full of them," Barbara says. "A few minutes later, it returned to take more fibers. Obviously, the bird was building a nest.

"We've left that old mop on our porch for 3 years now. Each spring, we watch more birds discover the advantages of its soft fibers. And to think that I almost threw it away!"

If you miss the nest-making process, there's another way to determine if black-capped chickadees are raising young nearby. In my southeastern Wisconsin yard, I look for this clue: bedraggled parents.

Keeping six to eight hungry balls of fluff fed is a full-time job, and it takes a toll on the adults. A fresh-looking chickadee at the feeders in summer tells me that it is a juvenile, though otherwise it looks like its parents.

The black-capped is the most common and widespread of the seven species of chickadees in North America. But all are fairly similar in appearance and display many of the same entertaining behaviors.

But don't just take my word for it. Set out a tube feeder of sunflower seeds to attract these little charmers, and you can see for yourself.

Backyard Birding Bio

Common Name: Black-capped chickadee.
Scientific Name: *Poecile atricapilla*.
Length: 5–1/4 inches.
Wingspan: 8 inches.
Distinctive Markings: Gray and buff feathers, bright-black bib and skullcap and white cheeks. Males and females look alike.
Distinctive Behavior: Acrobatic, friendly, curious and will often hang upside down. May become tame at bird feeders, and fly to an outstretched hand for seed.
Habitat: Woodlands, thickets, parks and wooded backyards.
Voice: Contact call is "chick-a-dee, dee, dee." In spring and early summer, the male's courtship song is "phee-be."
Nest: Both male and female dig a natural nesting cavity in dead tree trunks or branches. The nest may be lined with wool, fur, hair, moss or feathers. The six to eight white eggs with reddish-brown spots hatch in 12 to 13 days. They also will nest in old woodpecker holes or birdhouses with a 1-1/4-inch entrance.
Both parents then work to feed the nestlings. Pairs raise only one brood per year.
Diet: Primarily insects, but up to 50 percent of their diet may be plant matter, especially pine seeds.
Backyard Favorite: A tube-style bird feeder containing sunflower seeds, either cracked or in the shell.

■ Year-Round

GREEN THUMB

52

48

FORGET THE MOWING

Minnesota gardener sidelines her lawn mower, opting for lush gardens, ponds and blooming pathways.

By Vivette Botner
Field Editor, Duluth, Minnesota

Amazing! That's what I said the first time I saw Kathy Bomey's garden.

I was taking photos of another backyard nearby when the owner pointed out Kathy's home. Beautiful blooms, abundant shrubs and a picturesque pond covered the entire front yard. That was just the appetizer.

When I walked out back, I was awestruck again. What would have been a carpet of grass at just about any other house in this Duluth neighborhood was another spread of annuals, perennials, ground covers and shrubs.

"I hate to mow," Kathy ex-

DIFFERENT APPROACH. Kathy Bomey (inset) chose ponds (left) and flowers instead of a lawn.

COME SEE WHAT'S BLOOMING. Three snails adorn a colorful welcome sign in Kathy's garden (left)—just don't let these slug relatives eat the nearby hostas! Garden accents like these are a common feature in Kathy's yard. Above, trilliums and lady's slippers are wildflowers that thrive in the shade.

plains. "I started eliminating the lawn when I bought the house nearly 20 years ago."

The process was slow at first, she admits. But her project really got growing when she removed a dilapidated garage from the property.

"There was no way I was going to cover that space with more turf," she says. "I started buying plants that looked interesting and went on garden tours for new ideas."

> *"I'm not sure how I did it all, but I'm glad I did…"*

Today, only a tidbit of lawn is left, a mere 9- by 16-foot strip. The rest of her 75- by 150-foot lot is a complex web of gardens intertwined with paths and ponds.

One Stone at a Time

Rocks help define the rambling beds that blanket the property. Kathy hauled the majority of the stones herself, with some help from her sister-in-law and grandson.

"Every time I went on a trip, I'd bring back rocks for my garden," Kathy says. "Soon, whenever family or friends took vacations, they'd bring home more rocks. Once I had enough to create a flower bed, I'd get to work."

Although Kathy hired landscapers to install a 700-gallon water garden in the front yard, she learned from watching and built a smaller pond in back herself, even adding a waterfall.

"I'm not sure how I did it all, but I'm glad I did," she says with a laugh. "It's so peaceful. I can't imagine not having it."

The water garden in the front yard was nearly destroyed after a harsh winter, but Kathy decided to expand it rather than repair it. She nearly tripled its size to 2,000 gallons and added a 3-foot-high waterfall, a gurgling stream, fish, water lilies and other aquatic plants.

Countless Varieties

When visitors ask Kathy if there's a plant she doesn't have in her yard, she's hard-pressed to answer.

"I have so many," she says. "I planted quite a few varieties of shrubs, from weigelias to barberries, spirea and more. I think the weeping larch in front is one of my favorites. It's so dramatic, with its drooping branches."

To add color after many of the shrubs are finished flowering, Kathy tucks annuals in and around them.

"I particularly like Wave petunias because they'll wind around and up into the bushes, making it look like they're blooming again," Kathy says.

She also relies on lots of pansies, impatiens, marigolds, plus perennials and new favorites—ornamental grasses.

"Perennials, such as daylilies, purple coneflowers and hostas, are part of the mix. And you'll find between eight and 12 different kinds of ornamental grasses. They look interesting all year.

"I also have several container gardens of trilliums and lady's slippers stationed at the south end of the backyard where it's very shady. Those I change each year."

Containers aren't the only items that vary from one summer to the next. Kathy regularly "remodels" sections of her

FLORAL TAPESTRY. Flowers weave a colorful pattern in Kathy's yard (above). Several flower-lined walks (like the one at right) invite visitors to slow down and enjoy the garden, while also allowing easy access for flower bed maintenance.

backyard, moving rocks, plants and garden accents to new locations.

"Once every inch of property was used up, I began looking at the gardens and thinking about what I'd like to do differently. For example, I decided to move some ground cover plants in order to make room for roses, which I haven't grown before."

Ways to Save

To save money, Kathy starts most of her annuals from seed. She also works for a friend who owns a nursery.

"Instead of cash, I get paid in plants," she shares. "Honestly, though, I can't possibly put in enough hours to earn all of the ones I want."

Even though her gardens fade as the weather cools, Kathy still finds ways to keep her green thumb busy.

"I never consider autumn as a time for closing down my gardens for winter," she says. "I prefer to think of it as the season when I start planning for spring."

READER TIP

Landscapers installed the water garden in my front yard. But I learned the process by watching them and then built a smaller pond myself.

—Kathy Bomey, Duluth, Minnesota

GOING BANANAS

With determination, this gardener created a tropical escape in the Northeast.

By Nancy Moffett
Coopersburg, Pennsylvania

GROWING UP. It was the unlikely centerpiece of Jeff Hauck's tropical dream, but the banana (with Jeff, at top) thrived. A variety of vines (above) and other plants complete their paradise.

The Energizer Bunny has nothing on my husband, Jeff Hauck. He has always been interested in gardening, and constantly is adding trees, shrubs and flower beds to our yard. But I had my doubts the year he declared his plans to design a tropical garden near our backyard pool.

This may not sound difficult, except for the fact that we live in the Northeast and have a limited growing season. Nevertheless, Jeff dug into the project with dreams of creating a lush tropical-looking haven.

Planning Paradise

It was a cold day in January when Jeff came home with the first plant for our garden—a Japanese fiber banana (*Musa basjoo*). He bought it because it's supposed to be the hardiest of all bananas and survive in -20° weather when properly mulched. As I looked at the meager plant, however, I was skeptical it would ever make it outside. Shortly after, two of the leaves on the plant died and three more turned brown.

Jeff kept working toward his paradise, though. He searched stacks of seed catalogs and made notes, trying to decide what other plants would add heat to our Pennsylvania version of the tropics. Meanwhile, the banana plant was perking up and slowly growing in the light of one of our windows.

In the spring, Jeff sowed a variety of summer poinsettia (*Amaranthus tricolor*) and vine seeds in a temporary area by our kitchen window. He then built several 6-foot cedar trellises and two raised beds around our pool.

The banana plant, now a proud 20 inches tall, was the first thing to go into the soil. Surrounding it were a mixture of hibiscus, cannas and calla lilies, as well as a sprinkling of annuals like pink and white cleomes and a border of vincas.

In the second bed, Jeff planted Persian shield, verbena and morning glories. By then, the newly sprouted seeds were ready to go. He added the summer poinsettias between the two beds and found spots for the vines—cardinal climber, hyacinth bean, moonflower, love-in-a-puff and Spanish flag—along the homemade trellises.

Backyard Getaway

By midsummer, our tropical fantasy had become a reality. The true highlight was the banana plant. It grew 12 feet tall, and towered above the pool to create the perfect tropical setting. We spent many hours relaxing in the water, soaking up our spectacular view of paradise.

As soon as summer was over, Jeff was already making plans to improve our poolside retreat. He has his eye on an Arizona yucca, which resembles a small palm tree. He thinks it will be the perfect addition to the banana plant.

That's just how Jeff is…he keeps going and going!

THE FLOWER FARM

"Retired" farmers use their talents to produce a colorful crop of blooms.

By Ray Timmons, Holden, Missouri

My wife, Charlotte, and I used to coax crops from the earth on our small farm. When we retired, we could not get growing out of our systems, so we turned our energies to producing floral "crops" instead.

Over the last 15 years, we've created almost every kind of flower bed we could imagine, transforming our 4-acre farmstead into something truly fantastic.

An Annual Event

The first of May is when the real fun begins. That's when we start planting our colorful array of about 5,000 homegrown annuals.

We prefer annuals because they offer more color and a longer bloom period than most perennials. Plus, there are so many different varieties. This makes it easy to change the look of our flower beds from one year to the next.

To save money, we start most of our annuals from seed. We converted an old hog house into a small greenhouse, which creates the perfect conditions for our plants to thrive.

Some of our favorite flowers include marigolds, zinnias, rudbeckia, geraniums, begonias and petunias. We like these varieties for their abundant long-lasting flowers that look tidy with little deadheading.

To keep our flower beds full and vibrant all season, we al-

A BOUNTY OF BEAUTY. Every spring, Ray and Charlotte Timmons (left) plant 5,000 homegrown annuals on their 4-acre farmstead. They also have some unique flower beds, including (from top right) island plantings...an arch...and terraces.

low the volunteer plants that sprout up later in summer to grow. Also, we sow additional seeds a month or so after setting out the original bedding plants.

Bulbs and More

In addition to annuals, many of our beds boast a vibrant collection of spring-flowering bulbs. These harbingers of warmer weather may be more work to plant, but they provide a welcome abundance of showstopping color in an otherwise lifeless post-winter landscape.

One piece of equipment we've found to be a huge back-saver is a drill with a 24-inch bulb auger attachment. These are available at most home and garden stores. By using the auger to dig holes in our hard clay soil, we can easily plant up to 1,000 annuals or bulbs in a single day.

Despite our preference for annuals, we've found a spot for some pretty perennials in our flower beds, too. Purple coneflowers, butterfly weed, balloon flowers, roses, iris, poppy and daylilies all add a dazzling punch of color that we can count on season after season.

We especially like blue perennial salvia, which is hardy and coordinates well with the other colors in the garden. They also reseed themselves and are easy to transplant if it's necessary.

Flower Bed Frenzy

Every year, we add more flower beds to our yard. We've created beds that thrive on islands in the lake we dug ourselves (top right), others bordered with rocks or timbers, and still others on large stair-step terraces (above).

By far, the most unique garden feature is our "hill bed" (see photo above center). A rainbow-shaped flower bed arcs over a small pool with a waterfall and stream, and we planted mandevilla to grow along the graceful curve. We built the 7-foot-wide pool from an old fertilizer tank, which we lined with cedar, and then fashioned the edging and wood arch from treated plywood.

With all the beauty that blooms in our backyard, we enjoy sharing it. Friends and relatives often stop by to fish or paddleboat in the lake while admiring our blooming bounty, and the local garden club has included our yard on their tours.

We guess it proves that our *annuals* have a *perennially* positive effect on people. ◀

LOVE
GROWS A GARDEN

The union of hard work and devotion help this couple create a blooming paradise.

By Edna Manning, Saskatoon, Saskatchewan

NEAT PATHWAYS and colorful flower beds are the signature in Steve and Helen Fosty's yard. Above, stepping-stones accent a bed of lilies. At left, raised beds flank the pergola Steve built. They use their backyard greenhouse to start many of their annuals.

The neatly planted rows of flowers and orderly walkways in Steve and Helen Fosty's Saskatoon, Saskatchewan backyard seem to contradict the couple's relaxed attitude toward gardening.

"We don't spend all winter thinking about what we're going to plant and where," Helen says. "God didn't take time to color-coordinate, He just planted."

"We do the same, and it seems to work out," Steve adds.

The spectacular results—and numerous landscaping awards—speak volumes for their laid-back approach. It's obvious the two enjoy every moment they spend working side by side in the yard.

Helen explains their simple secret as "love and tender care."

A Blank Slate

Neither Steve nor Helen grew up with a gardening background, but when they purchased their property in 1981, their green thumbs grew and blossomed along with their yard.

"The property is large, and we had to do something with it," Steve says.

They removed some trees to open up space, leaving rows of pine and spruce running along two sides and surrounding their greenhouses.

"That first year we started with over 5,000 bedding plants in a single greenhouse," Helen says. "Now we're down to 2,800."

The Fostys prefer annuals because of the large selection, the season-long color, and how simple it is to alter the garden's look from year to year.

Their green thumbs grew and blossomed along with their yard.

One of the striking things about the Fostys' gardening style is the absence of untidy or neglected areas.

For example, in the shady nook under a stand of pines and spruces, Steve constructed two semicircular beds where hostas, ferns and elephant's ears thrive. Begonias and large pots of cannas add color. The bed is a beautiful use of an area that might otherwise be ignored.

Picture-Perfect Pergola

The focal point to the Fostys' yard is a large pergola and patio (photos opposite page) that Steve constructed. About 35 baskets and containers overflow with an assortment of petunias, geraniums and ivy. It is a favorite spot for the Fostys to relax and enjoy the entire yard.

A series of beds around the area feature low-growing annuals such as ageratum, salvia, petunias, gaillardia and pansies, planted among benches, birdbaths, gazing globes and the stepping-stones Steve makes.

Despite their preference for annuals, the couple has recently converted a few beds to perennials.

"We had a landscape designer come in and give us some ideas," Steve says. "We wanted some low-growing shrubs to provide continuous color, yet not block our view of the rest of the garden."

They chose dwarf European cranberrybush viburnum, variegated dogwood (which they plan to keep trimmed), golden spirea, miniature bleeding heart, mugo pine, gold potentilla and Little Princess spirea.

Other areas of their yard now feature a variety of perennials like silver mound, Veronica, juniper, Morden Fireglow

COLOR EVERYWHERE. Containers play a large role in the Fostys' yard. Above, they add instant height to an area. At top, pots brighten the shade without disturbing a tree's roots.

roses, coral bells, lady's mantle and wintergreen.

Near the back of their yard are the greenhouses for growing annuals, and six raised beds, largely for vegetables.

"We started with the raised beds and found they work well for a number of reasons, not the least of which is the ease of upkeep," Steve says.

The soil in raised beds warms up quicker in the spring, giving some plants a head start, he says. They provide better drainage and aeration, and offer more control over the soil conditions. Plus, working in raised beds is easier on the back during planting, weeding and harvesting.

More to See

A description of the Fostys' yard could go on and on. You'll find a small water feature next to the raised rock garden...lush ferns, hostas and colorful containers lining the front walkway...a thriving rose garden...prolific kiwi trees...and an arbor covered with mandevilla and passion flower vines.

It's enough to make passersby want to follow the wooden "Welcome" sign and enter this overflowing backyard retreat that the Fostys have so lovingly created.

"It's good to do these things together," Helen says. "It builds a bond."

Sounds like the "love and tender care" that nurtures their garden, nurtures their marriage as well.

SNIP, PLANT, GROW

Add to your garden without spending a cent.

By Melinda Myers, Contributing Editor

Taking cuttings is a great way to expand—or share—the beauty of any garden. Perhaps you'd like to preserve a flower with family history, increase your collection of favorite blooms or reproduce that hard-to-find plant.

Most gardeners have had success rooting leafy plants like coleus or philodendron. A short stem with leaves will quickly form roots in water, potting mix or vermiculite—and then you are well on your way to a full-sized plant.

The same does not hold true for trees and shrubs, however. With these plants, you'll need to pay more attention to timing and the type of cutting you take. And these factors will vary depending on the type of plant.

But with a little know-how, you'll soon be able to grow cuttings of plants like roses, lilacs, forsythias and spireas. The extra effort will be worth it.

Pay Attention to Patents

Before you take a cutting of that fancy new rose (like the one at right) or lilac, it's important to understand some of the laws of the plant world.

Many new varieties are patented. This means you cannot take a cutting from an existing plant to start a new one without the permission of the patent owner. This right is reserved for the company that spent time and money developing the new or unusual variety. If this is the case, a close look at the tag or growing information will reveal a patent number or note that the patent is pending.

Patents are good for about 20 years. After that, you are free to take cuttings and start your own plants. Although it may seem like an inconvenience, remember that respecting the patents helps support those who work to introduce new plants for us to enjoy.

When checking the tag, you also may see ® or ™ symbols. You can take cuttings and plant these varieties in your garden, as long as they are not patented.

If all this sounds too confusing, don't be intimidated. There are plenty of old family favorites and traditional garden beauties that aren't protected—and these make great candidates to grow from cuttings.

Getting Started

There are several types of cuttings you can use to propogate new trees and shrubs.

Hardwood cuttings are the key to starting plants like roses, forsythia, privet, olive, wisteria, spirea, hemlock and many other deciduous and needled trees and shrubs.

During the dormant season, which is late fall or winter, remove a 4- to 8-inch stem piece of the previous season's growth that contains two nodes—the place where leaves attach (see top right photo). Pack the cuttings in peat moss or sawdust and store them in a cool dark place until spring. As the weather warms, stick the cuttings—with the end that was closest to the roots down—in a flat of moist vermiculite, perlite or sand (see lower right photo). To increase the success for these types of cuttings, or any others, dip the end in rooting hormone first.

Summer is the time to take semihardwood cuttings—the new growth that's starting to harden up and mature. This works for varieties like holly, azaleas, pittosporum, euonymus, citrus, olive and other broadleaf evergreens and deciduous trees and shrubs.

Take 3- to 6-inch cuttings in the morning when the stems are firm and full of moisture. Remove the lower leaves and cut the remaining leaves in half to reduce moisture loss.

Then root semihardwood cuttings in moist vermiculite, perlite or sand in a shaded and humid location. Loosely cover the container with plastic to increase the humidity and monitor the temperature to prevent overheating.

Softwood cuttings from tender new growth are another way to propogate plants like lilacs, roses, forsythias, magnolias, weigela, spireas and fruit trees.

Take 3- to 5-inch cuttings early in the day and plant them right away for the best results. Root in a warm and moist rooting medium in a humid location that's out of direct sun (like in a cold frame).

No matter what kind of cuttings you're using, once they've rooted, you can treat them like bare-root plants and add them to your garden. Or, move them to a large container filled with well-draining potting mix. This allows the plants to develop stronger root systems before transplanting.

As you begin trying to grow trees and shrubs from cuttings, I do have some last words of wisdom: Professionals often spend years perfecting this process, so don't be disappointed if your cuttings don't root right away. Just keep trying!

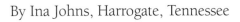

GROWING
IN CIRCLES

Gardener rounds up a lush new look for her once-barren backyard.

By Ina Johns, Harrogate, Tennessee

A small flower bed for irises and a few other perennials...that's what I had in mind when I decided to give gardening a try back in 1996. Little did I know that some 9 years later, I'd have a bounty of blooming beds all over our 1-acre backyard!

I've always loved flowers, but my only green-thumb activity after moving into our home in 1978 was planting a few marigolds, impatiens and geraniums next to the house. Still, I knew our expanse of half-dead grass lined with trees needed something.

My answer was to create a simple circular patch of irises

BLOOMS AROUND EVERY BEND. Ina Johns (above inset) created bright, curving flower beds that wind through her yard (top).

flanked by daisies, veronica, yarrow, phlox and purple coneflowers. The experience, from start to finish, was so gratifying that I couldn't wait to do it again.

You could say I've been gardening in circles ever since. A glance at our yard reveals that none of my beds have straight edges. All of the new gardens I've created are either round or oval.

The reason for this consistency is simple: To plan a new flower bed, I don't pull out paper and pencil or stakes and twine, I place a garden hose on the lawn in a pleasing shape. That way, I wind up with a gently curving outline. Then I etch out the edges with a shovel before my husband, Bill, uses the tractor to dig up the grass and add compost.

Learn from Mistakes

Nowadays, I generally have an idea what kind of flowers I want to plant in a new flower bed. But when I started, I'd go to the garden center and pick out whatever caught my eye.

After a few failures, I began to pay more attention to the conditions each plant preferred. I also started primarily focusing on perennials, both for their beauty and the fact that they come back year after year. I love that many varieties are

MANY HAPPY RETURNS. Pretty perennials and birdhouses dominate Ina's garden. Above: Purple coneflowers, ornamental grasses and sunflowers surround a birdhouse. Others like daylilies, lambs' ears and coreopsis (below) spread each year.

self-sowing and will spread throughout the garden with little effort from me.

I don't completely ignore annuals, however. I like to add them here and there for extra color, especially sunflowers, lantanas and petunias. I've learned to save the seeds and use them to start plants for the following growing season.

For the past several years, cultivating daylilies has become a passion. I love these easy-care flowers that provide pretty blooms from summer to fall. To date, I have planted over 125 daylilies, with plans to add even more.

Ornamental grasses have also caught my fancy. They add a sense of peacefulness to my gardens and seem to almost sing in the wind.

Another hobby of mine, thanks to my 19-year-old daughter, Ashley, is raising flowers and plants that attract butterflies and provide spots for these "flying flowers" to lay their eggs.

When Ashley was young, she used to collect caterpillars and care for them until they turned into butterflies. She got me interested back then, and today we have a patch of milkweed, which monarchs lay eggs on, as well as dill to attract black swallowtails. We wait in anticipation each year for caterpillars to emerge and watch them transform.

Character Building

My 27-year-old son, Shawn, contributes to my gardening efforts as well. He likes to build birdhouses out of old barn wood and perch them on posts in the midst of the flowers. He has also crafted wooden tepees for growing vines and rustic wheelbarrows that add so much character to our yard.

I like to make things for the garden, too, like wind chimes using old silverware. I've even fashioned one from dog tags and car gears and another by tying kitchen utensils to a tin teapot.

Probably the most interesting decoration that graces our yard is the old outhouse from my mother's place. I use it to store tools and display antiques. It's a real conversation piece.

One of the things I enjoy about our yard is that it constantly inspires new ideas. I know I started with a small plan, but now I just can't contain myself.

Every morning, I wake up knowing something different is waiting to be discovered. I guess you could say gardening is a never-ending joy that feeds my soul.

HER GARDEN
GROWS IN PERFECT HARMONY

By Judy Hominick, Dallas, Texas

Carolyn Bush is in perfect tune with her garden. You could say she's conducting a blooming symphony out her back door in Dallas, Texas, thanks to musical roots that have fed a growing love for gardening.

It all started when her interest in collecting stringed instruments from flea markets took a new twist. She spied an old tuba and had to add it to the mix.

"There was something about the shape of a tuba that made me think of flowers," says Carolyn, who planted the huge instrument in her garden out of necessity. "There was no room for it inside the house, so I put it outside. It kind of grew from there."

Soon a trombone found its way into another flower bed, standing tall among a

---

Gardening is a lot like music because nothing is ever static.

---

group of bush honeysuckle. When a small pond was added, a second tuba appeared, plus a bugle rising from the water next to a lizard's tail plant and Texas star hibiscus.

Working in Concert

Now, 15 musical instruments have taken root among nearly 200 different plants and trees in her yard. It's even certified as a Texas Wildscape Backyard Wildlife Habitat and as a Butterfly Habitat.

Music has always been a part of Carolyn's life…long before she thought of taking up gardening. Her father, a musician, planted that seed early on. And her mother, an organist, fertilized Carolyn's continued musical interests.

"I grew up with music", says Carolyn, who earned her certification as a Master Gardener in 2000. "Gardening is a lot like music because nothing is ever static. The seasons change, we try new plants that may or may not make it and continue to learn new things. It's another wonderful outlet for being creative."

For many years, Carolyn raised vegetables in her backyard until a cedar elm grew so large it began to cast some serious shade. Not that it mattered to this sentimental gardener…the lovely tree grew enough to be designated cochampion in the Texas Big Tree Registry.

But the additional shade forced Carolyn to make the tran-

BRASS AND BLOOMS. Carolyn Bush (inset, left) has assembled a band of instruments as unique additions in her Texas garden. Clockwise from left: Virginia creeper and impatiens surround a trio of clarinets…a solo tuba accents containers of impatiens…ferns and a saxophone work together in harmony.

No. 1 Green Thumb

sition from sunny to woodland backyard. She decided it was time for her yard to take on a more natural look.

Shrubs like the blue-berried mahonia, oakleaf hydrangea and strawberry bush helped anchor the garden. Turk's cap lily, obedient plant, St. John's wort and other shade-loving perennials started filling in the woodland setting. It wasn't long before birds, squirrels, butterflies, raccoons and possums were drawn to this peaceful retreat punctuated by retired instruments.

Carolyn designed the large garden with wandering in mind. Visitors are pleasantly surprised when they come upon a stand of clarinets forming a tepee beside purple coneflower. Accompanying a French horn are fall-blooming oxblood lilies, while wood fern plays a duet with a saxophone.

Carolyn's garden soon became a magnet for a young friend, Christin Colden, who, as a child was so drawn to the magical yard, that she adopted it as her secret garden.

Christin, now 16, fondly recalls those carefree days spent

acting out *Swan Lake* and the *Nutcracker*, with the enchanted instruments each playing a part.

"I used to spend hours there," says Christin. "I got involved with band partly because I loved the instruments in Carolyn's yard. Being there is like an old friend giving you a hug."

Like the roots of her many perennials, Carolyn's love of gardening and the arts has also spread to Christin's yard.

"A few years ago, Christin dug her own pond and surrounded it with gardens," reports Carolyn. "I like to think that perhaps my garden helped inspire her."

Carolyn continues to fine-tune her native and perennial plantings. They constantly change with the seasons, offering subtle shades of green in spring, occasional blooms in summer and stunning fall color. Together, they're a perfect melody.

And, with a bit of imagination, you can almost hear the strains of long-ago concerts blowing in the breeze.

Chapter 2

Bring It to the Table

This small-space, no-bend gardening method is just what the doctor ordered.

By Reilly Maginn, Daphne, Alabama

BEDSIDE MANNER. Reilly Maginn (left), a retired doctor, now cares for plants. His tabletop garden yields colorful and tasty results without bending or kneeling.

No doubt about it—downsizing to an apartment or condominium can seem like the end of gardening. After all, how can you raise bumper crops of veggies or armfuls of flowers without a sizable plot of soil?

Before you table all of your garden efforts, however, consider this—you can create a flourishing patch on top of a table just outside your back door. I like to call this method tabletop gardening, and it's truly amazing how much a 3-foot-square garden can yield!

What's more, this type of gardening is great for those of us who are white of hair and less than limber. Why? Because you no longer need to bend, kneel or squat. You can do all your green-thumb work in a comfortable and strain-free seated position (that's the retired doctor in me talking).

Don't Contain Yourself

So let's get started! First, you'll need a sturdy table that can hold about 50 pounds. Stay away from card tables—they may collapse under such weight.

You'll also need to gather containers to fit on top of your table. I often use old wooden ammunition boxes I find at an Army surplus store. They're a good size and already have open cracks in the bottom for drainage. Any kind of wooden box—or other container—will do, of course. Just check for drainage holes. If the container doesn't have any, drill your own.

Potting soil, a trowel, a watering can or bucket and a few dollar's worth of seeds are the only other tools necessary.

There's no call for shovels, rakes, hoes or wheelbarrows. And you won't have to spend hours in the hot sun weeding, hoeing or thinning plants. Only minimal upkeep is needed, and garden pests are the exception rather than the rule.

That means no dirty knees, aching back or sweaty blistered palms. It might sound too easy, but it's true—and tabletop gardening is fun!

Time to Sow

I like to place my table in a sunny spot that I walk past regularly, so it's easy to check the garden boxes. I fill my boxes with potting mix, dampen the mix and make shallow depressions about every 4 inches. Then I place a single seed in each depression and cover with a bit more mix.

For me, a square foot section yields about 16 plants—such as radishes, lettuce, beets or carrots—in a few short weeks. This is plenty of produce for a twosome to enjoy.

I train climbers like cucumbers and beans to grow up small wooden trellises nailed to the back of a box (see photo above center). Broccoli, tomatoes and other larger veggies still fit into the boxes as well. Devote a square foot of space to each plant.

If you'd rather raise flowers, these boxes will work, too. I've had a lot of success with zinnias and other small annuals, as well as herbs of all kinds.

The key to success is keeping it small. Believe me, tabletop gardening is easy, stress-free and affordable. Give it a try—I know you'll like it!

A WARM WELCOME

Pennsylvania couple happily shares their garden with visitors.

By Patrick Brezler, Waynesboro, Pennsylvania

Merle and Beulah Cordell don't want your money. This former farm couple graciously opens their garden to the public without asking for anything in return.

On average, more than 2,000 visitors stop by every year. Even tour buses have been known to make the drive down Grindstone Hill Road to their home just outside of Greencastle, Pennsylvania to see the spectacular flowers.

"We've had people come from England, Canada, California and almost every part of the eastern states," Beulah says. "There have also been visitors from Poland and Puerto Rico."

Merle loves checking the guest book that visitors sign and admits his favorite part of having the garden is the people it brings.

COME ON IN.
Merle and Beulah Cordell (left inset) believe in sharing. With a simple welcome sign (at right), they invite people in to tour their immense garden.

PLEASE SIGN
GUEST BOOK IN
THE MAILBOX

Their country road, which once saw the daily arrival of a milk truck, now greets visitors with a wall of beautiful colors. Massive hollyhocks, rose of Sharon shrubs and bee balm create a bold entryway and serve as a daily feast for bees and butterflies.

As you approach their farmstead, you'll see far more flowers than you would have imagined. The real showstoppers are red canna lilies (next page). These tall plants can reach 6 feet or more. The Cordells plant 18 varieties of the statuesque flowers—which they chose for their eye-catching nature.

"They're the showiest and they bloom from July to frost," Beulah says.

But there is a catch. Cannas are a tropical and subtropical species that don't survive winters in the North. That means the Cordells must dig up the rhizomes every year and care-

VIBRANT GREETING. The signature plants in the couple's garden are canna lilies (above, with marigolds and scarlet sage). They plant over 1,000 of them every year. Then they dig up the rhizomes to store them indoors over the winter.

fully store them over winter—a task that isn't easy on the back. Merle estimates they dig up and preserve 1,000 cannas every autumn to replant in spring.

Years in the Making

Adding cannas isn't the only change the couple has made since they purchased the farm in 1964. When they moved in, the only thing in the front yard was a tree stump with three hosta plants growing around it. Over time, they've created more than 50 flower beds that are are now scattered across the acre of land surrounding their house.

Beulah started gardening in the early years of their marriage. She raised four children, and Merle worked as a farmer, minister and geography teacher. But she still wanted an activity for her spare time. Gardening was the perfect fit.

"My husband was on the road a lot as a minister, so it gave me something to do," Beulah says.

She is quick to tell you that her favorites are the daylilies— a carefree bloomer. She gave up on roses early on because they required too much care.

Annual Display

A sea of annuals surrounds the sidewalk leading up to the Cordells' home. Beulah plants dozens of flats every year to form a colorful collage of marigolds, scarlet sage, impatiens and petunias, to name a few.

But that's only the preview to the main show on their expansive porch. It holds pot after pot of massive geraniums, a collection Beulah started when they first married.

"After years of trading plants with friends, I have just about every color," she says.

A local farmer gives Beulah the pots for her geraniums, and they never go unfilled. She jokes that she needs a bigger porch, but admits she would use the space to pack in more plants.

Times have changed for Merle and Beulah, but they are still young at heart. After 30 years of traveling around the country on a motorcycle, their daughter convinced them to trade it in for a safer mode of transportation. When the couple isn't in their garden, you might find them zipping around in a two-seater sports car.

As lifelong farmers, Merle and Beulah are accustomed to hard work. Even though they have sold the cows, it's obvious the two aren't ready to accept a rocking-chair way of life...you need only look at their garden for proof.

Editor's Note: *To visit the Cordells' garden, see the directions and map in the "Blooms" section at www.birdsandblooms. com.*

THE HEALING GARDEN

This couple's restful retreat grows strong hearts and spirits.

By Hilde Lange, Field Editor, Axtell, Nebraska

Sometimes, the answer to a prayer is just outside your back door. That's what Harriett and Doug McFeely (above inset) discovered years after they purchased 2-1/2 acres of cow pasture in Hastings, Nebraska.

They didn't know then that their unassuming plot of land would one day bring inspiration to others.

Now a beautiful garden called Country Meadows, the property is open to hundreds of visitors year-round. Many find the lush oasis the perfect backdrop for special occasions, while others come seeking solace.

It's also a godsend to Harriett, who had hoped for a way to stay home and take care of her aging mother. It was only after a few strangers came knocking on her door, asking to use the garden for a reunion and a wedding, that she realized her prayers had been answered...and a home business was born.

Blessed Bounty

Although Harriett humbly admits she's not a professional gardener, it's obvious she has one mighty green thumb. Years of hard work have transformed this once plain pasture into a garden thriving with yuccas, hostas, barberries, evergreens and many others.

There's also plenty of water. A 100-foot stream, two waterfalls and two ponds teeming with koi are inviting additions to the tranquil surroundings.

But it's the Three Trees Miracle Garden that's possibly the most captivating spot in the yard. It was inspired by garden visitors who have shared stories of how miracles have touched their lives.

A welcoming path leads guests to a grove of trees, where an arbor, pond and benches beckon. Harriett also records the stories, and sets out a plant and commemorative stone for each one.

A small chapel rests in the center of the garden. Bought at auction for $100, the old building was in dire need of repair. Formerly a farm summer kitchen, Harriett, with the help of a few friends and a volunteer carpenter, transformed it into the ideal place for reflection.

Personal Details

Everywhere you look, Harriett's garden is dedicated to friends and causes in her life.

A small rock garden, marked with a sign reading "Cody County," is a memorial to her famous cousin, U.S. scout Buffalo Bill Cody. The rocks are from Lookout Mountain in Colorado, where Bill and his wife are buried.

There's the Mothers Against Drunk Driving Memorial Garden, and a special Kids' Garden that's cared for by children with developmental disabilities.

Finally, a large broken fountain—a gift from a local group home—decorates the landscape. Although visitors often ask about it, Harriett has no plans to repair the fountain.

Instead, she says it's a reminder that we all may be "broken" in some way, but nature has the power to bring us peace, especially in places like Harriett's healing garden.

Faith Bemiss

PUT YOUR SOIL TO THE TEST

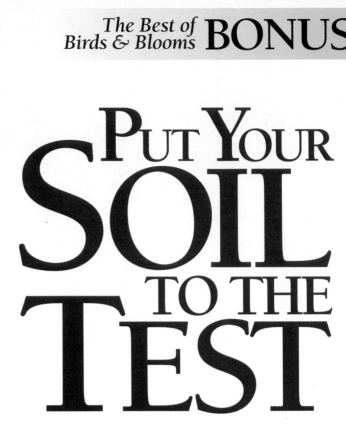

Here's how to get the "dirt" on your dirt.

By Melinda Myers, Contributing Editor

Even on my little city lot, the soil isn't consistent. Some areas are clay, some are loam and others are gritty and well-draining. Then there's that "mystery spot." I suspect it was once used to dispose of ashes, bottles and other debris.

All this variability in just one tiny lot. How can a home owner be sure they're doing the right thing when adding fertilizer and other amendments to their backyard soil?

The answer is simple—take a test. A soil test, that is. I promise, you won't even have to study.

The results from this simple lab analysis will take the guesswork out of what nutrients should be added to your backyard gardens and lawn.

"Soil tests may take a little time and cost a little money, but it's not a large expense compared to the amount of fertilizer you put on that may not be needed," says Sherry Combs, director of the Soil and Plant Analysis Lab at the University of Wisconsin in Madison.

Costs for soil tests vary depending on where you're located in the country, but you should basically get the information you need for around $15 for each test.

For your time and expense, you'll receive printed information that takes the mystery out of fertilizing. The recommendations save you time and money because you'll only add the nutrients your plants need.

Start from the Beginning

Your first task is to find a soil lab that's "state certified." That way, you know you'll receive accurate results.

Many states provide a public lab through their county Extension Service. If this isn't available in your area, check under "soil testing" in the yellow pages.

Soil tests can be taken any time, except when the ground is frozen. Sherry recommends jotting a note on the calendar to test in fall.

"That's when the soil is somewhat drier, which gives a longer window to take the samples," she says. "Spring samples usually are pretty wet, making turnaround time even longer because the soil has to dry out first before it can be tested.

"Plus, that's when the labs are busiest...gardeners are anxious to get results and into the garden."

Another time to soil test is when you're planning a new garden or landscape. Also, if your current gardens are looking sickly or just aren't as vibrant as they used to be, a soil test helps pinpoint any nutrient deficiencies.

"It's best to conduct several soil tests in a yard," Sherry says. "Because the front, backyard and gardens are used differently, separate tests should be conducted in each area."

It's especially important to conduct separate tests for problem areas in a yard.

Only as Good as Your Sample

The most critical step in soil analysis is in the sampling process.

"It's the most important part," Sherry says. "We recommend you take at least five samples from each area of the yard you're having tested." (See illustration above right.)

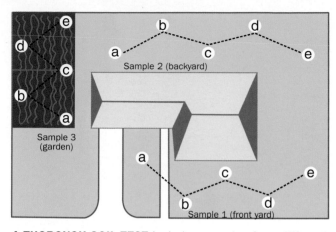

A THOROUGH SOIL TEST includes samples from different parts of a yard. Five samples (labeled a-e) are mixed from each area. This gives an "average" soil sample for each location.

A simple hand trowel works fine. Simply brush away any mulch or debris and take a slice of soil, starting at the surface, down to about 6 inches below ground level.

Collect several samples from the area being tested. Mix them in a clean bucket and let the soil dry for several days. Besides reducing the time it takes to analyze the soil, drying the soil first lightens the mailing load and costs.

Once in the mail (be sure to follow instructions carefully), enjoy your window of relaxation because when the test results are returned, you'll most likely want to immediately "dig in" and put them to use.

The results tell you everything you need to know about your soil, from its texture and pH levels to the nutrients it contains, plus the recommendations to improve it.

While soil testing is scientific, it really isn't daunting when you have the experts on your side. They'll give you the results and you'll reap the benefits of less work, less money spent and gardens that are noticeably more lush and productive. ✒

The Answers to a Soil Test

WHAT CAN YOU EXPECT when you send soil in for laboratory testing? The results include a whole lot of information on what your soil already contains and recommendations for improving it. Here are some typical factors that soil tests measure:

■ **Organic matter**—Organic matter, such as fallen leaves and decaying plant roots, influences water retention, provides some nutrients and feeds worms, insects and microorganisms that help improve the soil structure. Ideal soils contain about 5% organic matter.

It takes time to alter the level of organic mat-

ter in your soil because 100 pounds of organic material breaks down to 10 pounds the first year and only 1 pound the second year.

■ **Soil pH**—This tells you if your soil is acid, neutral or alkaline. It's also difficult to change. Though the difference in numbers may be small, it takes huge amounts of energy and materials to change them. Lime raises the pH in acid soils and sulfur lowers pH in alkaline soils. Don't add either without a soil test.

■ **Nitrogen**—Plants use nitrogen for growth.

Nitrogen dissipates through the soil quickly and is usually added regularly. Too much, however, isn't a good thing. It leads to thick green growth, fewer flowers and may damage your plants.

■ **Phosphorous and potassium**—Plants use these nutrients in smaller amounts. Unlike nitrogen, these move slowly through the soil. The test will tell how much to add, if any.

■ **Soluble salts**—This measurement reflects the amount of soluble chemicals, such as sodium, in the soil. A high level indicates over-fertilization, exposure to deicing salts or soils that are naturally rich in these chemicals.

■ **Calcium, magnesium and sulfur**—Many soils have adequate levels of all three, and some labs will test for them only if a deficiency is suspected.

RP Photo

87

74

76

70

Chapter 3

BACKYARD BIRD HAVEN

IT'S FOR THE BIRDS

This tree-filled yard tempts all types of feathered friends.

Chapter 3

A REAL TREE PARTY. It all started with a few trees—and turned into a backyard worthy of a celebration. Opposite page: Danny and Lisa's private "park" invites you to take a stroll. This page, clockwise from above: A cedar waxwing finds a backyard perch...Lisa spots a tiger swallowtail on a butterfly bush... a homemade fountain provides a place for birds to bathe.

Four-hundred pounds of birdseed is a lot to go through in one winter—even for nature lovers like Danny and Lisa Reed.

The couple always stocks six feeders to satisfy the hundreds of birds that flock to their tree- and flower-packed backyard in Hays, North Carolina.

But even Danny was amazed last winter when he realized just how much the birds had eaten.

"I counted the empty bags and I checked the receipts, and I just thought, *Wow*," he says.

"Wow" is exactly the word most people would use to describe the Reeds' 2-acre yard.

In the past 9 years, the industrious pair has planted hundreds of trees and flowers, converted their garage into a sunroom, and created their own backyard park (above left), complete with classic wood benches, a rock fountain and a jasmine-covered trellis.

Danny and Lisa love their private paradise—and so do the local finches, bluebirds, robins, hummingbirds, doves and wrens, many of which raise two broods or more in each of the couple's 20 birdhouses and surrounding trees.

"My wife and I are both from mountain areas, so we've

always had a soft spot for wild critters," Danny says. "We wanted our yard to be livable for us and for the animals and birds.

"It turned out great."

Trees for Two

When the Reeds first moved into their white ranch home, their yard had only three trees: a weeping willow, a poplar and a maple.

They kicked off their outdoor makeover by planting lines of Leland cypresses on both sides of their house, then enclosing the area by joining the two rows with a backyard slat-wood fence.

Since then, they have filled their lot with crape myrtles, weeping cherries, maples, apple and mimosa trees, English ivy and more.

From their plant-packed sunroom, the couple can look to their front yard—where the main attraction is a Yoshina cherry tree circled with mums, evening primrose and other blooms—or head out back for a stroll through their self-made park sectioned off by a split-rail fence.

Their yard also boasts an arbor with a swing, a miniature

READER TIP

Don't overlook trees if you're trying to find plants to attract hummingbirds. These tiny fliers love the sweet blooms of the mimosa trees in our backyard.
—**Danny and Lisa Reed, Hays, North Carolina**

windmill, several wooden wells, a banana plant that's taller than Danny…even a small vegetable garden, which they pack with tomatoes, potatoes and gourds (above).

"I told Lisa each thing I added to the yard would mean less grass I had to cut," Danny jokes.

But all joking aside, this pair truly works with Mother Nature in mind.

Danny compliments Lisa on her gentle touch with the flowers and genuine love for all living creatures. Lisa says she and Danny work together in the garden—and relax together in its beauty.

"A lot of evenings we'll just take a walk around the yard to look at what's blooming," she says.

Winter, Spring, Summer or Fall…

Danny and Lisa also love watching the wildlife that gathers in their yard. Hummingbirds feed on their mimosas and fight for spots on the feeders, and a couple of doves "practically live here," Danny adds.

"This year we're lucky enough to have a family of cedar waxwings, the type that look like they're wearing a mask," he says. "The tips of their tails are so yellow, just like they've been dipped in a can of paint."

Besides birds, the Reeds' plant display attracts butterflies and some four-legged creatures as well. Lisa says she loves to be outside with the wildlife, especially in spring.

She also loves summer, when she can bask in the heat of the North Carolina sun. Danny says he prefers fall.

It may not make their list of favorite seasons, but when winter approaches, at least one thing is certain: This couple better start stocking up on birdseed.

BATTLING BULLY BIRDS

By George Harrison, Contributing Editor

Photos: George Harrison

For those of us who feed birds, there's nothing more frustrating than a flock of so-called bully birds descending on our backyard feeders.

Not only do they eat the feeders clean in minutes, but their aggressive behavior also can discourage some of our favorite songbirds.

That's why controlling these species is one of the most common concerns among many *Birds & Blooms* readers.

For example, reader Georgia Wacker of Canton, Ohio wrote to ask for a solution to keep blackbirds and grackles from pillaging her bird feeders. And in Steger, Illinois, Mrs. Joseph Kraus says an invading swarm of house sparrows is eating her out of house and home.

European starlings are ruffling Wayne Taylor's feathers. These non-native birds are frightening away more desirable species from his Bethlehem, Pennsylvania yard.

Bully birds include blackbirds, grackles (above left), pigeons, European starlings (above center with red-bellied woodpecker) and house sparrows. The last three are non-native species and are not protected by law.

These hungry avian invaders are often attracted to a yard by the cheap wild birdseed mix or suet that's made available on the ground or in easy-access feeders.

If you're one of the people frustrated by the behavior of bully birds in your backyard, don't give up the fight. Here are some solutions that will help you keep these pest birds at bay, so you can continue feeding the birds you love.

■ **Lock Them Out.** Because virtually all bully birds are larger than more desirable birds, you can adapt your feeders to accommodate only smaller species.

Try enclosing the feeders with large-mesh hardware cloth or chicken wire with openings big enough to allow smaller birds to pass through (a 2-inch opening should do). This will exclude the large bully birds. You can also purchase caged-in tube or tray feeders at your local bird, hardware or garden store (like the feeder above with an American goldfinch). Just be sure to get one with the feeder portion located several inches inside the cage, so bullies can't reach the seed from the outside with their long bills.

■ **Outwit Starlings.** European starlings have a fondness for suet and often take over the feeders. Next time they're at your feeder, foil them by hanging the suet up and under a domed squirrel baffle.

Starlings are reluctant to go underneath any kind of cover and usually will avoid the hard-to-reach meal. A special starling-proof feeder, in which the suet can be eaten only from underneath, is also available in bird stores.

■ **Keep It Clean.** Some backyard birders have the greatest problems with bully birds that eat the cast-off seeds below hanging and post feeders. Pigeons are notorious for gathering in flocks underneath feeders for their meals.

The solution for this problem is to collect the fallen seeds in a deep container, such as a plastic garbage can or pail, that the pest birds cannot or will not get into. You can make a hole in the center of the container and place it right on your feeder pole.

■ **Feed Favorites.** Selective feeding is another way to control the kinds of birds that pillage feeders. Generally, bully birds prefer bread, corn, millet, wheat and sunflower seeds. To get rid of them, supply food they won't eat.

To feed finches, fill hanging tube feeders with only nyjer seed (thistle). For cardinals, chickadees and nuthatches, provide safflower seed in hopper or tray feeders.

If you do this, grackles, crows and blackbirds generally will look elsewhere for the foods they like. ✎

SETTING THE TABLE

Transform your yard into a bird haven with these tips from readers.

Easy Log Feeder

THIS PINE log peanut feeder (at right) is a favorite with our red-bellied, downy and hairy woodpeckers. Even better, it's a cinch to make!

Cut an 8-inch length of a small pine log (mine was 3-1/2 inches in diameter). Using a 1-inch spade bit, drill a series of 1-inch-deep holes around the log at roughly a 45-degree angle. Then fill each hole with peanuts, suet or your favorite combination of ingredients.

A few inches from the top of the log, drill a 1/4-inch hole through the log and thread it with a piece of 16-gauge galvanized wire, twisting it together at the ends to form a hanger.
—*Stefan Delloff, Pequannock, New Jersey*

A Grape Idea

WE LEARNED a while back that oranges could attract whole flocks of orioles, but our newest find is grape jelly!

We've observed the orioles eating this for several weeks, so we know they love it. In fact, most of them now go directly to the jelly and completely ignore the sugar-water mixture we provide.
—*Joe and Sharon Heynoski*
Erie, Pennsylvania

Birds of a Feather

DURING nesting season, I buy several packages of feathers from a craft store and scatter bright and drab colors alike under my maple tree. Within minutes, the sparrows arrive, pick them up and fly off to add the feathers to their nests.

The birds return time and again until all the feathers are gone—which only takes about 30 minutes. I've seen as many as 10 birds at a time bickering over the feathers.

I also put out bits of string, yarn, dog hair and slender strips of packing paper. They always use it all.
—*Carolann Lucente, Beavercreek, Ohio*

Strike Up the Band

WITH A LITTLE IMAGINATION, it seems almost anything can be transformed into a bird feeder.

When a friend was going to throw out a set of cymbals, my husband asked if he could have them. Placing one a few inches above the other (see photo above), he threaded the cymbals onto a steel rod. A nut above and below each one helped stabilize the feeder.

Now that we've filled it with sunflower seed, it's "drummed" up a lot of attention.
—*Audrey Kalivoda-Sanders*
Fairview, Tennessee

Snowman Serves Seed

WHEN MY TOWN was socked with 11 inches of snow, I came up with a fun way to feed the birds. I built a snowman with the usual details—scarf, earmuffs, derby and a carrot nose. Then I made arms from the stems of dried coneflowers and filled the top of its hat with birdseed.

A few days later, I was delighted to spy a chickadee pulling at seeds in the coneflower arms, while another nabbed food from the snowman's cap.
—*Lori Qualls*
Midland, Michigan

Sprouting a Birdbath

RHUBARB PLANTS provide the template for these colorful birdbaths (below). To make one, I curved a rhubarb leaf

over a mound of sand (to give it a nice shape), then covered the leaf with Quikrete Vinyl Concrete Patcher and allowed it to dry.

Then I turned the leaf over and carefully submerged it in water, soaking until the leaf tissues softened. Using a soft brush, I removed the remaining leaf membrane, digging it out in a few spots with a small pointed tool.

Once the leaf was completely dry, I was ready to paint. I used brightly colored craft paints and then added a coat of clear varnish, but you could seal it with polyurethane instead. If you use outdoor paint, and you can skip the sealing step entirely.

These rhubarb-leaf birdbaths are so much fun to make, and you can decorate them however you wish. I made 10 to give to friends as gifts. —*Yarda Ervin, Lansing, Michigan*

Fruitful Solution

WHEN WE MOVED to our home in the country, we decided to try to attract Baltimore orioles—something we'd never been able to do when we lived in the city.

My husband, John, built a "fruit table" to hold the sweet treats we knew would attract orioles and stationed it at the perfect vantage point in our yard.

As you can see from our photos (right), we were richly rewarded for our persistence. Not only did a flock of orioles fly in to enjoy the feast, but a male scarlet tanager (center) and a male rose-breasted grosbeak (bottom) also stopped by for a bite. The birds munched on our offerings of grape jelly, oranges, grapes and watermelon.

Thankfully, our brother-in-law, who loves to take pictures, happened to be visiting and captured these colorful sights on film. —*Linda Wysocki, Coal City, Illinois*

Hummingbird Beacon

YOU COULD SAY I roll out the red carpet for hummingbirds. I set a red plastic tablecloth in the yard to catch the attention of migrating hummers, so they know they should investigate. I anchor it with flowerpots at each corner, then drive in a tall metal garden stake to hold a hummingbird feeder.

You can find a red plastic tablecloth at a party store, but an old red oilcloth or a dyed bedsheet would work, too. Just find a spot that's clearly visible to birds flying above the treetops.

This trick brings many hummingbirds our way. In fall, we've had as many as 40 of them swarming our feeders as they make pit stops during their migration to warmer climates. —*Anne Speers, Conroe, Texas*

Ice Idea

WE'VE BEEN MAKING our own suet for years. The only difficulty was finding the right containers so we could freeze it in a size that fit our various suet holders.

That all changed when I worked on a craft project using ice cube trays. It dawned on me that the trays would make great containers for freezing suet.

The suet cubes pop right out, and it's easy to remove only the number you need. Plus, the cubes fit any size feeder, and the trays stack neatly without taking up a lot of space.

To make suet, I simply melt 2 cups of shortening and 2 cups of crunchy peanut butter in a saucepan over medium heat. While that's cooking, I mix together 4 cups of yellow cornmeal, 1 cup of sugar and 2 cups each of flour, nyjer (thistle) and instant oats in a large bowl.

I stir in the melted mixture, then spoon it into the trays and pop them in the freezer. That's all it takes to make six to seven trays of suet. —*Jerry and Kathy Hitzemann Everett, Washington*

Sugar-Water Shortcut

IN SUMMER, I have to fill my five large hummingbird feeders daily in order to keep up with the big appetites of these petite birds. And that means boiling up a lot of sugar water for the broad-tailed, rufous and occasional black-chinned hummers that visit us.

In order to cut down on the work and leave room in the refrigerator for our food, I now make a syrup with a one-to-one ratio of water and sugar. When I fill the feeders, I simply mix a cup of the syrup with 3 cups of water (to get the four-to-one ratio of water to sugar). It works great.

—*Carole Miller, Meeker, Colorado*

Bluebird Buffet

WE REMODELED a gazebo-style feeder in our yard to create an enclosed buffet that caters exclusively to our eastern bluebirds.

We covered the five openings with 1/8-inch-thick Plexiglas and drilled 1-1/2-inch holes on two of the sides to give the birds access. We also adjusted the top of the gazebo so we could easily remove it for filling.

Then we placed it on a fence post about 12 feet away from our bluebird house, filled it with a cup of mealworms and waited to see what would happen.

We were soon rewarded with the sight of a female bluebird entering the gazebo, grabbing a mouthful of worms and exiting (above right).

We never saw the male go inside the feeder, but we know the feeder worked well since we had to replenish the mealworms two to three times each day. —*Carmelite Moreau Diamondhead, Mississippi*

Sentimental Showpiece

THE OLD CONCRETE birdbath that once belonged to my grandfather had a large crack in the basin, making it both unusable and unattractive. I just couldn't throw it away, so my husband repaired the crack, then I dressed it up (right).

I lined the bowl with colorful pieces of tile and glass, along with some marbles, and glued them in place. Next, I used bathroom tile grout to fill in the spaces between the decorative pieces and finished the whole thing with concrete sealer.

Now we proudly display the birdbath in our yard. Grandpa would have loved the transformation. —*Judy TePastte*
Grand Rapids, Michigan

Nice and Easy

I GROUPED our finch feeders together in this special holder (left) that makes them easier to maintain and provides extra feeding spots, too.

I cut holes in five cedar boards, just a hair bigger than the diameter of the tube feeders. Then I assembled the boards in a hexagon shape, slid the tubes through the holders and screwed the caps on to keep the feeders in place. My design holds five feeders, but this idea would adapt easily to accommodate as many—or as few—as you'd like.

Filling the feeders is a snap because they're all in one place. And it's really something to see all the finches that come to visit. I've counted more than 35 birds feeding together at one time! —*Greg Tuggle, Hillsboro, Illinois*

Shooing Away Sparrows

FOR SEVERAL YEARS, I watched in frustration as sparrows chased the wrens away from my backyard. Then I came up with a simple solution, and it has worked well for the past several years.

In spring, I take down the feeder that holds mixed birdseed and put it away. I still offer the birds suet, nyjer and sunflower seeds, and I keep my hummingbird and oriole feeders out, too. For whatever reason, the sparrows soon leave my yard—and I still get to see all my favorite birds, including my beloved wrens.

Come fall, I put the mixed seed feeder back up and feed the sparrows and other species all winter long.
—*Mossie Peterson, Lowell, Indiana*

Creating a Sanctuary

WHILE WE typically see all kinds of birds at our backyard feeders, one spring they were overtaken by starlings, pigeons, squirrels and mallard ducks. At times, there were as many as 50 "bully birds" frequenting our yard! They would not leave until they consumed all the seed, and they scared away the smaller birds.

We finally took down the feeders and cleaned up the dropped seeds in an effort to discourage the varmints. The trouble was, the smaller birds were gone as well.

After a week of silence, I decided to create two "feeding sanctuaries" (see photo below) to hold our bird feeders and provide protection for the smaller birds.

For the top and bottom of each holder, I used 18- by 24-inch pieces of galvanized steel. The frames are pieces of lumber attached to the metal with screws.

I wrapped three sides with chicken wire, then cut four small holes on each side to create entrances that are perfect for lit-

tle birds, but keep out squirrels and larger birds. One side also features a hinged door, so we can easily refill and clean the feeders I placed inside.

The squirrels gave up after a few attempts to get at the feeders. And because the steel floor catches dropped seeds, we no longer have problems with ground feeders like pigeons, starlings or ducks.

What we have seen is the happy return of the smaller birds we enjoy so much. —*Dave and Barb Getz*
Greenwood, Indiana

Ribbons Do the Trick

AFTER SEEING a tip from a reader in a previous issue of *Birds & Blooms* about tying red ribbons onto hummingbird feeders to attract birds, I thought I'd give it a try.

We have several feeders, and I topped each one with a generous length of red ribbon. That did the trick. The photo (right) shows one feeder hanging near our front porch—see how busy it is!

Overall, I'd estimate we now have three or four times more hummingbirds at the feeders in summer than we did before. One feeder regularly attracts 20 to 25 birds at a time.
—*Ruth Lee, Frisco City, Alabama*

No-Weed Feed

TO PREVENT fallen birdseed from sprouting, I contacted experts to find out what to do. I learned a useful tip and wanted to pass it on to other readers.

Birdseed can be heated in a microwave oven to prevent the sprouting of weeds. For each pound of seed, microwave for 2 minutes at high power. The seeds can also be baked in a conventional oven by spreading a thin layer on a cookie sheet and baking at 250° for 30 minutes.

One more way to prevent sprouting is by using seeds out of the shell like hulled sunflower, cracked corn or peanut hearts.
—*Tom Kovach, Park Rapids, Minnesota*

Act of Diversion

IF YOU CAN'T BEAT them, feed them. At least that's what works for me when dealing with squirrels. To keep these critters away from my bird feeders, I divert them to a dining spot of their very own.

I put a screw eye into the end of a dried corncob, and then hang it on a shepherd's hook in my yard (left). I've learned to make sure the screw isn't too loose around the hook, though. These crafty creatures will figure out how to remove the hanging cob and be off with it in no time.
—*Mark Bozicevich*
Cordova, Texas

Sticky Situation

SINCE WOODEN peanut butter feeders are hard to clean and usually collect mildew, my son John and I decided to take action. We make our own feeders from PVC pipe (right). The body is constructed from 1-1/2-inch pipe, and the cups for peanut butter are 1-inch pieces attached to the body with PVC cement.

The feeders are quick to make and easy to clean, too. I coat the cut edges of the cups with clear lacquer or epoxy, which helps prevent mildew. And when it's time for a thorough scrubbing, the feeder fits in the upper section of the dishwasher.
—*Howard Williams, Athens, Georgia*

A Real Hit

I GET SO MANY suet-loving birds in my backyard that small suet feeders aren't practical. Instead, I bought a CD holder and added a board to the back and the bottom (left). Now I use large pieces of bulk suet, and the birds love it.
—*Kenneth Sabel*
Friendship, Wisconsin

War of the World

I HAVE WON most of my battles with the squirrels that try to eat from my bird feeders. My secret? I block squirrels from the feeders with various baffles—from plastic pumpkins to globes. Here are the results (above photos) from my latest victory.

In the first picture, the squirrel appears to be pondering its plan of attack. Next, it descends on its target, only to be left "spinning." The third picture shows the critter scurrying away in defeat.

I guess you could say the world got the best of this squirrel!
—*S.M. Kent, West Caldwell, New Jersey*

Window Feeder

WHEN MY husband and I moved into our first home, I was relatively new to feeding birds and certainly new to home ownership.

One of the first modifications we made to the house was removing an old window-unit air conditioner. We didn't get around to taking down its platform right away, and for that, I'm glad. As I was looking at it one day, I realized it would be a perfect place to feed birds.

I set out seed on this windowsill feeder, and we have close encounters with birds all the time. Children of all ages love to come to our home to see the birds up close. In this case, I guess procrastination was a good thing.
—*Susan Moussette*
Huntington, Massachusetts

Leave the Lights on

THIS YEAR, I wanted to try something different for our purple martin houses, so I went to a salvage yard for inspiration. There, I found a brass chandelier for $5.

After cleaning it up, we attached our gourd birdhouses to it and installed it on a retractable pole (below). The purple martins loved it!

They even ignored our other gourd birdhouses, and would only use the one on this hanger.

My bargain bin find turned out to be an attractive and functional addition to our backyard.
—*Judy Wolfe*
Dunnellon, Florida

They happily share their yard with birds and critters.

WHOSE HABITAT IS IT, ANYWAY?

By Marie Fletcher, Leoti, Kansas

Years ago, my husband, Ralph, and I moved to a new place on the south edge of a small western Kansas town. We planted a lot of shrubs, flowers and trees...not realizing how attractive we were making our 5 acres to the wildlife around us.

From our patio, we look over a miniature forest of staghorn sumac (top photo) that forms a natural canopy to cool the area in summer—and turns brilliant gold and red in fall.

A small redwood bridge arches over a homemade stream, making an entrance into the backyard. Beyond are a variety of trees, including Russian olive, black walnut, sunburst lo-cust, golden-rain tree, Scotch pine, ponderosa pine and red cedar.

Between the backyard and the small field to the west grow a variety of plums, plus choke cherries, elderberries, currants and mulberries.

To break the searing summer wind, we planted a 200-foot

LIVING IN HARMONY. Marie and Ralph Leoti (above inset) cre-ated a lush backyard wildlife habitat that includes plantings like larkspur (top) that grow near their "miniature forest" of staghorn sumac. Other plants that produce berries attract various birds.

ALL ARE WELCOME HERE. The Leotis enjoy watching the variety of wildlife that pass through their yard looking for food or shelter. From top near right: A young eastern cottontail peers through grasses...a pair of mule deer stop for a visit...an eastern black swallowtail feeds on coneflower... two juvenile western kingbirds find a protected perch.

hedge of lilacs on our southern boundary.

Those many plantings really enhanced *our* habitat. But as we sat on our patio enjoying the results of our work, we began to notice that we were not alone.

The Wild Kingdom

Eastern cottontail rabbits filtered into the yard from the grassy areas around our property. More and more birds started coming in to build their nests. To accommodate them, I put out birdbaths and pans filled with water.

American robins could not get enough of our elderberries and juniper berries, so I planted more.

Deer slipped in during the night or early morning hours to browse on the buffalo grass in the backyard. Pheasants began patrolling our lilac hedge, digging in the dead leaves and taking dirt baths. We could hear northern bobwhites doing their "bob white" call in the field. I put out scratch grain for them.

Realizing we catered to a variety of animals and birds, we decided to plant flowers that would attract butterflies as well. Soon, painted ladies, viceroys, red admirals and others were visiting. I saved milkweed wherever I saw it, because it's a favorite of monarch butterflies.

At first we referred to the animals, birds and butterflies as visitors, but now we've come to think of them more like extended family. They eat, drink and relax in *our* habitat...because it has become *their* habitat as well.

Natural Rewards

Of course, these animals do provide compensation for our hospitality—we get to enjoy the wonderful sights and sounds of our natural world.

There's the pleasure of seeing a beautiful male ring-necked pheasant strut his stuff alongside his more subtle mate...and hearing the songs of brown thrashers and northern mockingbirds.

There are flashes of color from American goldfinches, American robins and eastern towhees...and the soft coo of mourning doves and Eurasian collared-doves, plus the twitter of western kingbirds and a variety of others.

Of course, the backyard habitat is also occupied by a few less-desirable critters. A sleepy skunk occasionally follows the hedge back to its bed after a long night of hunting. We don't bother it, and the skunk ignores us.

Snakes are another matter. We added a small garden pond that provides water for birds and other animals, but it also attracted garter snakes. I frequently pluck these harmless snakes out of the pond with a pair of old kitchen tongs and carry them out into the field. Ralph teases that they simply slither back, and I suppose he's right.

In the end, it really doesn't matter what kind of wildlife comes passing through our backyard. We're just glad to be sharing it!

READER TIP

Birds love the plants in our backyard. The long lilac hedge we planted attracts all kinds of birds, and American robins can't get enough of our elderberries and juniper berries.

—**Marie Fletcher, Leoti, Kansas**

HOME TWEET HOME

Readers share their most creative birdhouses.

Fit for a King

"I LIVE for my birds," says Vic Robbins of Fleetwood, Pennsylvania. "I've been a commercial artist all my life and enjoy making gourd art and birdhouses. I'll try anything I feel is 'birdable.' My lion has rope for a mane and seedpods for eyes."

De-light-ful Gift

"ONE OF my hobbies is making birdhouses from old and weathered wood," says David Snyder from Port Orchard, Washington. "So when my wife's birthday approached one year, I thought a replica of the Coquille Lighthouse in Bandon, Oregon would make a great gift. Her mother used to play in the historic building as a child, so it's very special to my wife."

Two Was the Bear Minimum

"MOM LOVES Bluebirds, Dad loves chain saws. It's a rather strange pair of interests, you might say," writes daughter Kelsey Needham of Lawrence, Kansas. Her parents, Keith and Margaret, live in Mound City.

"Dad carved a 2-foot-tall bear birdhouse from a catalpa log and addressed every detail, including a clean-out door in back and a predator guard for the pole.

"Then he decided one bear wasn't enough, so he carved another—this one with overalls. On Christmas morning, Mom was surprised with the most unique birdhouses around."

Back to School

"USING a simple band saw and basic hand tools, this red-wood birdhouse took me 6 months to construct," writes Richard Gorthy of San Ramon, California. "It's a model of the one-room Tassajara schoolhouse in our area. I furnished the inside of the birdhouse with old-fashioned desks, bookshelves, a blackboard and a potbellied stove, leaving space in the 'attic' for birds to nest.

"Forty miniature daffodils adorn the outside, representing the hundreds that bloom on the school's grounds each spring."

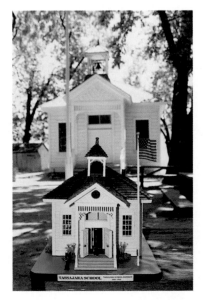

Double Vision

"THIS CHARMING birdhouse (above) is a replica of our home," says Linda Pratico of Rutland, Vermont. "My husband, Randy, fashioned it using leftover building materials from our house. Every bit is handmade, including the miniature shutters that accent each window."

Drilling It Home

"MY SON Kenneth had great fun making this one-of-a-kind oil rig birdhouse," says Maxine Bednar of Kouts, Indiana. "But it's the birds who have really struck pay dirt. Within an hour of setting up the house in my front yard, a pair of birds moved in."

Do Birds Prefer Chevys?

"OVER THE YEARS, I've built close to 500 nest boxes for bluebirds," says Len Vest of Chester, Virginia. "To challenge myself, I decided to build a house in the shape of a 1953 Chevy truck. I constructed all the parts from cedar and used a Dremel tool to make the curves. I worked on it for 5 months, and spent 800 hours in the shop."

This Barn Has Birds and Blooms

"MY HUSBAND, Randy, and I designed and built this multipurpose birdhouse and planter (below) based on the barn on his family's farm," writes Paula Simpson of Churchill, Ontario.

"There's a wren house on top, and two silos in back that are made from tube feeders. On the bottom is a flower box and a storage area for my small gardening tools. It sure brightens up the old satellite pole in our backyard."

Bedtime Reading

"MY BROTHER Bert Burmeister has become quite a birdhouse builder since he retired," explains Bonnie Chastain from Omaha, Nebraska.

"He built a workshop behind their home in Orlando, Florida, and he spends many hours there making creative birdhouses, like this stack of books. We think he's very talented!"

Taking a Break

"I RECENTLY started making mosaics from broken dishes, tiles, sea glass...whatever I can find," writes Janice Austin of Salinas, California. "I've loved bird-watching since a dear friend introduced me to it a number of years ago. So naturally, my favorite mosaic projects are birdhouses and feeders."

Up to the Challenge

"AFTER spotting an elaborate birdhouse while visiting our son in Bavaria, my wife asked if I could build one for her—only better," writes Gary Pomeroy of Springfield, Vermont.

"I took up the challenge, and after more than 30 hours at the work bench, I finished this birdhouse. There are two nesting compartments, one in front and another in back, and two balconies that hold seed. I used five different kinds of wood and added copper flashing to the roof peak and edges."

A Capitol Idea

TO CREATE this birdhouse, which I modeled after the U.S. Capitol in Washington, D.C., I started with a 5-gallon bucket and a plastic flowerpot," writes LaRoyce Shiver from Mobile, Alabama. "Then I added columns and the rest of the architectural features using wood and other materials.

"It has become quite popular with our backyard friends. Once the purple martins leave each year, squirrels move in and raise their families."

Hats Off!

"I WAS searching for unique gifts for the college friends I see only once a year, when I came up with the idea of red hat birdhouses," says Pam Fraser of Tallahassee, Florida. "We were all planning to wear red hats for our upcoming get-together, so I thought matching birdhouses would be fun.

"My dad, Ken Bope (above), who lives in Maggie Valley, North Carolina, loves to work with wood and happily agreed to design and make the houses. He crafted them so they'd open underneath for cleaning. The birdhouses were challenging, but he did a fantastic job!"

Full Steam Ahead

"MY FATHER, Patrick Holliday, has constructed several unique and beautiful birdhouses over the years, but I think this old-fashioned paddle-wheel boat is his best effort yet," writes Debbie Green from Palmyra, Missouri. "The birdhouse is stationed outside my cousin's restaurant, which overlooks the Illinois River in Hardin, Illinois."

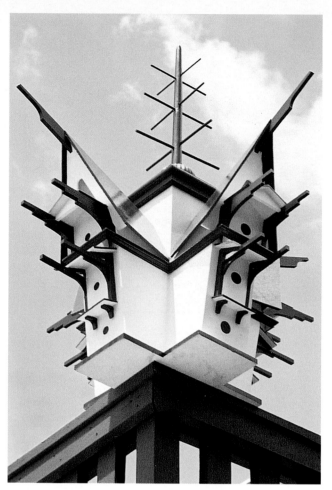

Victorian Villa

"IT TOOK 3 months, but I finally completed this Victorian-inspired birdhouse complex," says Ken Konvicka of Garland, Texas. "I based the design on a photo I took at Butchart Gardens in British Columbia. I was impressed with the structure, so I wanted to try making one myself.

"It seems like I took about 100 trips to the hardware store while building this project, but now it's ready for my backyard birds to enjoy."

A Birdhouse, to Boot

"MY OLD ski boots remind me of the good times I've had on the ski slopes," writes Richard Adamus from Penfield, New York. "So instead of throwing them away, I converted one into a birdhouse.

"I made the entrance hole with a large drill bit and capped the top of the boot with a block of wood."

Fanciful Fortress

"AFTER COMPLETING several other woodworking projects, I had a pile of scrap lumber on my hands, so I decided to build a birdhouse," explains Ken Hawkins of Decatur, Indiana.

"What I ended up with was more like a huge bird playhouse (below)! The building is 32 inches tall, 60 inches long and weighs about 50 pounds. It took me about 6 months to make it in my spare time."

Garden Musician

"I LOVE growing my own gourds and using them to create birdhouses," says Jo Ann Sutherland from Santaquin, Utah. "I was looking through all my gourds, hoping for inspiration for a project to add to my copper garden, when I located the perfect one. The shape of this gourd was just right for a kokopelli, which is the Native American musical figure that's popular in Southwestern art."

Bonnie Nance; inset: Faith Bemis

HOMEGROWN HOMES

Gourds are a natural choice for feeders and birdhouses.

By Bill Moore, Wentworth, New Hampshire

I f you're like me, there's no such thing as too many bird-houses. That's why I enjoy growing gourds. Once dry, gourds can easily be transformed into the perfect nesting spots.

Gourds are simple to grow, and so prolific that one crop is enough to create a housing glut. But that's no problem—I turn the surplus into unique bird feeders. After all, birds use hous-es only a couple of months a year, while feeders stay busy year-round.

For "homegrown" houses and feeders, look for seeds of any type of lagenaria gourd. The rounded, bottle-shaped varieties are often known as birdhouse or bottle gourds. Not surpris-ingly, they're the most popular choice for birdhouses and are becoming easy to find at garden centers (or see the list of sources on page 81). Some other types that will work well for this are swan, dolphin and dipper gourds.

From experience, I've learned a few hints that will help you cultivate a successful gourd crop.

HUNG OUT TO DRY. Growing gourds (left inset) is a great way to combine your interests of gardening and birding. After harvesting the gourds, allow them to dry by hanging them in a ventilated area (left). Then they're ready to be cleaned and converted into birdhouses, or even feeders (like the ones below).

Start with Seed

First of all, most of these gourds take about 120 days to ripen. Give them a head start by planting them indoors, 4 to 6 weeks before the last frost date in your area. I plant mine in peat pots so I can transplant them into the garden without disturbing the roots.

Put five seeds in each pot, a 1/2 inch deep, and place the pots under grow lights or on a sunny sill. When it's time to thin the seedlings to one per pot, use scissors. Pulling them out can damage the roots of the remaining plants.

When temperatures begin to warm, start hardening off the seedlings outdoors. During the day, place the pots in a shady spot. They can stay outside overnight as long as there's no threat of frost.

Then it's time to find a sunny planting site—and make it a big one. Space the plants 3 to 6 feet apart. That sounds like a lot, but trust me, these plants ramble!

For each seedling, dig a hole 18 inches wide and a foot deep, and amend the soil with organic matter. Once planted, surround the gourds with mulch to inhibit weeds and protect the shallow roots.

If your garden space for gourds is limited, just go vertical. This has advantages—it makes the gourds more uniform and less susceptible to slugs and fungal problems. However, gourds grown on trellises generally have straight necks. If you'd like the necks to curve, gently bend them after the gourds first emerge.

READER TIP

Give your gourds a head start by planting them indoors, 4 to 6 weeks before the last frost date in your area. Also, plant them in peat pots, so you can transplant them to the garden without disturbing the roots.

—Bill Moore, Wentworth, New Hampshire

The gourds are ready to harvest when the stems dry and turn brown. Cut the stem with pruning shears or a sharp knife, leaving about 6 inches attached to the gourd. Cutting the stem too close encourages rot.

All Dried Up

Gently wash and dry the gourds, then place them in a well-ventilated area to cure. An attic is ideal, but anyplace indoors works. Keep gourds in a single layer, not touching each other. Don't worry if the gourds get a little moldy—that's normal. However, discard any that become soft or wrinkled.

You'll know the gourds are dry when their color changes from green to tan, they become noticeably lighter weight and the seeds rattle. If you can use them as maracas, they're ready to go! Wash off the gourds and buff away any mold with a little sandpaper or steel wool.

Move-in Condition

To create a birdhouse or feeder, make an entryway with a hole saw. Then remove the seeds and dried pulp.

Drill a few small holes on top for ventilation, and in the bottom for drainage. If you'd like, insert a small stick or dowel under the entry hole for a perch, and affix it with waterproof glue.

To hang the gourd, hook the stem or neck over a branch, or anchor sturdy cord or twine through the top hole. Sometimes I get creative and add a second gourd as decoration (see photos above left).

The birds will love them, and you'll love the natural look and budget price.

Ready, Set...Gourd!

Gourd seeds are almost as easy to find as they are to grow. They're available from nurseries, garden centers and numerous catalog and on-line retailers. But if you can't find them in your local stores, here are a few sources to get you started:

Baker Creek Heirloom Seeds
2278 Baker Creed Rd.
Mansfield MO 65704
1-417/924-8917
www.rareseeds.com

Nichols Garden Nursery
1198 N. Pacific Hwy.
Albany OR 97321
1-800/422-3985
www.gardennursery.com

Pinetree Garden Seeds
P.O. Box 300
New Gloucester ME 04260
1-207/926-3400
www.superseeds.com

Onalee's Home-Grown Seeds
226 Benes Rd.
Brooksville FL 34604
1-352/544-2999
http://onaleeseeds. scifstore.com

Gourd organizations offer a wealth of information for both novice and experienced growers, including growing tips, craft ideas, information on gourd artisans and news about area gourd art shows and competitions.

To learn more, contact the American Gourd Society, P.O. Box 2186, Kokomo IN 46904 (*www.american gourdsociety.org*). Canadian residents should check with the Canadian Gourd Society, 44 Edgevalley Rd., Unit 48, London ON Canada N5Y 5P7 (*www.canadiangourd society1.homestead.com*).

MARTIN METROPOLIS

When it comes to attracting martins, no one does it better than these savvy Southerners.

By Laura Cartwright, Booneville, Mississippi

ROOMS FOR RENT. Over 600 purple martins (like the ones above inset) zip among a towering complex of gourd houses and apartments in this rural Mississippi yard (top). It's perhaps the largest and oldest martin colony in the United States.

Purple martins in the East largely depend on man-made housing. Near Booneville, Mississippi, *over 600* martins look to Luther and Joan Moorman for homes.

The martin colony on the Moormans' 107-acre farm may be the largest—and oldest—in the U.S.

"My father began putting up martin houses here in the '40s," Luther says. "I just kept adding them over the years. Now we have more than 300."

Growing Homes

It truly is a homegrown operation, since most of those houses are made from the gourds Luther raises each year.

He plants them in April, then lets the gourds grow as big as possible before harvesting. After frost kills the vines in late October, Luther lets the gourds dry.

"It takes a long time," he says. "At first they get moldy and look like they're rotten, but they finally dry out."

To prepare the gourds for martin homes, Luther and Joan use

WORTH THE EFFORT. Luther and Joan Moorman put a lot of care into their purple martin hobby. They grow gourds in their garden to make houses (above), then diligently check the homes (at right) to keep out nest raiders like European starlings.

an electric buffer to clean them to a beautiful shine. Then they cut a 2-3/4-inch entry hole in the short-necked gourds or cut the tip off the long-necked ones for a natural entryway.

After they remove the seeds and membranes, they apply a coat of waterproof sealant to the gourds. Luther also adds a small "awning" over each entry hole to help keep rain out.

Once they complete the gourd houses, they hang them among a large stand of poles that hold 16 houses each.

All of the poles have cables so Luther and Joan can raise and lower the racks to check the nests and clean the houses as needed. This allows them to keep European starlings in check. Otherwise, these non-native birds will push martins out of the homes.

And that's not the only martin challenger the Moormans have to fight. At the bottom of every pole is a disk-shaped guard that prevents snakes from climbing to the houses.

Helpful Hobby

All this may sound like a lot of work for a hobby, but Luther and Joan have always put plenty of effort into their outdoor activities. Until Luther was sidelined by back problems, he and Joan ran a lawn service business.

Their own yard still is a showplace of manicured grass and well-tended flower beds, surrounded by trees and shrubs. It's often filled with visitors during spring and summer, when birders come to marvel at the Moormans' purple martin majesty.

Luther and Joan are happy to share information about the birds with their guests.

He explains that martins have a very strong migratory instinct and arrive at the farm each year on February 11 or 12. After settling into the cozy gourd houses, female martins lay several eggs—three to eight per nest.

"As the eggs hatch, I've seen the males hanging upside down on the gourds," Luther says. "I figure they're making sure everything is okay.

"Purple martins eat only insects, so we don't have to buy any seed for them," Luther says. "When the babies grow a bit, the adult birds will bring dragonflies to feed them."

In July, when the young martins first come out of the gourds, it's something to see—there are hundreds of them!

"The adult birds try to keep the babies from coming back to the nest, but they don't always succeed," Luther says with a grin.

Time to Move on

The martins leave during the second week of August, as soon as the baby birds can fly, and migrate to Brazil and northern Argentina. Then the Moormans take down all of the houses—the gourds plus the larger "apartments"—for cleaning and storage. In January, the process starts over.

"I can't help but get excited when I put the houses up," Luther says. "Because I know that I'll soon be seeing my purple martins again."

READER TIP

We add small "awnings" over each gourd house entry hole to keep the rain out.

—Luther and Joan Moorman, Booneville, Mississippi

FANTASTIC FEEDERS

Winter Fuel

I'VE BEEN building feeders and houses for birds ever since I retired," says Dave Bott from Lacombe, Alberta. "This one is a replica of an old kerosene lantern. It's made entirely of wood, except for the glass globe. There are six feeding ports, which provide enough room for numerous birds, such as common redpolls."

Work of Art

"MY HUSBAND, Larry, spent more than 100 hours creating this beautiful feeder that's similar to the gazebo on our pond," writes Doris Tyler from Hartford City, Indiana. "It's built from western red cedar and features a double-curved copper roof."

Great Gift

"WE ARE avid bird-watchers and feed many birds in our yard," write Roy (left) and Vonnie Nelson of Murdock, Minnesota. "So you can imagine our delight when we received this elaborate bird feeder as a gift from a friend, John Hugo of Mason City, Iowa. We get quite a selection of birds visiting it for a meal."

Father Knows Best

"MY FATHER, Gene Lowe, enjoys taking care of the birds that visit his backyard. That's why he built them this lovely nine-port feeder," says Genia Turbyfield of Simpsonville, South Carolina.

"When my husband and I started to take up bird feeding ourselves, my dad went back to the wood shop and surprised us with our own handcrafted feeder. And guess what? Our birds love it, too!"

Eat Like a King

"MY GRANDSON and I built this castle bird feeder," writes Bob Dewitz from Williamsville, New York. "We added details like a satellite dish and a drawbridge, which we left open so birds could investigate under the seed tray."

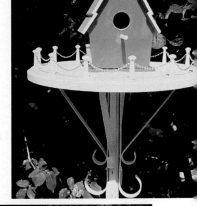

Backyard Cabin

"DURING OUR long winters, my husband, George, stays busy building feeders like this intricate cabin," says Carol Goodson from Worley, Idaho. "He doesn't use plans—just his imagination. On this one, the seed spills out the front door and down the steps.

"He builds birdhouses, too, and has filled our 2-1/2-acre property with a variety of houses, feeders and baths—all for the birds."

Victorian Charmer

"WHEN WE revamped our backyard with a Victorian cottage garden theme, my father, Larry Himenes (below, with my daughter Alexandra), made this wonderful birdhouse and feeder to go with it," says Laurie Swindell of San Lorenzo, California. "I sprinkle birdseed on the platform that encircles the house, and the birds seem to love it. I love it, too, because it was made with tender loving care by my father."

Whimsical Windmill

"THIS UNIQUE bird feeder is a replica of the DeZwaan, a 240-year-old working Dutch windmill that was sent to our town from the Netherlands," says Ken Dozeman from Holland, Michigan. "I copied its likeness by projecting the windmill's image onto a sheet of paper using slides I had made. Then I traced the image onto wood and cut it out. The large walkway that circles the landmark is the perfect place for seed."

A Sterling Effort

"I BUILT this rustic feeder for a neighbor whom my wife, Helen, and I often see on our daily walks," says Vernon Fellows of Peshastin, Washington. "I constructed it with scrap wood and aluminum roofing."

Feeding Frenzy

"GOLDFINCHES flock to this unique feeder my husband, Harold, built," writes Trudy Barnes of Centralia, Missouri. "It has a copper roof and a pan to catch any seeds that fall. There are small holes in the pieces of Plexiglas to allow access to the seed.

"The birds can dine from 10 feeding ports, including four where the finches feed upside down. The roof and the feeding portion both lift off, so it's easy to refill."

Ready for a Spin

"WHEN I get up every morning, the birds and squirrels are waiting for me to fill this Ferris wheel feeder," says Lenard Smith from Orange, Texas. "Each box-type 'seat' holds a cup of birdseed and has a drainage hole in the bottom.

I have two feeders like this. I keep one on the front porch, and the other in the yard near the swing where I like to relax. The squirrels have a ball on them."

Rocky Feeder

"MY BROTHER-IN-LAW Chris Jasan built this feeder (above) for my sister," says Kimberly Smith of Vacaville, California. "When I saw it, I knew that it was wonderfully unique with its river rock chimney and base. He even made a one-of-a-kind post for it using a tree trunk."

All Aboard the Feeder Train

"WE CAN'T FILL this dual bird and squirrel feeder fast enough," says Edward Shinkle of Ocala, Florida. "It's popular with all our backyard visitors.

"I got some of the feeder ideas from *Birds & Blooms*, and some are original creations. It has plenty of character with old license plates as roofs and two hanging feeders. But the real eye-catcher is the train, especially when there's a squirrel in the engineer's seat."

"Mort" Is a Different Sort

"I'D LIKE you to meet 'Mort,' the bird feeder I created from nearly all recycled materials (below)," writes Leonard Kuster of Green Bay, Wisconsin. "His body parts, shoes and hat were created from a fallen poplar tree. The pipe in his mouth is an ear of corn (picked clean by squirrels). The seed tray is a pie crust pan, and his teeth were made from a tomato sauce can."

Cactus Creation

"OUR FRIEND Tom Krieg constructed this uniquely shaped feeder for his home in Prescott Valley, Arizona," say Michael and Gloria Danek of Laingsburg, Michigan.

"As a retired engineer, he took special care with the design he crafted for his feathered friends. He formed it from long-lasting PVC pipe and drilled slightly angled holes to prevent the seed from spilling out. Tom has since passed away, but his wife, Ruby, continues to enjoy the variety of birds this saguaro cactus brings to their desert backyard."

WANT MORE BIRDS?

Here's the Menu:
Sunflower
Nyjer
Safflower
Suet Cake
Sugar Water

By George Harrison, Contributing Editor

Autumn is the time of the year when many backyarders think about feeding the beautiful songbirds in their neighborhoods. I'm not sure why this revelation happens this time of year—feeding birds year-round has many rewards.

Yet autumn is when birdseed sales are held and feeders are widely promoted to consumers…and I'm not talking about the feathered variety. You could say once the autumn winds hit, bird-feeding season is in high gear —people are buying birdseed by 50-pound bagfuls. But what kinds of foods attract the birds you most want in your backyard?

Black-oil sunflower seeds and out-of-shell sunflower meats are both excellent offerings for lots of birds.

Sunflower Seed—Top of the List

If you want to rely on just one type of seed that is most attractive to the greatest number of backyard birds, hands down sunflower seed is the right pick in any form—in the shell (black-oil or white-striped) or medium cracked out-of-the-shell meats. All forms of sunflower seeds are relished by finches, chickadees, nuthatches, grosbeaks, cardinals, jays and even some species of woodpeckers.

There's only one problem with sunflower seed—bully birds, such as blackbirds, European starlings and grackles, also love it, especially if it's served in a tray feeder.

There's a simple solution. Serve sunflower seeds from a feeder that allows only the smaller birds to enter the feeding chamber. These feeders are often called "exclusion feeders," with smaller perches, weight mechanisms or fencing to keep the larger birds out.

Nyjer Seed (Thistle)

If finches are your fancy, like the brilliant-yellow American goldfinches (left) that frequent my area, then you'll want to serve up this tiny, black seed some people call thistle. It's best served in a special tube feeder that has tiny ports to keep the small seeds from pouring out.

Chickadees love nyjer seed, too, and their acrobatic behavior allows them to extract the seeds from the tiny food ports. It's also a good choice if you're overrun by larger bully birds. They have a problem feeding from the tiny ports.

Safflower Seed

Though it may take some birds a little time to get acquainted with safflower seeds, northern cardinals, grosbeaks, mourning doves and house finches will frequent feeders that serve it. Because northern cardinals prefer a flat surface to stand on when eating, a tray feeder or hopper feeder with a wide rim makes it easier for them to eat safflower seed. Even chickadees will remove a single safflower seed and fly to a nearby branch to crack it open.

Perhaps best of all, squirrels don't like safflower seed! Consider switching to it if these rascals often pester your feeders.

Squirrels don't eat safflower!

Sugar Water

During spring and summer, sugar water mixed in the kitchen (one part sugar to four parts water, boil and cool before serving) is dynamite for feeding hummingbirds and orioles. Because most hummingbird feeders are made of red plastic, and oriole feeders of orange plastic, the sugar water doesn't even need to be colored to attract the birds' attention. Once these desirable birds find the feeder, it will be a challenge keeping it filled.

Nyjer seed

Chapter 3

"Mystery mixes" will not always attract your favorite feathered friends.

Suet Cakes

One of my pet peeves is the commercial suet cake selection in bird stores. Most suet cakes contain a smorgasbord of foods other than suet, such as berries, oranges and even insects. The most common extra ingredient in suet cakes is birdseed. Birds that eat suet, including woodpeckers, nuthatches, chickadees and titmice, eat it to get the energy that the suet offers, so all the extras are virtually useless. If they require seeds, berries or insects, they'll find those food items elsewhere. For my backyard, I purchase only pure suet cakes.

Wild Birdseed Mixes

This is often the "mystery mix" you'll find at grocery stores or on sale at the local discount store. It's usually a mix of lots of millet, cracked corn and very few sunflower seeds. The basic problem with these feed-all mixes is that they're not discriminating and may attract mostly undesirable birds and

Suet cakes: great for woodpeckers.

night critters, such as rats and raccoons. I recommend avoiding these do-all mixes, and stick with the specialty foods listed.

Feeding the most desired birds is probably much easier than you thought. Order off the right menu, and you're likely to see the birds you want feasting right outside your favorite picture window.

Feeders Hold More Than Food

There's more to filling feeders with the right seed to attract the birds you want. A feeder's shape, placement in the yard and distance above the ground will determine what kinds of birds actually use it. And yes, proper cover and habitat play an equally important role.

Here's a quick rundown of the most effective bird feeders:

Tray feeders, on a post or hanging, are open pantry shelves that attract most seed-eating birds. Problem is they also attract rain, snow and ice, so you have to maintain them more than other feeders.

Certain birds, such as cardinals, grosbeaks, bluebirds, woodpeckers and robins, will basically feed from only these types of feeders. Try to get one with screening or holes in the bottom for drainage to keep seed from spoiling.

Tube feeders are hanging cylinders with portholes and perches that are favored by small finches. Chickadees and nuthatches will use them, too.

If the bully birds figure out how to eat from a tube feeder, you may want to shorten the perches slightly, or enclose the feeder in a wire mesh that will allow only the little birds to get to the food. Commercially made exclusion feeders are available.

Hopper feeders, either on a post or hanging, are targeted to most kinds of seed-eating birds. They usually have an enclosed reservoir for seeds that slides food down to the open feeding tray below. The advantage is that the hopper keeps the seeds dry and always available to birds.

Suet feeders are usually small, square laminated cages that hold blocks of suet. They can hang on a tree trunk or be suspended from a branch. They're great for attracting woodpeckers, as well as titmice, chickadees and nuthatches.

Sugar-water feeders are for hummingbirds and orioles. Tanagers, finches and other birds may also use them. Simply keep them topped off with fresh, homemade sugar water…and stand back. ◂

First-Timer Shopping List

Getting started is the hardest part of backyard bird feeding. As soon as the proper food is served in an appropriate feeder in the right location, the birds are nearly guaranteed to come.

10-lb. bag of sunflower
5-lb. bag of nyjer
1 suet cake
1 hopper feeder (don't forget a squirrel baffle)
1 birdseed tube feeder
1 nyjer tube feeder
1 suet cage

'GLAD YOU ASKED!'

Birding expert answers your questions.

By George Harrison, Contributing Editor

Grosbeak Guest

I live in the Rocky Mountains and saw this colorful visitor (below) at my bird feeder one day. What is it?
—*Richard Loos, Granby, Colorado*

George: Your mystery bird is a male pine grosbeak, an inconspicuous bird that lives in the spruce and fir forests of the northern United States and Canada.

Often seen in small groups, its main diet in winter is berries. Though it's not rare to see pine grosbeaks in the forest, they only occasionally visit backyard bird feeders.

One-Year Lease

Last summer, a pair of bushtits raised a brood of four young in an elaborate, 9-inch-long pouch in my climbing rose. Will they use the nest again this year?
—*Bernice Lebeau, Whittier, California*

George: Most birds, including bushtits, do not use a nest for more than one brood. The exceptions are those birds that use birdhouses for nesting, such as bluebirds and chickadees.

There is a very good reason why birds that build nests in trees, shrubs or on the ground need a new nest for each brood. By the time the youngsters are ready to leave the nests, they've grown so much that the nest has expanded to accommodate their size. In doing so, the nest is unfit for another brood.

Cardinal Divide

Although we are longtime birders, we can't figure why there are no northern cardinals west of the continental divide. They seem to be so widespread in the East. Any ideas? —*Nancy Howard, Puyallup, Washington*

George: There are records of northern cardinals sighted in California and Nevada, and breeding records in western and southern Arizona and throughout Texas

However, you are correct that cardinals generally are not found west of the Rockies, probably because the habitat and food available are not suitable to this species.

With the popularity of backyard bird feeding, northern cardinals have already extended their historically southern range well into the North and West, and perhaps someday they will appear at a feeder in your yard in Washington.

Keeping a Neat Nest

I watched as this house wren (below) came and went from its nest all day. What is that object it's carrying away from the birdhouse?
—*Donna Neal Odenton, Maryland*

George: That white object is called a fecal sac. Nature has devised an extraordinary way to keep birds' nests clean by having nestlings pass their waste in a little white sac.

This makes it easy for the parent birds to carry it away from the nest in order to avoid attracting predators.

Pretty Mystery

I spotted this unusual little visitor (below) in my birdbath. What kind of bird is it? —Frances Collier
Ogdensburg, New York

George: Your mystery bird is an ovenbird, a member of the wood warbler family. Easy to identify by their markings, this bird's orange crown patch and a heavily streaked white breast make it a real standout.

Like other members of the warbler family, the ovenbird migrates in the fall to spend winter in the warmth of southern Mexico and Central America.

The stout ovenbird gets its name from the shape of its domed nest, which resembles an oven. Usually found on the leaf-covered forest floor, the neatly formed nest is typically made with grass, leaves and twigs.

Keeping It Clean

How can I protect the inside of my wooden bird feeder from water damage and mold, and what's the best method for cleaning out old birdseed?

—Beatrice Bailey, Newcomb, New York

George: Start by trying to prevent water from getting into your feeder. You can mount a dome above it to keep out the rain, snow and, perhaps, even squirrels. If wind continues to blow rain and snow into the feeder, try applying caulk to the corners and cracks where the moisture is entering.

To clean it, a good shot from a garden or pressure hose will wash away the old clumps of seed.

Buzz Off

Do you have advice to keep flies away from oriole feeders? I bought a feeder that holds grape jelly and fruit, but, unfortunately, the bugs seem more interested in it than the birds are. —Karina Alpers
La Porte City, Iowa

George: Switch to sugar water to attract and keep orioles throughout the summer and into September.

Sugar water (one part sugar to four parts water, boil then cool mixture before serving) in an orange, plastic oriole feeder is easy to maintain and will attract a minimum number of bees and flies. These feeders are available at most birding stores.

Don't Go, Goldfinch

American goldfinches appear at my feeders near the end of April, then disappear about 2 weeks later. How can I convince these birds to stick around?

—Doug Goodgion, Falls Church, Virginia

George: In May, American goldfinches may move from your backyard to habitat that's more suitable to their nesting needs. They seek out fields with plenty of thistle plants, which they use to build nests and feed young.

All you can do to keep them around is offer the foods they prefer, such as nyjer (thistle) or sunflower seeds in the shell or medium cracked.

Also, it's possible that these finches have been in your backyard before April as well. Their olive-brown winter plumage is so dramatically different from the yellow summer plumage they begin to sport in spring, that it's possible they have been visiting your feeders incognito.

Strange-Looking Sack

I found this strange object (below) near our farm. It was originally hanging from one of our cottonwood trees. Can you tell me what it is?

—Karen Provost, Navarre, Ohio

George: It appears to be the nest of a Baltimore oriole.

An oriole nest is made in the shape of a pouch with the entrance at the top. But the female oriole weaves the nest in such a way that it can close up like a purse, sometimes concealing its identity as a nest.

Often suspended from a branch near the top of a tree, the female incorporates various plant fibers and hair into the nest. This woven sack can be as deep as 8 inches.

Frequently, Baltimore orioles will return to the same territory in subsequent years, though they seldom reuse old nests.

Mealtime for Mockers

I always see northern mockingbirds at my birdbath, but never at my feeder. What types of food should I set out for them? —Wilma Mitchell, Fayetteville, Tennessee

George: Northern mockingbirds are omnivorous, with about half of their diet consisting of various insects, such as beetles, ants, bees, butterflies, wasps and grasshoppers.

But mockingbirds are also quite fond of both wild and cultivated fruit. If you want to attract them to your bird feeder, simply place small pieces of fruit on a tray feeder or inside an empty grapefruit half. Pieces of apples or citrus, or grapes and berries are an open invitation for mockers to dine.

Mystery Visitor

I spotted this unusual bird (below) at my backyard finch feeder. I was able to get several good pictures, but still can't identify it. Can you? —Mikelyn Burnell
Kimball, Michigan

George: This unusual species is a European goldfinch, a common bird in Britain and Europe. Like American goldfinches, it will eat sunflower seeds and nyjer at bird feeders.

Unlike the American goldfinch, the European species does not change plumages in winter, so the red on its face gives it a spectacular appearance year-round. Also, the sexes look alike, so we can't speculate if your visitor was a male or female.

Many attempts have been made to introduce this species into North America, but none have been successful. The bird that appeared at your feeder was probably an escaped pet.

Where Do Swallows Go?

I've always wondered where barn swallows migrate. Do they ever return to their original place of birth?
—Lola Carlson, Bowdoin, Maine

George: All swallows, including barn swallows, are long-distance migrators. Barn swallows abandon their breeding range in the fall to wing their way through the Caribbean to spend winter in Central and South America. A few may irregularly winter as far north as southern Florida and the southwestern United States.

They usually return to the same general area where they were raised. Most nest within 20 miles of their birthplace, while some even nest much closer.

Out of the Ashes

Several hummingbirds visit my yard to feed from the flowers and feeders. However, they also seem to relish the ash piles from my paper burner. Why is the ash so popular with these hummingbirds?
—Ruby Barth, Reedsport, Oregon

George: Although I have never seen hummingbirds feed from an ash pile, I suspect the ashes offer a mineral they need for laying eggs. A bird's reproduction cycle often requires special nutrients it must acquire prior to laying eggs.

Changing Tastes?

I've noticed the woodpeckers in my backyard eating sunflower seeds, while the black-capped chickadees have developed a taste for nyjer. Can birds learn to eat new kinds of food?
—Lillian Marcotte
Hartland, Vermont

George: Yes, many species of birds are eating new foods as they adapt to what's available at bird feeders.

Some other changes I've heard include finches and doves eating safflower seeds, and American robins feasting on cracked sunflower. Dark-eyed juncos, which typically feed on the ground, are flying up to eat sunflower seeds off tray feeders.

And while it's a fairly common sight today, orioles, house finches and tanagers didn't used to sip sugar water from backyard hummingbird feeders.

These adaptations not only help increase the populations of these birds, but also allow them to pioneer into new regions.

Ants in Your Feathers?

I witnessed blue jays taking large red ants in their bills and rubbing them under their wings and on other parts of their bodies. Why would they do this?
—Thomas Kintz, Homosassa Springs, Florida

George: Blue jays and many other species will use crushed ants to rid their bodies of parasites. The ants contain formic acid that will kill parasites or cause them to abandon birds. Some birds will also roll on anthills to obtain the same relief from parasites.

Table for One

Many birds visit my feeders, often in pairs. However, the males of some species, such as indigo buntings and rose-breasted grosbeaks, always arrive solo. Why don't I see them with a mate? —Debby Videto
Bowden, West Virginia

George: There's more than one answer to your question. First, if it's nesting season, the females may be incubating eggs or feeding young.

The other possibility is that, in some cases, the males and females look so different from one another that they may not appear to be a pair. For example, the rose-breasted grosbeak female looks like a brown-striped sparrow, and the female indigo bunting is light brown with little or no blue in her feathers.

Finally, it's common behavior among many species for males and females to feed and bathe separately during the breeding season. This may help defend the pair from being preyed upon at the same time.

Long Live the Birds?

What is the life expectancy of common backyard birds, such as northern cardinals, bluebirds, mourning doves, chickadees and towhees?

—*Yvonne Dragonette, Beverly Hills, Florida*

George: If a backyard bird survives its first year, and 80 percent do not, the bird may live an average of 5 or 6 years.

The first year is the most hazardous for birds. From nestlings to fledglings to inexperienced juveniles, these young birds face a wild world fraught with danger.

Averages aside, some backyard species have lived much longer. For example, records show that a northern cardinal lived in the wild 13-1/2 years; a mourning dove lived 10 years; and a black-capped chickadee reached 12 years, 5 months.

Soak Up the Sun

I spotted this greater roadrunner at the Red Rock Visitor Center in Nevada. I followed it around for a bit, then it sprawled itself on the patio in this strange position (below). What is it doing? —*Peggy Hamlen Las Vegas, Nevada*

George: This is a very interesting and colorful photograph of a greater roadrunner sunning itself. Birds will do this in very hot conditions to help rid their feathers and bodies of parasites. The insects cannot stand the heat, and leave the bird. When they are sunning, the birds are also absorbing vitamin D, which is essential to their health.

Whip-poor-will Watch

Is it my imagination, or is the whip-poor-will population diminishing? Is there anything we can do to protect these birds? —*Keith Etzel Shippenville, Pennsylvania*

George: You are not imagining it. Whip-poor-will numbers have declined dramatically in recent decades due to loss of their wooded habitat in both summer and winter ranges, pesticides that kill the insects they eat, and nocturnal predators, such as great horned owls, that hunt them.

They are on the watch list, but not yet endangered. One of the only things people can do to help is to save the mature woodland habitat where whip-poor-wills live.

Editor's Note: Learn more about whip-poor-wills in "Top Billing" on pages 22-23.

Why the Cold Shoulder?

Every winter, I put out plenty of suet and birdseed. A few birds visit my backyard, but not like they do in summer. What's the problem? —*Margo Magwood Kitchener, Ontario*

George: Most people who feed backyard birds find that winter is the busiest time of the year. The fact that you don't have more activity in winter may have something to with the amount of evergreen habitat in your yard.

When the leaves of deciduous trees disappear in the fall, a yard without evergreens provides no adequate cover for birds to use when they are threatened by predators or inclement weather.

You can correct this by planting some pines, spruces and firs near the feeders to reestablish a comfort level for the birds that visit in winter. A quick fix would be to stand an old Christmas tree near your feeder. This will provide some temporary cover for the birds.

"Hairy" Hawk

My husband and I believe this backyard visitor (below) was a young red-tailed hawk. However, a friend of ours said it can't be because they won't stay close to humans, and their feathers don't go as far down on their legs. Can you clear up this mystery?

—*Jill Johns, Perrysville, Ohio*

George: You and your husband were right in your identification. This bird is a juvenile red-tailed hawk, which is apparent because of its lack of red tail, and the abundance of white on its breast and upper legs.

All red-tails have feathers on their upper legs, but your photograph makes it look like they extend down farther than they really do. These birds actually have yellow featherless legs from the knee joint down to the toes.

Red-tailed hawks commonly nest in mature forests in rural subdivisions, and are used to humans in their habitat. Because this bird is a juvenile, perhaps just out of the nest, it may not yet have acquired a strong fear of people.

FLYING FLOWERS

114

Photos: monarch, Richard Shiell/Dembinsky Photo Assoc.; red-spotted purple, Richard Day/Daybreak Imagery; painted lady, Donna and Tom Krischan; luna, Nancy Rotenberg

RED-SPOTTED PURPLE

Here's a beautiful butterfly that's surely a colorful character. The red-spotted purple's wings are awash in several vibrant shades, making it one of the most attractive flying flowers in North America.

A member of the admiral family, this butterfly's distinctive hues vary depending on your point of view. When viewed from the underside (at left), its scalloped wings are brown with blue and white edges, and distinctive brick-red spots cluster around the border markings.

The view from above (see photo below) is surprisingly different. The topside wings are black with a brilliant-blue to blue-green iridescence most noticeable in bright sunlight. Spanning 3 to 4 inches, these lovely butterflies are hard to miss.

Their coloring isn't only beautiful, it helps them survive. That's because they look a lot like the foul-tasting pipevine swallowtail, which birds will not eat.

The red-spotted purple is most active from early spring to fall and shows up almost anywhere from southern New England to central Florida and west to Colorado, Nebraska and the Dakotas. It's also found in canyons and arroyos dotting the Southwest and northern Mexico.

Their caterpillars are mottled creamy gray with a pair of prominent brush-like bristles behind their head (below right). They'll eat the leaves of a number of host trees, including willows, poplars, aspens, apples, cherries and hawthorns. Adult butterflies are attracted to nectar, fruits and sap.

Red-spotted purples are seen in fields, forests and along shorelines, roads and paths. But keep your eyes open. They also feed in gardens with plenty of nectar-producing plants.

POINT OF VIEW. The red-spotted purple takes on different looks, depending on how it's perched. Its underside (far left) is brownish with red spots, while the top of its wings (left) are bright blue. Their caterpillars (above) are mottled gray.

Skip Moody/Dembinsky Photo Assoc.

Richard Day/Daybreak Imagery

97

Rick Poley

Larry Ditto/KAC Productions

These distinctive fliers show their stripes.

ZEBRA LONGWING

Tom Allen   Kevin Barry

There's no question how this striking beauty got its name. The pale-yellow, zebra-like stripes on its wings are impossible to miss. The butterfly's long, narrow wings, measuring about 3-1/2 inches across, are distinctive as well.

This year-round resident of southern Texas and Florida frequents forest edges, thickets and flower gardens. If you vacation at Walt Disney World in Orlando, Florida, you might notice longwings gracefully flitting among the flowers there. What's more, these butterflies are easy to observe, since they fly slowly and don't easily startle.

Zebra longwings will venture north during the summer months to places like Georgia, South Carolina, Nebraska and Colorado and, on rare occasions, southern California.

Many butterfly houses at public gardens, museums and zoos also include the attractive zebra longwing in their collections. So no matter where you live, chances are you don't have to travel far to see one.

Time Is on Their Side

In addition to their attractive coloration, these fliers exhibit a number of other noteworthy traits. For instance, they return to the same spot each night to roost in clusters for protection. And unlike many species that survive only a few weeks, adult zebra longwings have life spans as long as 3 months.

There are a few good reasons zebra longwings are so long-lived. First, they rely solely on native passionflowers as host plants for their offspring. Since they are closely tied to their host plant, they usually don't stray far from them.

Also, females lay only a few eggs per passionflower, and may lay far fewer eggs each day than many other butterfly species. Female longwings definitely need to survive longer to deposit the 1,000 or so eggs they produce during their lifetimes.

Why don't females lay more eggs on each host plant? For one thing, zebra longwing caterpillars are very hungry after they hatch and will compete for the few leaves available on the vine. Spreading them out increases their chances of becoming butterflies and reduces predation on the caterpillars and eggs.

The passionflower isn't the most hospitable home either. The plant's nectar attracts ants and parasitic wasps, both of which will eat longwing eggs and caterpillars. To protect her eggs, the female tries to lay them on the growing tips of the passionflower vine, a spot that has little nectar and few predators.

Flying Flower Facts

Common Name: Zebra longwing.
Scientific Name: *Heliconius charitonius*.
Family: Brushfoots.
Wingspan: 2-1/2 to 3-5/8 inches.
Distinctive Markings: Long narrow wings are black with yellow stripes. Undersides have crimson dots at the base of the wings.
Distinctive Behavior: Zebra longwings are one of only a few butterfly species known to eat pollen in addition to nectar. Pollen gives them protein and provides energy.
Habitat: Forest edges, woodlands and flower gardens.
Caterpillar: Bluish to white with a white head and six rows of black branched spines on its body. Grows about 1-5/8 inches long.
Host Plant: Native passionflowers.

□ Summer
■ Year-Round

A BLACK-AND-WHITE BEAUTY. The zebra longwing caterpillar's white body is marked with rows of black branched spines. This one (right) is feeding on a native passionflower.

Rick Poley

Eye-Catching Caterpillars

Just like its parents, the zebra longwing caterpillar is distinctive in appearance, with a white body and multiple rows of black spines. It spends its time munching on the leaves of the passionflower vine where it hatched, absorbing the toxin these tropical bloomers contain.

Although this toxin doesn't harm the caterpillars, it does make them unpalatable, even into adulthood. In fact, the butterflies' bright stripes serve as a warning for predators to stay away.

Eventually, each caterpillar forms a spiny mottled chrysalis with metallic spots on the sides, and attaches it to the underside of a passionflower leaf with silken strings. Ten to 14 days later, the chrysalis becomes transparent, splits open and an adult butterfly emerges. Once its wings are dry, the zebra longwing is ready to fly—attracting attention wherever it goes.

WHITE PEACOCK

With a name like "peacock," you expect to see something pretty flashy—and the white peacock butterfly definitely delivers!

From its large, silvery-white wings outlined in orange to the intricate pattern of brown and orange scrawls—and small, black eyespots that highlight them—this butterfly is a standout beauty.

A member of the brush-footed family, the white peacock is a close relative of the buckeye butterfly. It is fairly small, with a wingspan of about 2-3/8 inches.

While it prefers the humid climates of southern Florida and Texas, it sometimes shows up in surprising locales. These butterflies have wandered as far north as Missouri and Kansas, North Carolina and even Massachusetts.

However, the white peacock isn't very hardy, so it tends to stick close to the Deep South and other balmy areas. The butterflies can also be found in the tropics of Central and South America.

One behavior that makes this butterfly unique is that it's active year-round, due to the warm climates, rather than finding a protective spot to overwinter as a caterpillar or chrysalis like many other butterfly species do.

Look for this fanciful flier in swampy spots, along shorelines and near water, in weedy fields and in places where the ground has been disturbed. Pay close attention to flowers like bacopa and verbenas, too. The butterflies prefer the nectar these blooms produce.

Don't expect a white peacock to perch on you, though. This beauty is people-shy. It isn't a strong flier and often flies in a low and erratic manner.

Females lay pale-yellow eggs on water hyssop and ruellia leaves. The eggs hatch into spiny black caterpillars with silver spots that avidly feed on their host plants.

Each caterpillar (right inset) forms a smooth, green chrysalis that darkens with age…until the graceful fair-winged beauty emerges.

Photos: Jim Yokajty/The Image Finders; inset, Tom Allen

READER TIP

Look for this year-round southern flier in swampy spots, along shorelines and near water, in weedy fields and in places where the ground has been disturbed.

MONARCH

Majestic beauty reigns from coast to coast.

Ask almost anyone to name a butterfly they know, and chances are, "monarch" will be the response you hear most often. It's no wonder—these distinctive fliers are found almost everywhere!

Ranging from southern Canada to the mountains of central Mexico, from California to the East Coast, and all points in between, the monarch is as abundant as is it widespread. And the flier's large size and striking orange-and-black wings make it easy to spot.

The monarch is a year-round resident in southern California, southern Florida and Hawaii, but it isn't a permanent fixture in colder climates, thanks to its preference for temperatures above 60°. Monarchs living in northern areas head to the far South, Southwest or Mexico as soon as chilly weather begins to set in.

In fact, monarchs are the only butterflies that regularly migrate from north to south as birds do. You might see thousands of them roosting in trees during fall as they make their way to warmer locales for the winter.

Pacific Grove, California plays host to countless numbers of the species, earning it the nickname "Butterfly Town, USA." Florida, Texas and Mexico are also destinations for these kings of the road. (For more on monarch migration, see pages 104-105.)

Flight of Fancy

Watching a monarch fly is a real treat—whether it's hurriedly zipping by or leisurely gliding along, occasionally stopping to sip nectar from aster, verbena, ironweed, sedum, zinnia and butterfly bush flowers. The butterfly is quite approachable, so it's easy to get close and observe its behavior.

Monarchs are commonly found in city and suburban gardens, as well as open prairies, weedy fields, pastures, roadsides, rugged foothills and marshes. If you want to attract some to your yard, install a butterfly feeder filled with sugar water or plant the flowers they prefer—and be sure to add several milkweed plants also.

Why milkweed? Because this regal butterfly is a member of the milkweed butterfly family, a clan that lays eggs on milkweed plants.

READER TIP

To attract this beauty to your yard, install a butterfly feeder with sugar water or plant nectar-filled flowers. And don't forget the milkweed!

Richard Shiell/Dembinsky Photo Assoc.

AN AMAZING PROCESS. The metamorphosis of a monarch from caterpillar to adult butterfly is a remarkable process to witness. First, the caterpillar hangs upside down in the shape of a 'J' (1) until it slowly sheds its skin (2) to enter the chrysalis stage. Within an hour, the soft casing hardens to form a protective shell (3). Nine to 14 days later, the chrysalis becomes clear and splits open so the adult can emerge (4). After allowing its wings to dry (5), the monarch is ready to take flight.

Metamorphosis photos: Richard Day/Daybreak Imagery

The plants serve as the major food for monarch caterpillars, with an important added benefit—the poison found in milkweeds provides a lifetime of protection from predators. As the caterpillars munch on milkweeds, they store the plants' toxins in their bodies, transferring the noxious chemicals into the butterflies they become.

Visual Clues

The adult monarchs' vivid wing markings serve as a warning to birds and other predators. Inexperienced hunters that decide to eat one quickly learn that these beauties don't make a tasty meal!

The message a monarch's wings send is so effective that the viceroy species of butterfly mimics its markings as a defense mechanism.

Monarch caterpillars are as stunning as their parents, with bold yellow and black stripes covering their plump white bodies and two antennae-like filaments crowning each end. They grow to about 2 inches long.

When it's time to begin the transformation, each caterpillar forms a delicate-looking jade green chrysalis that becomes increasingly transparent. (See photo series above right.) After 2 weeks, a butterfly emerges…and the cycle of life continues.

Flying Flower Facts

Common Name: Monarch.
Scientific Name: *Danaus plexippus*.
Family: Milkweed.
Wingspan: 3-1/2 to 4 inches.
Distinctive Markings: Bright orange with multiple black veins. Wings are edged in black with white speckles.
Distinctive Behavior: Caterpillars dine on milkweed plants. Adult butterflies migrate north and south.
Habitat: Widespread during migration, from cities to suburban gardens to rural fields and mountain pastures. When breeding (before the southward migration), they prefer open areas with plenty of milkweed plants.
Caterpillar: White with yellow and black stripes, measuring up to 2 inches long.
Host Plant: Milkweed.

Summer
Year-Round

Kathy Adams Clark/KAC Productions

MYSTERIOUS MONARCHS

This butterfly's migration is nothing short of amazing.

By Tom Allen, Contributing Editor

Many butterflies from around the world migrate each year, but no butterfly can match the incredible journey of the monarch.

In autumn, these regal butterflies travel up to 2,000 miles over 2 months. Those from east of the Rocky Mountains head to a 30-by-50-mile patch of forest in the mountains of south-central Mexico, and those west of the Rockies winter in southern California. The only exception is a nonmigratory population in southern Florida. There, monarchs continue to breed and produce caterpillars year-round.

Butterflies in "Training"

But monarchs just don't flap their wings and head south. With a cruising speed of 12 mph, they would be exhausted after a short journey if they didn't adequately prepare. In fact, many monarchs arrive in Mexico five times fatter than when they started in their summer range.

So how do they do it? First of all, it's important to know there are three to six generations of monarchs each year, and only one of those generations makes the preparations to migrate. The monarchs that emerge in spring and summer live only 4 to 5 weeks and simply produce the next generation.

Then, as autumn approaches, the butterflies sense the temperature change and shortening daylight. This signals the caterpillars that develop in fall to delay maturing into adults, allowing

Robert E. Barber/Unicorn Stock Photos

and the next generation completes the journey back to their original summer range.

No Map, No Guide

One of the great mysteries of this journey is that no monarch making the trip has ever traveled the route before. How they know where to go and how to get there continues to baffle the scientific world.

Although they may not have understood it, this migratory phenomenon was well known to the regions' ancient cultures. Monarchs and other butterflies appear on pre-Columbian Meso-American Indian art and embroidery. Yet, the monarchs' wintering grounds were not discovered by modern scientists until the mid-1970s.

Mysterious as it may be, there are several theories about how and why the monarchs migrate.

One theory is that the monarch originally was a tropical species that followed its main food source, milkweed, as the plant became more common in the North after the last ice age. Unable to withstand cold winters, the butterfly would head south each winter and return north in spring.

There's a possible explanation for the location of their concentrated wintering sites as well.

While the butterflies can't withstand freezing temperatures, neither can they remain in warm climates where they would be active and deplete their stored fat reserves. This might also cause them to use up milkweed in an area, since the warm weather could trigger continued mating and egg laying.

That's why the temperate climate in their mountain roosting sites high in the Sierra Nevada range is perfect for them. The butterflies can remain semidormant for winter, living off their fat stores. Although the monarchs do not feed during hibernation, they do require moisture, which they get in the high-elevation coniferous forests.

A Delicate Balance

Due to the concentrated roosting sites, when local people began harvesting forest trees for timber, it placed the wintering monarchs in grave danger. Even removing a few trees changes the forest's critical temperature—making the nights frostier and the days warmer, which altered the environment the butterflies needed to hibernate.

A cry for help came from conservationists around the world and forced the Mexican government to take action. News quickly spread of the monarch's plight. Unfortunately, this attracted droves of visitors to the area, and thousands of butterflies that fell from the trees were trampled.

In recent years however, the Mexican government has taken steps to protect the monarch's wintering grounds. In 1986, the country established a preserve to protect the area. And slowly but surely, tourism and guided walks are replacing the need to harvest timber as a means of supporting the local economy.

With ongoing preservation and concern, the monarch will have a bright future...and continue to intrigue butterfly enthusiasts for a long time to come.

extra time to begin storing large fat reserves for the journey south.

When the newly hatched adult butterflies take flight in fall, they head for warmer areas as quickly as possible, feeding and storing fat as they go. They fly south by riding on wind and thermal currents, even if it is not a direct route.

As they get farther south, they become more selective and ride higher on the thermals to conserve energy. Once they reach Texas and the Gulf of Mexico, they begin a more direct route and fly closer to the ground, unless the winds are blowing in the right direction. While traveling across the Gulf, they rest on any structures they can find, such as oil rigs and ships.

When they arrive at their mountainous roosting sites in Mexico and California, the butterflies congregate in huge groups, numbering in the hundreds of thousands. The orange-and-black striped beauties often cover entire groves of trees—dangling from every branch and limb (see photo above). There, at elevations of 10,000 feet, they remain semidormant for the winter.

As winter ends, the butterflies increase their activity and fly farther and farther from the colony until they begin to return north. They then mate and lay their eggs along the route,

Flying Flowers

PIPEVINE
SWALLOWTAIL

At first glance, the pipevine swallowtail isn't as flashy as its swallowtail cousins.

But once the sun strikes those inky unmarked wings, watch out! This flier's plain appearance disappears in a burst of brilliant, iridescent blue with a smattering of white spots. The underwings, featuring orange and white spots atop shimmering sapphire markings, are more flamboyant without the help of sunlight.

The pipevine's appearance has little bearing on its name,

however. The moniker stems from the fact that its caterpillar's sole source of food is, naturally, the pipevine. And fittingly, it's the only kind of plant the adult female will use to lay her rust-colored eggs.

Aside from nutrition, these plants also offer something else—protection. Pipevines contain noxious chemicals that the caterpillar tolerates and stores in its body. If an animal eats the caterpillar or adult butterfly, the toxins will make it sick. Experienced predators know that the pipevine's markings

A RED FLAG. The pipevine swallowtail's markings serve as a warning to predators that it contains toxins. Even the caterpillar (above) sports fleshy tubercles, which give it a formidable look.

indicate illness, and they stay away.

This defense mechanism is so effective, several other butterfly species mimic the adult pipevine's underwing markings. Female spicebush swallowtails, some female eastern tiger swallowtails, female eastern black swallowtails, female Diana fritillaries and red-spotted purples are among the copycats with similar wing markings.

The pipevine swallowtail caterpillar has another form of security. Its rusty-black body is studded with red or black fleshy tubercles, giving it a formidable appearance.

You'll likely see this graceful butterfly throughout most of the eastern U.S., north into southern Ontario and as far west as Arizona, California and Oregon, thanks to the spread of pipevine plants, which have become popular with gardeners.

Aside from flower beds, the pipevine swallowtail is a common sight in open woodlands, canyons, meadows, orchards and roadsides, and can be found throughout most of the eastern U.S., north into southern Ontario and as far west as Arizona, California and Oregon, thanks to the spread of pipevine plants.

Despite its size—this flying flower's wingspan can reach a huge 5 inches—it's speedy, moving with rapid and shallow wing beats. The pipevine also tends to flutter its wings while feeding, making it difficult to photograph.

READER TIP

This graceful flier prefers to sip nectar from plants like honeysuckle, orchid, butterfly bush, azalea, lilac, thistle and swamp milkweed. Its host plant is pipevine.

'GLAD YOU ASKED!'

Our butterfly expert answers your questions.

Winged Wonder

I spotted this striped butterfly (above) perched on a pine tree in my yard. It looks like a tiger swallowtail, but I didn't think these butterflies were in this part of the country. Can you tell me what kind it is?

—Jeanne Hardy, Paulden, Arizona

Tom: The butterfly is a female two-tailed swallowtail. This butterfly, which occurs throughout the western United States, is very similar to the common tiger swallowtail, but can be easily distinguished by the double tails on its hind wings.

You can tell this one is a female because it has a large amount of blue on the hind wing. This is also a good way to identify a female tiger swallowtail.

Make Your Own Nectar

I purchased a butterfly feeder to help attract more butterflies to my garden. I already make my own hummingbird nectar. Can I use this recipe to feed butterflies? —Niceta Field, Ray, Michigan

Tom: While hummingbird nectar typically is a 4-to-1 ratio of water to sugar, butterfly nectar is a bit weaker. Try a 10 percent sugar-water solution (about 1 part sugar to 10 parts water), and add a pinch of multivitamins, if you'd like, from a children's vitamin capsule. Or, use Gatorade with a little sugar added—about 1/2 teaspoon of sugar per cup.

One word of advice, though. You'll want to have some sort of trap to keep ants from taking over the sweet liquid.

Another thing to keep in mind is that butterflies are attracted to flowers by the amount of ultraviolet reflection they emit. Since some colors emit better than others, certain feeders may not emit the correct wavelengths to attract butterflies. Purple, lavender, orange and red usually work well, but you'll just have to try them.

In addition to feeders, there are a few other simple ways to attract butterflies. You can put bananas or fermented fruit in your feeder to attract butterflies like mourning cloaks, anglewings or tortoiseshells.

Also, don't forget the flowers. Because of the differences in UV reflections, some flowers are better than others. One to try is lavender or purple butterfly bush (*Buddleia*), which should attract fritillaries and swallowtails.

Group Shot

I snapped this picture (below) at a resting area in a nearby national forest. I believe there are three different species of butterflies here. Why are they grouped together like this? There did not appear to be any water on the ground. —Bill Campbell
Kingsport, Tennessee

Tom: This activity is called "puddling" and it's a common sight, especially during early spring in wooded areas of the Appalachian Mountains and elsewhere. Newly emerged male butterflies of several species will gather at moist spots to sip minerals and salts from the wet soil.

Although you mentioned that there didn't appear to be water on the surface, all the butterflies need is a slightly damp area from which to extract the collected minerals.

In your photo, the two dominant species are tiger swallowtails and pipevine swallowtails. They have also been joined by one or two spicebush swallowtails and a few duskywing skippers.

A Blooming Mystery

This royal walnut moth was in my garden early one morning (below). I've never seen this kind of flying flower on my blooms before. Was this a rare sighting?
— *Paul Wolf, Hanover, Pennsylvania*

Tom: The royal walnut is also known as the hickory horned devil because of the long horns on the caterpillar. This flier belongs to the same family as other large moths such as the luna and cecropia.

This moth is fairly common in your area, especially where hickory and black walnut trees are found. However, it's not a flier that visits flowers. These moths do not have mouths for feeding, so you're not likely to see it on a bloom.

Home Sweet Home?

I have two butterfly houses, but I'm not sure where to hang them. Do these houses really attract butterflies? — *Donna Hoppes, Pendleton, Indiana*

Tom: Butterfly houses are more of a garden decoration than a way to attract butterflies to your yard.

Although a few butterfly species seek shelter for winter hibernation or a shady roost during the hot summer, most butterflies usually rest on vegetation or in trees.

However, if you put your houses in a protected area near woodlands, you could attract a mourning cloak or question mark to them. And in areas where Milbert's tortoiseshells are found, a butterfly house might be effective, since these butterflies hibernate in large groups.

Be aware that butterfly houses also make good homes for wasps and hornets.

Butterfly Assistance

Four monarch caterpillars recently hatched on my milkweed, and I've noticed some ants and aphids on the plant, too. Do monarchs need these insects, or should I get rid of them?
— *Mrs. John Mecozzi*
Camarillo, California

Tom: Many butterflies in the hairstreak and blue families have a cooperative relationship with ants. The ants protect the caterpillars from predators, and in return, the ants feed on a sugary solution the caterpillars secrete.

However, monarch caterpillars don't secrete a sugary solution, and they don't need protection, either, because the milkweed they eat produces toxins that ward off predators.

So while the ants and aphids don't pose a threat to the caterpillars, they could be a problem for your milkweed. You can deal with the pests by applying a little soapy water to the plant when the caterpillars aren't present.

ATTRACTING BUTTERFLIES

By Tom Allen, Contributing Editor

It seems everyone wants to know how to attract butterflies to their gardens. It's one of the most common questions I hear. But before you can create a successful habitat for butterflies, you need to consider your own "habitat."

Are there features like open fields, wooded areas or wetlands? What region is it? What's the climate like? All of these factors determine what butterfly species inhabit the area around your home, as well as the types of plants you can grow to attract them.

Time to Play Host

A good place to start is with the foods—or host plants—that butterflies require during the caterpillar stage. Most butterflies, especially females, do not stray far from host plants.

The most well-known example of this is milkweed, the host plant for monarchs and a great nectar source, too. Some other examples are everlastings for American ladies, clovers for sulphur butterflies, and tulip trees, ash or choke cherry for tiger swallowtails.

In addition, you also need to be aware of some of the characteristics of the butterflies you'd like to attract.

Monarchs migrate in fall, therefore it helps to plant late bloomers for them, such as asters or chrysanthemums.

Another important trait to consider is the length of a butterfly's proboscis—what they use to sip nectar.

Some butterflies, including swallowtails and skippers, have a long proboscis and can reach into deep-throated flowers, such as cardinal flower, honeysuckle, bee balm and azalea.

Other species, especially small ones (like the acadian hairstreak above), can only reach into flowers with short corollas. So planting milkweed (including butterfly weed), purple coneflower, blazing star, phlox, buckwheat, butterfly bush and lilac will attract them.

Butterfly Buffet

In addition, there are a number of butterfly species that don't like flower nectar as a food source. These are the anglewings, the admirals and the tortoiseshells, to name a few.

They are mainly sap feeders and get their nutrients from tree wounds, rotting fruit and even animal dung. To attract them, you can set out various crushed ripe fruits and allow them to ferment.

While no one can attract all the butterflies that are common to their region, planting a few of the flowers mentioned here should increase the fluttering activity in any backyard.

CLOUDED SULPHUR

Have you ever seen a pair of small yellow butterflies spiraling upward in the air? Then you've witnessed one of the spectacular behaviors of the common sulphur, also known as the clouded sulphur.

While this behavior might *look* romantic, the truth is the female sulphur is rejecting the male. The male will pursue the female a bit longer, but eventually he'll head off in search of a more receptive mate.

Common sulphurs often bask in the sun with their wings closed. The undersides of the wings (at right) feature two silvery spots encircled in red, which helps distinguish them from other sulphurs.

The tops of the wings are yellow for all males and most females, particularly those that live in southern regions. You may spot white females in cold climates.

Regardless of color, females' wings have light-black borders with yellow dots, while males' wings have solid, ink-black borders (like the one above). Their wingspan typically is 1-3/8 to 2 inches.

Male common sulphurs are often confused with orange sulphurs (also known as alfalfa sulphurs) because they look almost identical. The butterflies, however, have no trouble telling each other apart—whether it's due to ultraviolet colors we can't see or the production of certain chemicals, called pheromones.

These butterflies are common in western Canada and across most of the United States. They prefer open areas, such as meadows, parks and large backyards. They like clover, dandelions and wildflowers for nectar, and the females usually select clover or alfalfa as host plants for their chartreuse eggs.

The common sulphur caterpillar is small and green with light side stripes and darker back stripes (inset at right). Each one forms a bright-green chrysalis in fall that protects it over the winter months.

Common sulphurs are active from March to November. They often congregate around puddles to collect salts and other nutrients. In fact, creating an area of damp sand or soil in your yard is a great way to coax these sunny flying flowers to pay you a visit.

Richard Shiell; lower inset, Tom Allen; top, Ken Thommes

VERY HUNGRY CATERPILLARS

You can't have your plants and butterflies, too... or can you?

By Gilbert S. Grant
Sneads Ferry, North Carolina

SOMEONE has been eating my garden!

Although I enjoy the beauty of a butterfly flitting among my flowers, I was still shocked to discover that a group of black swallowtail caterpillars had been munching away on my precious fennel and dill.

Of course, in order to have those adult jewels flying through the garden, we must welcome a few caterpillars as they dine on their host plants. These plants provide a place for the female butterflies to lay eggs, and then supply food for the growing caterpillars.

So my solution to that hungry group of black swallowtail caterpillars? Plant more fennel!

Now, I have enough plants for me and the caterpillars to enjoy. On occasion, I've noticed as many as 20 caterpillars eating the spread I have offered.

I applied this same lesson to the other common caterpillar plants in my yard.

For instance, in late summer, passionflower vines appear in some of my flower beds, and are soon visited by female gulf fritillaries and variegated fritillaries in search of a place to lay eggs. Since I have a lot of these vines, I don't mind when I see the colorful caterpillars (like the one top right) eating the leaves. Later, the butterflies (top far right) are a delight as they fly among the lantanas in late summer and early fall.

I've also noticed that another prevalent butterfly—the common buckeye—prefers my toadflax and snapdragons, so I added more plantings of those as well.

To be able to enjoy winged jewels like these, we must accept the damage the caterpillars sometimes cause. With extra plantings, we can enjoy both our flowers and the colorful *flying* flowers they attract.

Nancy Rotenberg

WANT BUTTERFLIES? START AT THE BEGINNING

Attract "flying flowers" by selecting plants to feed caterpillars.

By Tom Allen, Contributing Editor

Top photos: John and Gloria Tveten/KAC Productions

TIME TO DINE. Caterpillars (like the monarch, far left) see your garden as a big buffet. Select the right plants to attract certain species, like passionflower for gulf fritillary caterpillars (above left), which will transform into beautiful adults (above).

One of the best ways to attract butterflies is to fill your garden with plants for caterpillars to eat. You can even combine the plants into a butterfly and caterpillar garden.

You don't need to worry that the caterpillars will destroy all your plants. That's a common misconception.

Most garden butterfly species lay only one or two eggs on each host plant before moving on to look for another plant. As a result, the caterpillars don't appear in large enough numbers to cause great harm to any single plant. In addition, very few butterflies lay their eggs in clusters, as several moths are known to do.

In fact, moth caterpillars often are responsible for the plant damage gardeners find. While some moths can be a welcome backyard addition, such as the attractive hawk moths or Saturn moths, many can be quite destructive. A good example is the eastern tent caterpillar that appears in early spring and consumes cherry tree foliage to the very last leaf.

Be a Good Host

Knowing the proper host plants is the secret to attracting butterflies. A good place to start is with black swallowtails, a species found throughout much of the United States. This butterfly is easy to please and will feed on plants in the carrot family. While they especially like fennel, they will also lay their eggs on dill, carrots and parsley.

Plant a variety of these so the caterpillars spread around your garden, ensuring some survive potential predators to become adult butterflies. Plus, it leaves plants for you, too.

If you live in a warmer climate, try passionflowers to appeal to gulf fritillaries and zebra longwings. Use native plants if possible for these species, since the butterflies will not feed on some of the hybrid passionflowers. Two favored types are maypops and corky-stemmed passionflower, both native to the South.

Plant your passionflowers in sunlit areas to attract gulf fritillaries, or in the shade for zebra longwings. Add several along fences or on a trellis, and there will be enough to go around.

Variegated fritillaries also use passionflowers as a host, but they seek out flax, pansies and violets as well.

A Blooming Favorite

Violets are a popular host plant for many fritillary butterflies. In addition to the variegated species, violets will attract great spangled, Aphrodite and Atlantis fritillaries—all common in the eastern U.S.—as well as most of the western fritillaries (like the callipe, Mormon and zerene).

So no matter where you live, adding violets in shady garden spots (just don't let them invade your lawn) should catch the attention of members of this family. You may see the fritillaries in summer, but the caterpillars won't show up until the following spring.

There are many other common host plants you can add to your garden, including milkweed to attract monarchs or everlastings for American ladies. Just see the list (below) to get started.

16 Plants for Caterpillars

To attract butterflies, host plants are a good place to start. These plants provide a spot for butterflies to lay their eggs, and they also offer food for the caterpillars. Butterfly expert Tom Allen recommends the following "sweet 16" to attract some common species.

Rick and Nora Bowers/KAC Productions

Richard Shiell

1. Aster—Pearl crescent
2. Everlasting—American lady (at right)
3. Carrot—Black swallowtail
4. Choke or black cherry— Tiger swallowtail
5. Dill—Black swallowtail
6. False nettle—Red admiral, eastern comma
7. Fennel—Black swallowtail
8. Flax—Variegated fritillary
9. Milkweed—Monarch
10. Pansy—Variegated fritillary
11. Parsley—Black swallowtail (at right)
12. Passionflower—Gulf fritillary, zebra longwing, variegated fritillary
13. Snapdragon—Common buckeye
14. Toadflax—Common buckeye
15. Violet—Most fritillaries
16. Willow—Viceroy, western tiger swallowtail, red-spotted purple, mourning cloak

LUNA MOTH

These elegant creatures shine in the moonlight.

You won't find this beautiful "flying flower" basking in the sun—it's nocturnal by nature. In fact, its name, luna, is Latin for "moon."

This spectacular creature has lovely pale-green wings that can measure more than 4 inches across, making it hard to miss, even in the moonlight. It gets its name from the fact that it's active at night, like most moths, but also because of the silvery, crescent moon-shaped eyespots on its wings.

Those eyespots aren't for decoration, however. They serve as a protective disguise, fooling predators into thinking it's a much larger animal.

If the eyespots don't dupe an animal on the prowl, the luna relies on another trick. Its head is so well covered by its wings that hunters often misjudge their target and go after the long curving tails on the luna's hind wings instead. This gives the moth a chance to escape.

Widespread Beauties

Its large wings make the luna a strong flier, and this species is quite common throughout its range in the eastern United States and southern Canada. It's attracted to bright light, so it isn't unusual to see one resting on the side of house or a tree.

Readers Robin and David Byard of Somerset, Pennsylvania recall the luna that perched on a hanging basket of flowers in their yard.

"I awoke one morning in May to find this beautiful moth clinging to the basket," Robin says. "It remained there for 2 days before flying off."

GET A GOOD LOOK. The feathery antennae and stout body of this luna (left) help observers distinguish it from butterflies. Below, lunas perch with their wings open, often near a bright light at night.

Many people who spot a luna erroneously believe it's a butterfly instead of a moth. Although moths tend to have duller wing colors than butterflies, that's certainly not the case with the luna.

The best way to separate moths from butterflies is to examine their antennae. Moths usually have feathery or filament-like antennae with fine tips, while butterfly antennae always end with a club or knob. Moths, especially the larger ones, also generally are more robust than butterflies.

Fly by Night

Like many large moths, the luna will only survive for a few days once it emerges from its cocoon as an adult. It will quickly attract a mate, then the female immediately begins laying eggs on the leaves of trees such as paper birch, sweet gum, hickory, walnut, persimmon and sumac.

The luna caterpillar is lime green with a thin, yellow line on each side and tiny orange spots. It has a hearty appetite and will grow to be about 3 inches long. It needs to store plenty of energy, because once it's a moth, it stops eating entirely. The adult luna doesn't even have a mouth.

The caterpillar eventually turns reddish before spinning a brown, papery cocoon, often among leaves on the ground below a tree.

In the northern parts of its range, luna moths typically emerge between May and July. In the South, there may be as many as three generations of these moths from March into September.

–Flying Flower Facts

Common Name: Luna moth.
Scientific Name: *Actias luna*.
Family: Giant silkworm.
Wingspan: 3 to 4-1/2 inches.
Distinctive Markings: Pale-green wings with two sets of silvery eyespots. They have dark-colored margins along the front of their forewings and long tails on their hind wings.
Distinctive Behavior: Strong fliers that are attracted to light.
Habitat: In deciduous woodlands.
Caterpillar: Green with a yellow stripe down each side, tiny orange spots and hairs along back. Grows to be about 3 inches long.
Host Plants: A variety of deciduous trees, including paper birch, persimmon, sweet gum, hickory, walnut and sumac.

Year-Round

IN THE BEGINNING. The lime-green luna caterpillar (top) eats voraciously and grows to about 3 inches before spinning a papery cocoon (above) among leaves on the ground.

Flying Flowers

QUEEN

It may look like a monarch, but this regal beauty is actually a cousin of that well-known flier. The queen butterfly bears monarch-like markings, including black veins and white spots along the edges of its wings and on its body. But this species is slightly smaller, with a wingspan of about 3-3/8 inches (compared to a monarch's 4-inch span), and noticeably different in color—it's more mahogany brown than orange.

The queen is no fan of cold temperatures and typically keeps to the southern United States from Nevada east to Missouri, southern Georgia and the Carolinas and south through Florida. It is a common sight in the Sonoran Desert in Arizona, California and Mexico, and can be found in South America, too.

The queen may also visit northern states like Massachusetts, Illinois or Idaho if the weather is unusually warm.

When in flight, queen butterflies take several strong wing flaps, followed by a leisurely glide. Look for them in open areas like brush-filled fields, grassy roadsides, prairies, meadows, deserts and open waterways.

Queens are only active when it's warm and sunny. On cool mornings, you might spot one basking in the sun to raise its body temperature and gain enough heat to fly.

Like monarchs, queens are milkweed butterflies, named for their preference for this plant. Females lay eggs *only* on milkweed, typically producing several broods from April to November.

The caterpillars that hatch sport bright bands of white, black and yellow, with three pairs of black "tentacles" (see bottom photo at right). They munch entirely on milkweed leaves, which provide both nutrition and protection in the form of a toxin that doesn't bother the caterpillars, but makes them taste terrible, even after they've become butterflies. Most birds and other predators simply leave queens and other milkweed butterflies alone.

Each caterpillar completes its metamorphosis inside a 1-inch-long, bright-green chrysalis suspended from a nearby leaf, stem or twig. The delicate, winged creature that emerges dines on the nectar of many plants, including milkweed, goldenrod, aster, daisy and thistle.

A HEALTHY DIET. Like its monarch cousin, the queen butterfly gets protection from toxins in the milkweed it eats. These butterflies are found in the southern United States.

BANDED HAIRSTREAK

Unlike other butterflies with striking colors or intricate patterns, the banded hairstreak is a study in subtle beauty.

Viewed from above, its small 1- to 1-1/2-inch-wide wings are a rich, sooty black. But that's a rare sight, since this species rests with its wings closed, displaying the more interesting undersides.

Even so, the patterns underneath are quite simple. They consist mainly of several rows of black dashes outlined in white, a small splash of orange along the bottom outer edge, and a patch of blue positioned above the thin white and black tail on each hind wing.

Another small, almost unnoticeable tail sits a bit above the longer one, usually in line with the smattering of orange.

The only distinction between males and females is the small oval area along the upper inside edge of the male's forewing, which the female lacks. Otherwise, they are almost identical.

Rick and Nora Bowers/KAC Productions

Tom Allen

This quiet beauty prefers life among the trees.

Richard Day/Daybreak Imagery

Common Denominator

And speaking of similarities, several cousins so closely resemble the banded hairstreak, it can be challenging to tell them apart. These related butterflies include the striped, king's, hickory and Edward's hairstreaks.

You don't have to rely on wing coloration alone to pick a banded hairstreak out of the crowd, however. Sheer numbers are on its side, since it's the most common of the bunch, thanks to its widespread range and ability to adapt to a variety of habitats.

You'll find this flier from Nova Scotia and Maine to North Dakota and southeastern Saskatchewan, as far south as Texas and Florida, and just about all points in between. Chances are, if you think you've seen a banded hairstreak, you're right.

It also engages in hard-to-miss behavior. This territorial insect responds to every banded hairstreak that enters the area it calls home, and it will charge after the intruder in an effort to drive it away. Sometimes, as many as six may be spotted chasing each other.

Also, look for males perched during daylight hours on shrubs and tree branches located near the ground, where they have the best chance of finding a mate.

EYE OF THE BEHOLDER. Though subtle, this flying flower displays plenty of beauty. Clockwise from far left, the banded hairstreak rests its wings...two hairstreaks feed on butterfly weed ...a pupa waits for spring...a caterpillar munches on a leaf.

Into the Woods

The graceful creature prefers to flit about hickory, walnut or oak forests or hot oak-filled canyons in the westernmost reaches of its range. It will frequent forest edges and clearings, roadsides and city parks, too, as long as hickories, walnuts and oaks grow nearby.

The trees are important because they serve as hosts for banded hairstreak caterpillars. Adult females lay beige or pale-lavendar eggs on twigs during the summer, and the larvae hatch the following spring.

The caterpillars vary in color from brown to green or white, with dark blotches on the head and tail. Some even have yellow stripes along each side. They dine on spring growth, including catkins and leaves, before each forms a hairy, mottled, brownish-pink chrysalis that is tightly fastened to a leaf or twig with a sturdy silken string.

The butterflies emerge in late spring and early summer, and can be found sipping nectar from milkweed, dogbane, daisies, sumac, meadowsweet, white sweet clover and yarrow—when they aren't chasing each other, that is!

So if you live near the woods in southern Canada or the eastern U.S., keep your eyes peeled for this quiet beauty—and get ready to bask in its understated yet breathtaking glory. ✦

Flying Flower Facts

Common Name: Banded hairstreak.
Scientific Name: *Satyrium calanus*.
Family: Gossamer wing.
Wingspan: 1 to 1-1/2 to inches.
Distinctive Markings: Undersides of wings have black dashes outlined in white, an orange patch toward the bottom and a blue area above a thin, black tail.
Distinctive Behavior: Adult butterflies are very territorial and will chase any newcomer. Males can be found during the day perched on low shrubs and tree branches, watching for females. It rests with wings in upright position.
Habitat: Deciduous forests containing oak, hickory or walnut trees, woodland clearings, roadsides and city parks.
Caterpillar: Yellowish-green or brown with dark blotches at either end. May have yellow stripes and dashes.
Host Plants: Oak, walnut and hickory trees.

Year-Round

Tom Allen

READER TIP

This flying flower is at home in any open land-scape. Look for it feeding on thistles, asters, sun-flowers, zinnias, mallows and various legumes.

PAINTED LADY

As ornate and colorful as the Victorian-style home that shares its name, the painted lady butterfly makes a grand impression everywhere it appears. And this beauty, also known as the "cosmopolite," gets around. It's the most widespread butterfly in the world!

The painted lady can be found on every continent except Antarctica and Australia. A permanent resident of the Sonoran deserts in Mexico and the southwestern U.S., this flier travels northward during March and April, either in scattered numbers or impressive swarms. It permeates the countryside from coast to coast and moves well into Canada until the first hard frost, usually in October.

Unable to survive freezing temperatures, its annual trek is one way. However, the painted lady's prevalence in all parts of the country during warm weather virtually ensures anyone the chance to see this well-traveled creature.

The painted lady isn't too hard to pick out of a crowd. Its recognizable wings are highly patterned and measure 2 to 2-1/2 inches across. On top, they are salmon orange with striking black and white markings (left). The hue is pinker underneath (top inset), where the wings are covered in an elaborately colored web with a row of four to five small bluish eyespots.

It looks very similar to the less common American lady butterfly (sometimes called the American painted lady), which has two large eyespots on its underwings.

At home in any open landscape, this butterfly is as likely to grace an alpine meadow as it is to flit about a coastal garden or an urban park. You might spot it feeding on thistles, asters, sunflowers, zinnias, mallows and various legumes.

When it comes to selecting a host plant for its eggs, the female painted lady most often chooses a thistle or a related plant. The caterpillars (lower inset) that hatch are eye-catching and measure about 1-1/4 inches in length.

These larvae are dark colored with a yellow stripe, and all have short white or gray spines. The lavender-brown chrysalis each caterpillar forms is bumpy and measures just less than 1 inch.

There often are two broods of these butterflies each summer, assuring plenty of painted ladies for all to admire.

SPLIT PERSONALITY. Although the painted lady displays showy colors on both side of its wings, the markings are so different that you may think they belong to two different butterflies.

124

127

138

152

134

BLOOMING BEAUTY

Photos: rose and dahlia, Alan and Linda Detrick; poppy, Mark E. Gibson/The Image Finders; allium, Nancy Rotenberg; sunflower, Dianne Dietrich Leis

ROSES

Take your pick—any of these classic beauties will be the crowning glory in your garden.

There's a good reason the rose is often referred to as "the queen of the garden." It has long been prized, not only for its unmatched beauty, but also for its healing properties, delicate flavor and sweet fragrance. And with so many shapes, colors and sizes to choose from, this bloomer stands out in any form.

Roses have been around for ages. Ancient fossils of early roses have turned up in Montana, while active cultivation of the flower started in Greece and Asia more recently—about 3,000 years ago!

Since medieval times, roses have been used as food and medicine. Healers believed roses could cure all kinds of ailments. Their nutritional value was confirmed during World War II when scientists discovered rose hips contain more vitamin C than most fruits or vegetables.

So Many Choices

There are literally *thousands* of roses available to modern gardeners. Luckily, these beauties are divided into distinct categories. Some of the most popular ones include:

Old roses are varieties that were introduced before 1867. These fragrant types include gallica, damask, bourbon and tea roses. They're hardy, disease resistant and easy to grow, but not as showy as newer types.

Hybrid tea roses are the most popular rose. Their flowers are showy and look wonderful in arrangements. They can be more susceptible to disease, however, and need protection from cold winters.

Floribunda roses are a cross between hybrid teas and a low-growing hedge variety called polyantha. These tend to be shrubbier in form and grow 2 to 3 feet tall, producing clusters of blossoms.

Grandiflora types were created by combining long-stemmed hybrid teas and the clustered flowers of floribundas. These roses can grow as tall as 6 feet.

Shrub roses are large full plants that can be hybrids or naturally occurring natives. They're hardy in almost every Plant Hardiness Zone and often fragrant. Some new types are repeat bloomers.

Climbers produce long stems called canes that need to be supported, making them ideal for trellises, arbors and walls.

Which Rose Is for You?

When choosing roses, you need to keep in mind three factors: your soil conditions, the amount of time you have to care for the plant and where you want to use it.

"If you want cut flowers, hybrid tea roses or grandifloras are good choices. Shrub roses, on the other hand, make the garden look great with little care," says Diane Brueckman, rosarian for the Missouri Botanical Gardens in St. Louis. "The best advice is to contact your local rose society and ask what varieties do well in your area."

You can also narrow the field by focusing on the traits you're after, such as scent, stem color or rose hips.

"Damask and alba roses and their hybrids are very fragrant. So are old-fashioned tea roses," offers Stephen Scanniello of Barnegat, New Jersey, who has authored numerous books on roses, including *Roses of America* and *Rose Companions*.

Diane has a few fragrant favorites, too. "I'm a big fan of the

Richard Shiell; opposite page: Alan and Linda Detrick

FALL IN LOVE. Who can resist the timeless elegance of roses, like the red Chrysler Imperial hybrid tea rose (at left)? These bloomers perform best when mixed with other flowers in the garden. Above, a red climbing rose and yellow miniatures make a colorful border with purple irises and evening primrose.

David Austin English roses, especially Pilgrim, a yellow, medium-sized shrub rose," she says. "A floribunda called Apricot Nectar is a good choice, as is Peter Mayle Romantica and Westerland, a climber."

Some roses, such as Mutabalis or Red Meidleind, offer colorful canes or fall foliage.

Abundant rose hips are an added bonus for other types. These rose "fruits" will brighten your garden after the blooms have faded, plus they provide food for the birds. Diane and Stephen both recommend any of the rugosa rose varieties for this purpose.

"Many of the native rose species will produce hips, including prairie, Carolina, Virginia and Arkansas roses," Stephen

ROSES ARE RED... and yellow and pink and white and orange. With hundreds of varieties, there's a rose color, shape or size to suit just about anyone. Clockwise from left: Ramblin' Red clambers up a building...Constance Spry, a David Austin English rose...the open flowers of *Rosa sericea*, a yellow shrub rose.

In addition, Diane suggests selecting a spot among your other flowers that receives morning sun, which helps dry the foliage and reduces the risk of disease.

"In areas with hot summers, spots with eastern exposures are best in order to prevent burning and damage from intense afternoon sun," she says. "You'll also have better luck intermingling roses with other plants."

Roses are available as bare-root plants or in containers. It's best to plant bare-root roses in spring while the plant is still dormant—and right after you've soaked the roots overnight. Container plants can go in the garden anytime during the growing season.

Many roses are grafted, a process that attaches a bud from a desired plant onto a hardier root system. The bud graft is easy to spot—it's the swollen knob with branches sprouting from it. To protect the graft in northern regions, plant it 1 to 2 inches below the soil surface. Southern gardeners should keep it even to 2 inches above the surface.

Make the planting hole twice as large as the roots. To avoid disturbing the roots of container plants, cut away the pot rather than pulling out the rose.

Roses are thirsty, and it's important to water them deeply to soak the top 6 to 8 inches of soil. Direct the water at the base of the plant and away from the foliage in order to prevent mildew and black spot. And don't forget the mulch. This will help conserve soil moisture.

Some rose varieties, like hybrid teas, are heavy feeders and require fertilization three to four times during the summer. Shrub, climbing, old rose and floribunda types don't need that much—just give them a dose in spring. Repeat bloomers benefit from an extra application after the first round of blossoms.

If the temperatures in your area drop below 10° in winter, you'll want to protect your hybrid roses after the first week of freezing temperatures. One method is to pile about 10 inches of soil loosely around the base of the plant.

"All in all, roses give you a big bang for your buck," says Diane. "They aren't that expensive, will produce all season long and last for years with a little care."

adds. "Some gardeners don't like the fact that these only bloom once. If that bothers you, try rugosa Scabrosa, which blooms multiple times."

A Little TLC

Ready to get planting? Before you do, Stephen suggests you carefully select your site.

"Make sure it gets 5 to 6 hours of sun, and the ground is a well-mixed combination of compost and soil," he says.

Plant Profile

Common Name: Rose.
Botanical Name: *Rosa*.
Bloom Time: Early summer to autumn.
Hardiness: All zones—check individual varieties for specific hardiness.
Flower Colors: A wide palette, including white, red, pink, cream, yellow, orange, magenta, purple, lavender, tan and brown.

Flower Shape: Single, semi-double or double blooms in many shapes, including flat, cupped, rounded, high-centered, urn-shaped, rosette and pompom.
Height: Varies widely, from 6-inch ground covers to 20-foot climbers.
Spread: 12 to 18 inches or more.
Light Needs: Full sun.
Soil Type: Moist and well draining.
Special Care: Pruning varies with the type of rose and your climate. In general,

shrub roses and climbers need the least pruning. On established shrubs, remove damaged or dead canes before growth begins in spring. Wait until after the first blooms of the season to prune climbing roses.

On hybrid teas, remove any winter-damaged canes in spring. You can also shape and control the size by pruning the remaining stems to anywhere between 12 and 24 inches in height.

CALIFORNIA POPPIES

Bask in the glow of these golden perennials.

Sweeping across the arid foothills and valleys west of the Sierra Nevada, an endless sea of golden-orange California poppies light up the scenic landscape each spring.

The sight captivates travelers today, just as it did centuries ago, when American Indian tribes living in the area collected the sunny, yet potentially poisonous, blooms as an herbal source. Later, Spanish mariners discovered hillsides ablaze with these brilliant poppies, giving them the most appropriate name—*copa de oro*, or "cup of gold".

Today, they're simply known as California poppies (*Eschscholzia californica*), a fitting name for a plant the state of California adopted as its official flower in 1903.

This fiery beauty is by no means confined to the Golden

Blooming Beauty

State. In fact, they've made their way to far corners of the world in a most unusual way.

After the gold mines in California were "played out" in the late 1800s, miners left the U.S. for Chile, New Zealand and Australia. Inadvertently, they took poppies with them. The ships they sailed needed ballast, so they used local sand, which just happened to be littered with poppy seeds. Now, California poppies are common in these far-flung lands.

In the U.S., California poppies naturally appear in pastures, grassy slopes, vacant lots and along roadways. Rich soil and humid conditions don't suit this tough plant, which is why California poppies are most at home in the West. Specimens crop up in garden beds from southern California to southern Washington and other western states as well.

Lively Offspring

In the wild, California poppies produce 2-inch-wide, satiny, cup-like flowers in shades of pale yellow to deep, golden orange (see the photo at far right). Bloom time generally runs from spring through summer.

Hybrid varieties are available in lots of flower shapes and

Faith Bemiss

AWASH WITH COLOR. When California poppies burst into bloom, the vibrant-orange flowers sometimes stretch as far as the eye can see in fields along the West Coast (see photo below). But these flowers are equally colorful in the home landscape. There are a variety of hues available, from hybrid shades of pink (right) to the typical orange (far right).

Bob Coury/Unicorn Stock Photos

This fiery beauty is by no means confined to the Golden State.

for the color of their flowers, such as Cherry Ripe, Milky White and Purple Violet.

Keep in mind that when these hybrids reseed, you may be disappointed that they lose their unique coloring. The blooms typically revert back to the orange or yellow of their wild ancestors.

And all California poppy blossoms will only open in bright sunlight, closing at night and on cloudy days.

California poppy's blue-green foliage is lacy and small, characteristics that allow it to thrive in arid conditions. The leaves don't have much surface area for water to evaporate. This helps it conserve moisture.

Another trait that guarantees growing success is that California poppies aren't picky when it comes to soil. It doesn't like wet roots, so be sure they're planted in well-draining soil. But if the dirt is dry or poor in terms of organic material, poppies will still do very well.

Add a Casual Flair

The tall, nodding blooms are ideal in rock and cottage gardens, rather than formal flower beds. If you do choose to include them in a well-manicured garden, be ready to remove some of the spent flowers regularly to limit reseeding so the plants don't take over.

Poppies don't transplant well, so to grow them, pick a sunny spot and broadcast the tiny seeds across the soil where you want them to root. Sow seeds in fall or mid-spring in areas with mild winters. The plants will act as perennials and self-sow each year. In colder regions, treat California poppies as annuals, planting their seeds each spring.

Be sure to keep the soil moist until the seeds germinate. Then sit back and enjoy the view when these wildflowers bloom in a blaze of glory!

Editor's Note: Tennessee gardeners should check with their local county Extension service before planting California poppies, as they're considered invasive in some areas.

colors. The Sunset strain has single blooms, while Mission Bells and Ballerina both sport fuller semi-double or double blooms with frilled and fluted petals.

The Thai Silk line is compact at 8 to 10 inches tall and has fluted bronze-tinged flowers ranging from yellow to orange, red, pink, rose, cream and white. Other cultivars are named

READER TIP

These tall, nodding blooms are ideal in rock and cottage gardens, rather than formal flower beds.

Plant Profile

Common Name: California poppy.
Botanical Name: *Eschscholzia californica*.
Bloom Time: Summer.
Hardiness: Perennial in its native habitat, or grow as an annual in all zones.
Flower Colors: Orange, red, rose, purple, yellow, pink, cream and white.
Flower Shape: Four-petal, cup-like blossoms measure 1 to 2 inches across.
Height: 8 to 15 inches.
Spread: 9 to 15 inches.
Light Needs: Full sun.
Soil Type: Well-draining; thrives in poor and dry soil.
Planting: Sow seeds directly on soil in fall or winter in mild climates; sow in spring in cold climates.

HOSTA HAVEN

This reader has eyes for only one kind of plant in his backyard.

By Frederick Ryan, Schenectady, New York

LOVIN' THOSE LEAVES. Ten years of hard work have paid off for Frederick Ryan (below left). He has collected more than 200 varieties of hostas in his backyard, and has added many personal touches along the way that bring attention to his favorite plants. Frederick creates his own planters, like 'V'-shaped ones (above right), and circular and wooden step designs (top left). He also uses unique lighting to make the plants shine.

Ten years ago, I fell in love.

A thunderstorm had just passed through town, and I was out driving around. As I turned the corner, I spotted a bed of radiant hostas glistening in the soft sunlight after the storm.

I had never been a gardener—my hobbies were hot rods and airplanes, not flowers and dirt. But a month later, I still couldn't stop thinking about those hostas, so I broke down and went to a local greenhouse.

Today, I have more than 200 varieties of hostas, and I wouldn't have it any other way.

Wetland to Green Land

Long before I acquired my home, the backyard was like a swamp. A fisherman from my area had lived in the house, and he filled the yard with water so he could practice casting.

I was just a young boy when my parents bought the house from him. I still remember helping my dad fill in the area—it took 27 dump truck loads of soil.

Over the years, my mother put in a few flowers here and there, but the yard didn't see much gardening activity. Even when I inherited the house nearly 20 years ago, I had very little interest in doing any planting. I mowed the grass, and that was it. But once those hostas caught my eye, I was hooked.

I don't have a lot of space to work with, since the yard is only 50 by 75 feet. However, I've made the most of it.

Building a Collection

I have 18 wooden planters, all of which I designed and built myself. My 'V'-shaped creations are probably the most eye-catching. I wanted them to look as if they were barely balanc-

ing on each end (see photo above).

Since I consider myself a romantic, I also built a large heart-shaped planter. It took me a month to finish it. I started by laying out the shape with a rope, and then little by little, it came together. Now, I joke that a piece of my heart will always be in my backyard.

I've never been big on names. I probably couldn't tell you the official names for most of my hostas. I do keep a running planting list, though, which is how my collection has grown.

As a car enthusiast, I often go cruising for a couple of hours at a time. In past trips, if I saw a nursery along the way, I stopped to check out their hostas. When I found one not on my list, I bought it. Then I couldn't wait to bring my new treat home to enjoy.

After years of doing this, my space is filled, but I still find plenty of other projects to keep me busy with the plants. One of these is lighting.

Lights, Hostas, Action

I've always been fascinated by the way lights can emphasize the different features on a car. I decided the same concept could work with my hostas, so I bought some lights at a home improvement store and got to work on my plan.

Now I have dozens of custom-made lights among the plants that help give them an enchanting nighttime glow. My proudest beams are the nine lanterns I made myself. I created them using two lights and red plastic. In the daytime they look clear, but at night the top half shines a beautiful candy-apple red.

People often ask why I'm so infatuated with hostas. I can't explain it, other than I like their reliability. Hostas take care of themselves, and they come back year after year.

You can't ask for much more than that.

Editor's Note: Hostas in raised containers are more susceptible to the damaging effects of winter weather. Some gardeners may need to provide additional insulation for the roots. One common method is to surround the containers with bales of straw for winter.

HELIOTROPE

This annual is a scent-sational garden addition.

By Kathleen Zimmer-Anderson, Waukesha, Wisconsin

Some say the fragrance of heliotrope reminds them of cherry pie, while others claim the blooms' scent resembles talcum powder…vanilla…cloves…or even licorice.

Whatever comes to mind when you take a whiff, this colorful bedding plant certainly is one of the most aromatic annuals around. It's no surprise that heliotrope flowers once served as a main ingredient in colognes, perfumes, soaps and powders.

The plant also was a favorite among Victorian-era gardeners, although its popularity faded a bit during the 20th century. Heliotropes have begun to make a comeback, however, and are getting easier to find at many garden centers.

Sun Lover

Heliotrope serves as a woody perennial in its native Peru, but is unable to withstand winters in North America. Here,

HEAVEN SCENT. Heliotropes are best known for their fragrance—which resembles cherry pie, vanilla or licorice, depending on who you talk to. Its purple clusters (left) rise above textured leaves. The upright annual works well with a variety of other plants in borders or containers (lower right).

it works as an annual for backyard gardeners.

The shrubby specimen derives its name from two Greek words—*helios*, which translates into sun, and *trope*, meaning turn. The moniker came about thanks to a legend that describes how the flower heads turn to face the sun. That myth might not be completely true, but there's no doubt the plant thrives in bright locations.

Its nicely textured, dark-green leaves create a perfect backdrop for eye-catching masses of tiny tubular blooms that come in a variety of hues, from light blue to rich violet, lavender or white.

Aside from filling a border area, flower bed or rock garden with loads of color, heliotrope is ideal in window boxes, containers or hanging baskets. It partners well with a variety of other flowers, including verbena, geraniums, dusty miller and petunias.

This pretty plant has another appealing feature—its sweet nectar attracts the attention of "flying flowers" like hummingbirds and butterflies.

Hot Growing Hints

Heliotrope can either be grown from seed or from plants purchased at a garden center. However, because heliotrope is so sensitive to cold, it's best to wait at least 2 to 3 weeks after the last frost date before placing the plants in your garden, so the soil has enough time to warm.

Select a spot that receives full to partial sun with moist well-draining soil. Space the plants about 12 inches apart and water thoroughly.

After the heliotropes become established, you'll want to water them whenever the top 1 to 2 inches of soil just begins to dry. If you've added a heliotrope to a container, check it daily and water when the top few inches start to dry out. Conditions that are too dry or too moist will result in unhappy plants.

Container-grown heliotropes also benefit from a little fertilizer. You can add a slow-release version when you first fill the container with soil, or use a liquid fertilizer for flowering plants throughout the growing season.

Pinch to Grow Inches

Nothing's prettier than bushy heliotropes in a container or a flower bed. To encourage them to fill out, pinch back the growing tips of the young plants. If they start to look scrag-

gly later on, another round of pinching will help shape them again.

Deadheading fading flower clusters is another task that yields lovely results. Not only will you remove unattractive spent flowers, you'll promote better blooming from summer into fall.

If you'd like to preserve your container heliotropes over winter, you can bring them indoors before the weather becomes cold. Place the plants in a cool, sunny spot and water regularly.

While the bloomers are relatively pest-free, white flies, spider mites, aphids or mealy bugs can be a problem on plants wintering indoors. If you notice any of these critters, use an insecticidal soap to banish the pests.

As soon as the risk of frost has passed, your heliotropes can head outdoors again—and you can enjoy another sweet season of fragrant flowers!

Plant Profile

Common Name: Heliotrope.
Botanical Name: *Heliotropium arborescens.*
Bloom Time: From summer until the first frost.
Hardiness: Annual.
Flower Colors: Blue, violet, lavender and white.
Flower Shape: Clusters of tiny tubular blooms.
Height: 12 to 24 inches.
Spread: 12 to 15 inches.
Light Needs: Partial to full sun.
Soil Type: Rich and moist.
Planting: Place container-grown plants in the garden 2 to 3 weeks after the last frost date—when the ground and air have had enough time to warm.

You also can propagate your own seeds. Sow them in moist sterile potting mix about 10 to 12 weeks before the last spring frost in your area. Barely cover the seeds with soil, then keep the soil moist and at room temperature (about 70°). The seeds will germinate in about 3 weeks.

Prize Picks: Marine bears 6-inch-wide clusters of deep, violet-blue flowers and is the most readily available variety. (That, and the similar Mini Marine, are the cultivars pictured on these pages.) Atlantis is a particularly fragrant species, while White Lady and Alba produce lovely white blossoms. Light Eyes offers distinctive lavender blooms with light centers.

Derek Fell

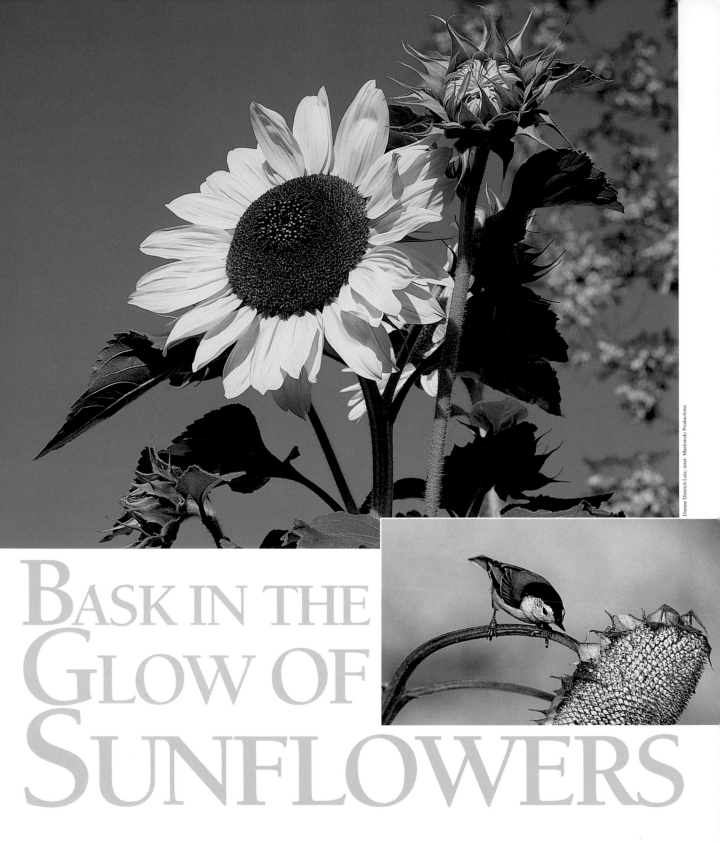

BASK IN THE GLOW OF SUNFLOWERS

These bright blooms are a longtime garden favorite for all ages.

By Kathleen Zimmer-Anderson, Waukesha, Wisconsin

Alan and Linda Detrick

Alan and Linda Detrick

Gay Bumgarner

TOWERING TREASURE. The warm glow of sunflowers will brighten any garden. This beauty also attracts birds, like the white-breasted nuthatch (far left inset) and adds statuesque prominence to backyards with flowers that soar as high as 15 feet. Numerous varieties are available, including (above, from left) Floristan, Music Box and Teddy Bear.

I've always thought of sunflowers as kings of the garden. When I was a young girl, my dad and I tucked sunflower seeds into the earth and tended them until the plants towered majestically overhead.

Nothing else quite measured up to those sturdy-stalked beauties. And the rewards as summer progressed into fall fed both body and soul—amazing flowers and tasty seeds for my brothers and me to munch on. Sunflowers symbolized goodness.

I still feel that way today, which is why I make a point to plant sunflowers with my daughters each spring. Listening to Olivia and Abigail "ooh" and "aah" as the seedlings nudge their way out of the soil and sprout tall and strong is a treat...and I experience the same childhood thrill.

Without a doubt, sunflowers are particularly well suited for teaching youngsters the joys of gardening, mostly because the large seeds are easy to plant, they require just a little TLC, and the results are speedy and stunning. But that doesn't mean more serious gardeners should ignore these sunny specimens.

Universal Appeal

Today, sunflower hybrids come in a wider range of shapes and sizes than ever before, virtually ensuring that you can find one to fit into almost any style flower bed. The colors of the flowers have expanded well beyond yellow to include red, purple, rust and even white.

Among the annual varieties you can choose from, Mammoth Russian and Russian Giant produce traditional 10-inch-wide golden flowers on top of tough stalks that rise as high as 15 feet. Sunspot is a more diminutive cousin, bearing similar sized blooms on 2-foot-tall stems.

The flowers of the 4- to 5-foot-tall Ring of Fire are 5 inches wide and very colorful, from the rich-brown center to the circle of red petals outlined by another circle of warm, yellow petals. Autumn Fire, another midsized variety, has blossoms that range in color from rich mahogany to lemon, gold and bronze, while the Italian White variety fea-

tures unusual dark-centered, creamy blooms.

Teddy Bear is a compact cultivar that grows a mere 2 feet tall with 5-inch-wide double flowers. Music Box, a 2-foot-tall, multibranched type, yields a crop of blooms in a slew of shades, including some bicolor combinations.

You also can find dwarf varieties at garden centers in late summer that are perfect for containers or planting in bare spots in your garden. These mini sunflowers match up nicely with mums, pumpkins and asters to create an attractive fall display.

Want something more permanent? Give a perennial sunflower (*Helianthus multiflorus*) like Flore Pleno a try. This double-flowered variety thrives in Zones 4 to 9 and develops 5- to 6-foot-tall stalks with sizable, dark-green leaves, as well as a profusion of brilliant-yellow, dahlia-like blooms that last well into September.

A host of other perennial varieties are available as well, including Capenoch Star and Lodden Gold, both of which produce lovely, lush flowers year after year that are perfect for cutting and in arrangements.

A native plant in North and South America, people have used the sunflower as both a decoration and a source of food for centuries. The Incas in Peru actually worshipped sunflowers. Other Indian tribes were more practical in their approach to the plant, using it in cooking, as hair accents and to make paint.

Multipurpose Posy

Early pioneers spun and wove fibers from the stalk into fabric, used the petals to make dye and discovered the whole plant provided food for people and animals alike. Many sowed sunflowers right next to their sod houses or cabins in the belief that the plants warded off malaria.

Modern fans of sunflowers often rely on

Alan and Linda Detrick

SUNNY DISPOSITION. With more than 70 species to choose from, you're sure to find a sunflower to love. Traditional varieties tower over the backyard with their sunny flowers (below). Perennials like Flore Pleno (left) return year after year. The Vanilla Ice hybrid shows its cool colors (bottom).

Nancy Rotenberg

them to lend height to a flower bed or to attract butterflies and hummingbirds. Many also harvest the seeds to fill bird feeders during the winter months.

Keeping hungry critters away from the flower heads can be a challenge. In fact, I vividly remember the year we lost our entire crop to the marauding chipmunks who lived in the stone wall that edged my parents' garden.

But there is an animal-friendly solution to this situation. Simply cover the flowers loosely with cheesecloth or netting, and you'll discourage squirrels, chipmunks and other scavengers.

Start the harvesting process when the backs of the flower heads turn brown. You can cut them, leaving 1 to 2 feet of the stems attached. Hang the heads upside down until they are completely dry and brown. Then the seeds will be ready and can be roasted or saved for the birds.

Green-Thumb Care

Growing these showy yet incredibly resilient flowers is a cinch. They will withstand both heat and drought and require only the most basic upkeep.

Pick a spot that receives full sun and has moderately fertile, well-drained soil. You can plant the seeds directly in the ground about 6 inches apart once all danger of frost has passed—or you can start seeds indoors in moist seed starter mix 4 to 6 weeks earlier. Keep the temperature between 68° and 86°, water regularly and seedlings will appear in 10 to 14 days. Transplant hardened-off seedlings outdoors after the last frost.

When seedlings are about 3 inches tall, thin them to a spacing of 18 to 24 inches between each plant. Then water from time to time when the top few inches of soil become crumbly. If you've chosen a taller variety, you could stake the stem as it grows to prevent the plant from bending or breaking, either under its own weight or in very windy conditions.

You might notice that the leaves turn spotty or white. This is caused by leaf spot or powdery mildew, conditions that are unsightly but not fatal. To cover up the leaves, you can plant slightly shorter flowers in front. Aphids can also cause minor damage but won't really do much harm. Otherwise, sunflowers are fairly pest- and disease-free.

In fact, it's almost impossible to find a friendlier blossom

to grow in your garden. So start thinking now about what varieties you'd like to include in the mix next spring. You can even enlist the little ones to help you sow seeds when the time comes, and turn sunflower cultivation into a full family affair.

Plant Profile

Mark Turner

Common Name: Sunflower.
Botanical Name: *Helianthus annuus.*
Bloom Time: Summer to first frost.
Hardiness: Annual; perennial types hardy in Zones 4 to 9, depending on variety.
Flower Colors: Typically yellow with dark centers. Some hybrids bear red, purple or white hues.
Flower Shape: Showy, daisy-like blooms that consist of colorful florets surrounding a dark center. Some double-flowered varieties resemble mums or dahlias.
Height: 15 inches to 15 feet.
Spread: 1 to 2 feet.
Light Needs: Full sun.
Soil Type: Moderately rich and well-draining.
Planting: For annuals, sow seeds 6 inches apart after danger of frost has passed. Thin seedlings when they are 3 inches tall, leaving 18 to 24 inches between plants.
Attracts: A variety of hummingbirds and butterflies will feed from the flowers. Later, squirrels and birds will eat the seeds.

Chapter 5

MYSTERIOUS PLANT CHANGES

Why flowers unexpectedly change color or form.

By Melinda Myers, Contributing Editor

Gardening is full of surprises. One of the most puzzling is when flowers unexpectedly change color or form. I hear from many gardeners who wonder why this happens—a purple patch of flowers that becomes yellow; an oddball red bloom on a white-flowering plant; or flowers that take on the characteristics of the surrounding plants (like the striped tulips above).

Although it may seem like the work of mischievous garden gnomes, there typically are three possible reasons for such plant changes: mutations (also called "sports"), hybridizing, or offspring plants that exhibit different features than the parents. To determine what caused these changes in your yard, start by examining the plant's history.

A Sporting Chance

For instance, reader Dawn Scheppke of Eau Claire, Wisconsin reported that when she planted purple irises in her flower bed of yellow ones, several irises emerged as *purple and yellow* the following spring.

Since the two irises didn't have time to cross-pollinate (that would take longer than a single season), some of the irises probably sported, a spontaneous mutation from the parent plant…though the timing is oddly coincidental.

When flower growers discover a sport, they often propagate them and sell the new plants for their unique size, color or flavor. The golden delicious apple is a tasty example of a plant that first emerged as a sport.

Many variegated plants also are the result of sports. But sometimes, these plants revert back to the parent plants' original color and form.

That's what happened in Phyllis Felton's garden in Castle Creek, New York. She wrote to ask about her variegated hostas that are turning solid green.

Unfortunately, there's nothing a gardener can do to stop this process. Just enjoy the new surprises each season.

Plant changes also occur through hybridizing—when two plants cross-pollinate. This results in a reshuffling of genetic material, with the offspring taking on various characteristics from both parent plants.

Jane Elliott of Manchester, New Jersey experienced a somewhat different dilemma. A division of her blue balloon flowers turned white after she transplanted them.

While this may be a sport, it could also be the result of the offspring not growing true from seed—a common problem with hybrid plants, which typically don't produce seeds that carry the genetic material needed to grow an exact copy of the parent plant.

It's possible the transplanted portion died, but then dormant seeds in the soil sprouted and grew. These seedlings didn't come true from seed, causing the resulting flower color to be white instead of blue.

Other Explanations

Donna Schubert of Republic, Ohio knows that grafted roses—including most hybrid teas—also can change color. For 7 years, her rosebush boasted orange blossoms. Then one year, red roses appeared on the same plant.

This happened because propagators graft a single bud of the desirable rose, orange in this case, onto a hardy root system. If part of the grafted portion dies, often as the result of cold temperatures, the hardy rootstock will take over.

Believe it or not, diseases can also cause changes in plant characteristics. Europe's 17th-century tulip craze, known as Tulipmania, was the result of a virus. The disease infected a plant, causing a yellow streak to develop in a red flower. The resulting bloom caused people to go gaga trying to obtain the unique bulbs.

The bottom line when it comes to plant changes? Remove the new plants if you don't like them or if they compete with your desirable plants. Or leave them be.

You just might end up with a sport or a hybrid that's better than the plant you purchased.

Scott E. Zinck

Nancy Rotenberg

HAVE A BALL WITH EYE-CATCHING ALLIUM

Add a colorful bounce to your garden with this pretty perennial.

If you want to add a colorful bounce to your garden, there's no better bloomer than allium. This pretty perennial is a winning selection for almost any yard. The allium's flower head is its most striking feature. You've likely admired an allium's globe-shaped cluster of flowers in late spring or early summer. These "ball-headed" flowers (above) range in size from 3/4 inch to 12 inches wide, depending on the variety.

Other types of allium produce loose flower heads, called "tufted" (above far right), with upright or drooping blooms that tend to be smaller but are no less dramatic.

This native of the Northern Hemisphere has more than 700 varieties to its name, providing gardeners with a huge roster of shapes, sizes and colors. You'll find specimens that grow 5 feet tall, petite versions that reach a mere 6 inches, some with interesting foliage or uniquely colored blossoms.

Alliums include edible onions, garlic and chives. Often referred to as ornamental or flowering onions, the name "allium" comes from the Latin word for that pungent vegetable.

Find real proof of the perennial bulb's genetic roots when you crush a leaf. Take a whiff, and you'll encounter an onion-like scent. The blossoms, however, tend to be pleasantly fragrant.

Despite its smelly lineage, it has long been considered a good luck charm. Even today, some believe the yellow-flowered *Allium moly*, also known as lily leek or golden garlic, will bring good fortune to those who cultivate it.

Loyal Fans

Gardeners today find other good reasons to plant this flower. Not only can you find an allium to suit almost any spot

Donna and Tom Krischan

You don't need to do much maintenance to keep alliums looking their best. If you experience a rainy spring or summer, hold off on watering the plants, or they will become waterlogged and bulb rot can occur. You can also mulch the plants in the fall, after the soil freezes, to provide extra protection from frost heaving or early sprouting.

Divide and Multiply

If your alliums start to look overcrowded, simply divide them in autumn.

You can propagate those that bear seeds by placing the seeds in moist peat moss and refrigerating for 4 weeks. Then remove the seeds from the peat moss and sow in a potting or seed-starting mix. Keep the mix warm and moist. Once sprouted, move seedlings to a sunny window or under artificial growing lights. Just be sure all danger of frost has passed before planting the hardened-off transplants into the garden.

Many varieties drop their own seeds—the easiest way for them to multiply.

Once you have a few alliums in your yard, don't be surprised if these superstar flower clusters attract the attention of a few new fans.

in the garden, the enchanting plant is easy to grow and is readily available as bulbs or container-grown plants.

Most alliums need full sun, although a few varieties will tolerate partial shade. Well-drained soil is the other important requirement—bulbs will rot in standing water. If your soil contains clay, work organic material into it to improve drainage.

Plant these beauties outdoors in fall when temperatures become consistently cool. Place bulbs at a depth about two to three times their vertical diameter, but no deeper than 4 inches. Spacing depends on the variety.

Most alliums look wonderful when combined with other perennials, from purple coneflowers to roses. The only exception is the giant allium. Its large flower head is such a standout it can look out of place with the wrong plants.

Try pairing it up with an equally bold plant like yucca or surrounding it with a finer textured flower like threadleaf coreopsis.

Because many alliums bloom later in the spring, they can serve as a "bridge" between early crocuses and daffodils and summer flowers like daylilies, phlox and yarrow.

Most varieties of allium work well as cut flowers (any onion scent fades once the stems are in water). They last a long time in fresh arrangements and dry well for year-round use.

Plant Profile

Common Names: Allium, flowering onion and ornamental onion.
Botanical Name: *Allium species*.
Bloom Time: Late spring to fall.
Hardiness: Zones 2 to 8.
Flower Colors: White, purple, blue, pink and yellow.
Flower Shape: Small star-, bell- or cup-shaped flowers grow in round clusters (ball-headed), or loose upright or drooping clusters (tufted). Flower heads range from 3/4 inch to 12 inches across.
Height: 6 inches to 5 feet.
Spread: 12 to 18 inches or more.
Light Needs: Full sun; some varieties tolerate partial shade.
Soil Type: Well-draining.
Planting: Plant bulbs in fall at a depth two to three times their vertical diameter, but no deeper than 4 inches.
Prize Picks: Giant allium (*Allium giganteum*) grows 3 to 4 feet tall with a striking 6-inch purple flower head. Drumstick chives (below, *Allium spaerocephalon*) produce small tightly packed purple flower heads on 3-foot stems. Ornamental onion (*Allium seneceus* 'Glaucum') features grayish green foliage with 1-inch pink or purple flowers on a plant 6 inches tall.

Michael Shedlock

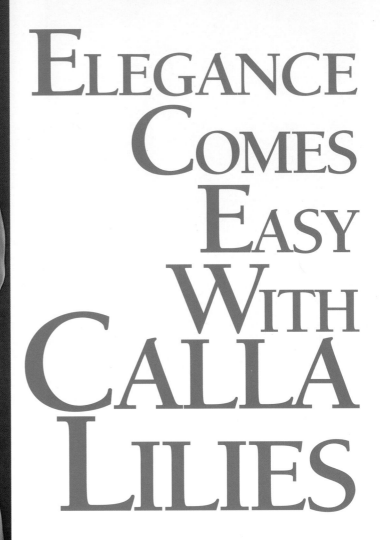

ELEGANCE COMES EASY WITH CALLA LILIES

By Kathleen Zimmer-Anderson
Waukesha, Wisconsin

From the origin of its name to the graceful flower it produces, the calla lily has "lovely" written all over it! "Calla" comes from the Greek word *kalos*, which translates into "beauty"—and this bloomer certainly is a knockout.

Its lance-shaped, glossy green leaves provide the perfect backdrop as it produces dramatic flowers in spring and summer.

That swirling white petal most think of as the flower is actually a protective leaf known as a spathe, while the golden spike at its center, called a spadix, holds the plant's tiny blossoms.

White is the most common color for the flower-like spathe, but a number of hybrids in shades of yellow, pink or red are also available today. Most produce a wonderful fragrance, too.

SOPHISTICATED SWIRLS. Calla lilies lend a touch of elegance to any backyard garden. Its whirled petal is actually a leaf that protects the tiny blossoms on the center spike. New varieties add to the possibilities with spotted foliage (left) or red flowers (far right).

A symbol of timeless purity, long-lasting calla lilies are often seen in bridal bouquets and other floral arrangements, leading many gardeners to mistakenly assume it's a delicate hothouse plant that can be grown only indoors.

Tough Enough

But that isn't the case. The calla lily is hardy enough to brighten a shady spot in your garden without much fuss.

This native of southern and eastern Africa grows in the wild there along lakes, near streams and in swamps, indicating that it's comfortable in moist conditions.

In North American backyards, the lilies will thrive in shallow pools or ponds and look spectacular when planted in or near water gardens.

That doesn't mean you need to have a water feature in your yard in order to successfully cultivate callas. You can mix them in your flower beds with annuals and perennials in partial or full shade—or even plant them in full sun, as long as you keep the soil moist.

Calla lilies like rich, moist soil that drains well, so if you have clay soil, add organic matter to promote drainage. Do the same for sandy soil to improve water retention.

Northern gardeners may want to get a jump on the season by planting rhizomes indoors in mid-March. Place them in a container filled with well-draining potting mix, then cover with about 3 inches of soil. Water sparingly until you notice green shoots peeking through the surface, then water more generously and add fertilizer. Be sure to keep the soil moist.

Moving Outdoors

You can move them to the yard, gradually acclimating them to outdoor weather, then transplant into the garden once the threat of frost has passed.

Or plant rhizomes directly in the garden once you're sure temperatures will stay well above freezing. Place them about 4 inches deep and about 18 inches apart.

Another option is to purchase potted calla lilies from the garden center and transplant them in your garden. You should plant them at the same level

they were growing in the container.

Once the plants are in the garden, you don't need to do too much to maintain their graceful appearance. Remove faded flowers for a tidy look and water regularly if the weather turns dry.

R. Todd Davis

Plant Profile

Common Names: Calla lily, arum lily, garden calla and trumpet lily.
Botanical Name: *Zantedeschia* species.
Bloom Time: From late spring to early summer.
Hardiness: Annuals; except common calla lily, which is a tender perennial in Zones 8 and above.
Bloom Colors: White, yellow, pink and red.
Flower Shape: Tiny flowers on a large spike at the center of a flower-like leaf called a spathe.
Height: 12 to 36 inches.
Spread: 8 to 24 inches.
Light Needs: Partial to full shade; will tolerate full sun if soil is kept moist.
Soil Type: Moist and well-draining.
Prize Picks: Hardier and more sun tolerant than other *Zantedeschia aethiopica* varieties, Crowborough produces large 4- to 6-inch-long spathes, while Little Gem is ideal for tight quarters, reaching 12 to 18 inches in height.

Common calla lilies (*Zantedeschia aethiopica*) perform like perennials in warmer areas (Zones 8 or higher) and can remain in the garden all year long. But for locations that experience cold winters, the rhizomes need to be dug up right after the first light frost. Store them in peat moss or perlite in a cool (about 50°) spot.

Two other prevalent types, spotted calla lily (*Zantedeschia albomaculata*) and golden calla lily (*Zantedeschia elliottiana*), are more susceptible to the cold and must be preserved indoors for winter, or replanted each year.

Winter Blooms

Want to enjoy the attractive plant all year long? Consider keeping potted calla lilies in a warm, sunny window during winter and water just enough to prevent the soil from completely drying out.

Increase water as the days become longer and the sunshine grows stronger in the spring and summer. Then set containers outside once warm temperatures return.

You can even place the plants, container and all, directly into your garden. Dig a hole roughly the same depth as the container, and set the pot in the hole. Make sure the lip of the pot is even with the soil's surface.

Then sit back and enjoy the beauty that will abound in your yard as these stylish plants put forth blossom after gorgeous blossom.

More than 16,000 daylilies provide nonstop flowers in this Texas garden.

By Wendy Rudnicki
Friendswood, Texas

A FLOWER
A DAY

For Pearland, Texas residents Paula and Leon Payne, their interest in daylilies started in 1987 with a few yellow blooms.

It almost stopped there.

"I read an article in a magazine about all these different colored daylilies we'd never seen, and we started trying to find them, but we couldn't," Paula says. "I called some of the gardening radio shows and they didn't know, either. So we just sort of gave up."

About 8 months later, however, the National Daylily Convention hit Houston, Texas—and Paula found a list in the newspaper of sources for a multihued variety of daylilies. She and her husband bought about $100 worth.

"We thought we broke the bank!" Leon exclaims. "The very next year, I started hybridizing a little bit, and our garden just kept growing."

Growing Paynes

Today, the Paynes grow about 800 different varieties of daylilies—and more than 16,000 daylily plants in all!

In 1995, Leon and Paula bought the two lots behind their house and started their business: Paynes in the Grass Daylily Farm. They sell both full-grown daylilies and daylily seedlings.

"We had so many flowers, we had to do something," Leon explains.

"It was a hobby that got out of control," Paula adds.

About 9 years ago, Paula and Leon even helped start a daylily club in their area. The Lone Star Daylily Society sponsors plant sales, flower shows and garden tours, and is

a recognized club of the American Hemerocallis Society.

The botanical name for daylilies is *Hemerocallis*, which is derived from the Greek word for beauty. If you visit the Paynes, you will see why the name fits. Garden areas surround their home on all four sides, displaying a mix of bright perennials to show how stunning daylilies can be alone or when blended with other plants and flowers.

In the early '90s, Leon and Paula applied to have their garden added to a list of AHS display gardens. The vice president of their AHS region inspected their place to make sure they had a variety of well-marked daylilies. They did, and today, the Paynes' garden is one of more than 325 display gardens in the United States and Canada.

"We invite people to come even if they don't want to buy anything," Paula says. "We always hope we can get someone else interested in daylilies."

Days in the Making

Leon—who worked as a NASA aerospace engineer for 35 years—attributes his involvement with daylilies to the challenge of trying to develop a better daylily by hybridizing.

"It's easy to get a lot of seedlings, but to get the right one, the one that you're trying to get, that takes a lot of practice," he says.

To hybridize a flower, the Paynes take the pollen from one daylily and dust it onto another. If it works, the result is a seedpod, which they use to collect seeds for planting.

Unfortunately, it doesn't always work.

The Paynes care for about 8,000 seedlings a year, but usually only get

A BUDDING HOBBY. Leon and Paula Payne (left inset) started growing daylilies (like the one at far left) for their beauty. Now they enjoy creating new hybrids as well. Their collection includes about 800 varieties and 16,000 plants in a huge garden (top left) behind their home (above left). They also add daylilies among perennials like purple coneflowers and mealycup salvia (above) to show how well the different plants complement each other.

about 100 worth trying again. Planting, harvesting and other duties keep them busy, though. Some months, they get up at 5 a.m. and work until dark!

Square Dance at Sunset?

The couple registered three new daylilies in 2002: Square-dancer's Curtsy, Sunset Illusion and Rodeo Clown. Since then, they have registered three more: Line Dancer, Lone Star Wagon Wheel and Halloween Masquerade, which is Paula's favorite and won an AHS award in 2003.

"It's an orange daylily with a black edge and eye," Paula explains. "When people see it, they know it. It's great to grow a daylily that you can recognize without a nametag."

But for the Paynes, there are rewards beyond registering a new daylily or seeing the enthusiasm on the faces of their visitors.

"What my husband likes," Paula says, "is to go out in the morning when the seedlings start blooming, and know he's the first person in the world to ever see that flower bloom."

Editor's Note: For information from the American Hemerocallis Society about how to properly plant and care for daylilies, visit its Web site at *www.daylilies.org*.

> ## READER TIP
>
> To hybridize a daylily, take the pollen from one flower and dust it onto another. If it works, the result is a seedpod.
>
>
>
> **—Paula and Leon Payne, Pearland, Texas**

MORNING GLORY

This climbing annual greets each day with fresh-faced and fuss-free blooms.

By Margene Whitler Hucek, Keswick, Virginia

Photos this page: David Cavagnaro

WINNING STREAKS. Variegated leaves and multicolored flowers are just some of the traits to consider when selecting a morning glory for your yard. Two striking varieties are *Ipomoea nil* 'Mt. Fuji' (above left) and *Ipomoea tricolor* 'Flying Saucers' (above right). There also are several dwarf types that work in smaller planting spaces like hanging baskets or window boxes.

Morning glories conjure up images of lazy summer days, when time is best spent relaxing under an old oak tree, drinking iced tea and enjoying the fruits of my springtime labors. The tomatoes are ripe…there's corn to be picked…and my morning glories are in full bloom, providing an enchanting show well into autumn.

Each spring, I plant a morning glory called Heavenly Blue (like the one at far left) near a pillar in my vegetable garden and along the nearby picket fence. We can see that spot from our dining area and enjoy the incredible blue blooms it produces all season.

Hummingbirds often flit about the azure beauties, feeding on the flowers' sweet nectar. They even rest on the vines from time to time.

Common morning glories climb up and over our mailbox. Their funnel-shaped flowers range from deep purple to bluish purple or red with white throats. Like all morning glories, these blooms last only a day—but because the vine is so prolific, it continuously creates a colorful welcome for friends, family…and our mail carrier!

Family Ties

Morning glories belong to the *Convolvulaceae* family, a large group of vines that includes the sweet potato. In fact, the family name comes from a Latin word that means "to entwine," accurately describing the climbing abilities of most members of this family.

The morning glories commonly grown in gardens go by the botanical names of *Ipomoea purpurea* or *Ipomoea tricolor*, which has many cultivars.

In rural England, the morning glory was once known as "life of man" because its blooming pattern resembles that of a person's life—budding in the morning, full bloom at midday and wilting by evening.

Because these plants devote

no energy to building strong upright stems, they grow quite rapidly. They can reach 10 to 20 feet in a single season. Giving it adequate support, such as a post, trellis, fence or wall, is vital. I use guides—either string or thin bamboo sticks—to direct young plants to the main support.

If your support surface is smooth, provide wire or string "handholds" for the vine to cling to as it grows. Don't worry about the wire or string looking unsightly, though. The fast-growing climber quickly covers up these makeshift handholds.

Morning glories are a good choice if you're looking for a seasonal screen to add privacy to a porch or patio. The speedy climbers will provide attractive temporary cover to a doorway or part of your yard that will eventually be shaded by trees.

They're also ideal for small gardens since their growth is mostly vertical. But even if you have plenty of space, encouraging a few morning glories to climb up a trellis or other upright structure will add extra dimension to your garden.

Although not as common, you can let your morning glories climb up and over stumps or large rocks (a big bonus if there's an area of your yard that needs some work).

Be careful to limit your plantings to areas that can handle the vine's vigorous growth habits—they can easily smother more fragile flowers or greenery.

You'll Love These Blooms

However you use the vines, the dramatic, 4- to 6-inch-wide heart-shaped, green leaves make a delightful backdrop for the elegant, funnel-like flowers. Depending on the variety you choose, these blooms can

---

READER TIP

Morning glory seeds have tough outer coats, so it's best to soak them in warm water overnight before planting. This encourages speedier germination.

—**Margene Whitler Hucek, Keswick, Virginia**

Bonnie Nance

ALL WRAPPED UP. Morning glories need some sort of support to cling to as they grow. But the plants aren't picky—the vines will wrap around anything, even an old rusty seat (above).

transplant well. Look for a space in your yard that receives full sun and make sure the soil drains well—these beauties don't tolerate wet conditions.

If you don't have a good spot in your yard to grow morning glories, consider using containers. Just provide support for the vines and remember to water.

Morning glory seeds have tough outer coats, so it's best to soak them in warm water overnight before planting. This encourages speedier germination.

Plant seeds 6 inches apart, covering them with a 1/4 inch of soil. Thin 3-inch-tall plants so they stand about 12 inches apart, then step back and watch them grow! You'll soon have an abundance of blooms.

Morning glories will self-sow, and the resulting blooms usually revert to a purple or reddish flower. (Note: In some areas, this vigor has made them a noxious weed. Check with your county Extension service before adding them to your landscape.) I like to leave some vines in the garden over winter, since finches come looking for seeds in fall.

Pests are few for this vigorous plant, although beetles may cause some problems in late summer. You can control those critters with insecticidal soap.

Ease of care is yet another reason gardeners like morning glories. They do best without fertilizer, which will encourage vine growth at the expense of flower production. And they tolerate dry weather, although a drought may reduce the number of blossoms.

When my husband and I rented homes during the early years of our marriage, I couldn't afford to invest in costly perennials and had to rely on budget-friendly annuals like morning glories for a burst of summer color.

Now that we've settled in our own home, I delight in having beds of phlox, peonies and roses...but I still make room for morning glories. I find there's no better way to start a day than with these colorful blooms twining around my door.

measure as much as 5 inches across and are available in a range of colors, although blue and purple are the shades most gardeners associate with morning glories.

Aside from the two I prefer to plant in my garden, there are plenty of other selections, including the red blooms of cardinal climber (*Ipomoea* x *multifida*) and star glory (*Ipomoea quamoclit*), or Spanish flag (*Ipomoea lobata*), a shade-tolerant type with narrow, crimson blooms that mature to yellow and orange.

Another popular variety is moonflower (*Ipomoea alba*), which opens its white blooms during the evening hours. There also are some dwarf varieties that require no support and are especially attractive when used in window boxes or hanging planters.

Sowing Know-How

Morning glories are tropical natives and survive winters only in very warm climates. In North America, they are grown as annuals.

It is best to sow seeds directly in the garden after the soil warms to about 65°. That's because morning glories don't

Plant Profile

Common Name: Morning glory.
Botanical Name: *Ipomoea* species.
Bloom Time: Summer until first frost.
Hardiness: Annual.
Flower Colors: Blue, white, purple, pink and red.
Flower Shape: Funnel- or trumpet-shaped blooms.
Height: Vines range from 6 to 20 feet in length.
Light Needs: Full sun.
Soil Type: Moderately fertile and well draining.
Propagating: Plant presoaked seeds directly in the ground after the soil has warmed and the threat of frost has passed. Space the seeds 6 inches apart, then thin 3-inch-tall plants to 12 inches apart.
Prize Picks: The sky-blue flowers of Heavenly Blue are appealing, as are the white blooms of Pearly Gates and the bicolored Flying Saucers. All three are cultivars of *Ipomoea tricolor*. Hummingbirds are attracted to red Scarlett O'Hara and Crimson Rambler. Moonflower (*Ipomoea alba*) is a fragrant night-blooming variety.
Caution: All plant parts are toxic if ingested.

Chapter 5

Steve Terrill

Mark Turner

THE SKY'S THE LIMIT

Things are looking up with this "vine" way to elevate your landscape.

By Jeff Nowak, Executive Editor

Vine-ally, a simple solution to expanding your gardens without having to break large areas of ground—or even a sweat. All you have to do is think *up* rather than *out* and let climbing vines do the rest.

Vines pack a visual punch that will hit you square between the eyes. These plants give your garden new dimension, add vibrant color to your landscape and are a practical problem solver for many unsightly situations.

Looking to hide the trash cans on the side of your house? Let a vine climb a trellis strategically placed in front of them. Want to blend your chain-link fence into the landscape? A nice flowering vine will give it a natural look without sacrificing function. Have a stump that's too expensive to remove and too big to take out yourself? Plant a vine—it's nature's camouflage. Running out of planting space? Go vertical!

There are plenty of other reasons to select vines for your landscape. Early-blooming sweet peas chase away the chill of winter...Virginia creeper adds beautiful fall color...trumpet vine invites hummingbirds...and grapes are a favorite nesting and feeding site for northern cardinals.

Perfect Planning

But before charging off to the nearest nursery or garden center to pick out the first vine that comes to mind, it's best to plan before you purchase.

There are so many vines to choose from, it would be impossible to list them all (our short list in the box at far right

GET A GRIP. Each vine has its own method of climbing. Virginia creeper (at left) scales upward using strong hold fasts, which act like natural suction cups. Scarlet runner beans (right) use their main stems to twine around supports.

will get you started). However, all vines fall into one of three groups—annuals, perennials or woody vines.

Annuals, such as cypress vine, grow from seed each year. Perennials, like passionflower, die to the ground in winter, but sprout again in spring from the same roots. Woody vines, like wisteria, stand all year.

"One clever gardening trick is to mix annual vines with woody vines," says plant expert and contributing editor Melinda Myers. "Initially, woody vines don't grow very fast. So the annual vines can provide more immediate cover and color.

"It's fun to mix different vines together, such as clematis planted near a climbing rose (below)," she adds. "Together, they really brighten up a yard."

Most landscape vines grow upward, so it's important to understand how they climb and what types of support structures best suit their needs.

Some vines, such as honeysuckle, twine their way up, wrapping around and around as they grow. Others, like passionflower, send out tendrils to grab on. Some, such as climbing

Chapter 5

VERSATILE VINES. There are many ways to use vines to add height to your landscape. You can combine two varieties like clematis and rose (below left) for a burst of color, or use them solo to let unique vines like wisteria (right) shine. No matter what types you choose, however, make sure to provide proper support, from strings for morning glory to sturdy structures for wisteria.

Steve Terrill

hydrangea, have aerial roots, while Virginia creeper and others use hold fasts that serve as natural suction cups.

Selecting Support

A lightweight trellis is perfect for the twisting vines of clematis, but no match for a vigorous climbing rose, which is more suited to a heavier arbor.

If you're a fan of the dangling purple clusters of a blooming wisteria (at right), make sure you have a Herculean structure to support its incredible weight. We're talking major timbers that are located well away from your house, so the vigorous vine doesn't wreak havoc on rain gutters and downspouts.

Any of the clinging vines, like Boston ivy, are perfect plants to green-up brick walls. But be careful if you have a wooden house. Your siding could rot from the trapped moisture, and many of the hold fasts are so strong they can damage the wood.

Use Your Imagination

Elaborate structures are not necessary for planting vines in your backyard. Annuals, like morning glories, are the perfect answer for flimsy fences and lightweight arbors. In fact, they'll even grow on supports as simple as netting or strings.

"My husband, Jim, stretches strong cord diagonally from the ground to the top of our wraparound porch," says Angela Griffin Hatchett from Altoona, Alabama.

"Then he crisscrosses it going the other way. This gives the morning glories plenty of support as they reach toward the sun."

Vines also are great plants to enjoy with children because many grow extremely fast. Make a simple tepee from bamboo poles and let scarlet runner beans cover it for a neat summer hideout.

And if you're not a builder, a simple 4 x 4 post in the middle of a perennial garden is enough to provide a vertical break to your landscape. Just anchor it and stagger a few nails every 6 to 8 inches, so the vine has something to hang onto.

12 Picks to Elevate Your Landscape

Here's a short list of vines that will liven up your landscape. Check with your county Extension service (listed in the government section of your local telephone directory) before planting these vines. Make sure they're not too vigorous in your area. Also ask for recommendations for vines that do well in your climate.

Vine	Planting Zones	Maximum Height	Notes
American bittersweet (*Celastrus scandens*)	3-8	30 feet	Woody and heavy twining vine; fruits provide fall to winter interest.
Clematis (*Clematis* species)	4-9	6-20 feet	Perennial and woody twining climbers with prolific flowers.
Climbing hydrangea (*Hydrangea petiolaris*)	4-9	50 feet	Woody with aerial roots; clusters of white flowers; tolerates shade.
Confederate jasmine (*Trachelospermum jasminoides*)	9-10	20 feet	Woody twining evergreen; fragrant in summer with white flowers; can be wintered indoors.
Mandevilla (*Mandevilla splendens*)	Annual	10-20 feet	Twining vine used as annual with lovely trumpet flowers; can be wintered indoors.
Morning glory (*Ipomoea* species)	Annual	10-12 feet	Fast-growing annual twining vine; flowers open in the morning.
Passionflower (*Passiflora* species)	6-9	6-30 feet	Perennial with tendrils to help climb; host plant to several butterflies.
Scarlet runner bean (*Phaseolus coccineus*)	Annual	5 feet	Annual trailing plant that will climb; red flowers with edible beans.
Sweet pea (*Lathyrus odoratus*)	Annual	6-8 feet	Annual twining vine with fragrant flowers; sow seeds in autumn or early spring.
Trumpet vine (*Campsis radicans*)	5-9	30 feet	Woody vine that clings by aerial roots; flowers attract hummingbirds.
Virginia creeper and Boston ivy (*Parthenocissus* species)	3-9	50-70 feet	Woody climbers with strong hold fasts; vibrant in autumn; can be aggressive.
Wisteria (*Wisteria* species)	6-9	28 feet	Woody twining climber with dangling flowers; needs strong support.

RUSSIAN SAGE

This aromatic and elegant perennial is a real winner.

Richard Shiell

By Stacy Tornio, Associate Editor

The description of Russian sage may sound lofty, but it won't let you down. This perennial promises to be low-maintenance and grow in a variety of soils...and provide eye-catching beauty besides!

It's no wonder the Perennial Plant Association named Russian sage as the Perennial Plant of the Year in 1995. This charmer earned the honor for its striking stems of lavender-blue flowers, long blooming season and easy care.

Russian sage has gray-green leaves and silvery stems, which add to its lovely elegance, but the real treat arrives in late summer. This is when the plant bursts forth with small, lavender-blue flowers, aligned in gentle spiral clusters along the stems.

Like garden sage, Russian sage is part of the mint family, and its scent lives up to the name. The light, sage-like fragrance of the plant is easy to detect in the garden, and the leaves release a lovely aroma when crushed.

A Russian botanist chose the plant's botanical name, *Perovskia atriplicifolia*, in the 1800s to honor B.A. Perovski, the governor of a Russian providence. The plant's origins are in central Asia near Afghanistan and Pakistan.

A Versatile Choice

Though many gardeners use Russian sage as a filler plant, it certainly has the presence to shine alone. At maturity, it reaches 3 to 4 feet tall and spreads another 3 feet wide. This makes it perfect as a mass planting to fill in a large space or for a colorful backdrop to other plants.

Choosing companion flowers for Russian sage is as easy as selecting your favorite color. It's hard to go wrong—Russian sage will complement just about any plant. In addition, the extensive blooming season of Russian sage makes it a popular pairing for both summer and autumn perennials.

Purple coneflowers and black-eyed Susans are a couple of the common choices. Others that work well include daylily, bee balm, garden phlox, coreopsis and aster. Just make sure

PURPLE HAZE. With long stems of lavender-blue flowers, Russian sage can shine alone (above left) or share the spotlight. Above, Russian sage accents Joe Pye weed, porcupine grass, daylilies and rudbeckia. The plant's delicate blooms (above right) last from summer until autumn.

Plant Profile

Common Name: Russian sage.
Botanical Name: *Perovskia atriplicifolia.*
Bloom Time: Summer to early fall.
Hardiness: Zones 4 to 9.
Flower Color: Lavender blue.
Flower Shape: Small, tubular flowers on panicles.
Height: 2 to 4 feet.
Spread: 3 to 4 feet.
Light Needs: Full sun.
Soil Type: Well-draining.
Planting: Start bare-root plants in early spring or container plants throughout the growing season.
Prize Picks: Blue Spire has deeper purple blooms; Little Spire works well in small spaces, reaching only 30 inches tall.

the size of the plant you choose is enough to stand up to Russian sage's big and billowy nature.

Most Russian sage plants are self-supporting, but tend to grow loose and open. To encourage stiff growth, try pruning the plants halfway back in June. Or, enjoy its freedom and accent it with other large companion plants.

Up, Up and Away

To add Russian sage to your garden, start bare-root plants in spring or use container-grown perennials throughout the growing season, spacing the plants 30 to 36 inches apart. They will tolerate most soil conditions, including rocky areas.

As you're growing new plantings, make sure to give them plenty of water, but don't overdo it on the fertilizer. Excess fertilization can often lead to floppy stems and meager flowers.

Once you've established Russian sage, the majority of your work is done. As long as it's in well-drained soil where

it gets plenty of sun, Russian sage often blooms from July through October without any maintenance, and it also withstands drought. You don't have to worry about pests or diseases either, which don't bother this plant.

Although Russian sage is categorized as a perennial, its outstretched demeanor makes it quite shrub-like. By late fall, its stems become woody, but you can continue to enjoy the plant throughout winter. The silver stems create a beautiful seasonal show.

Once spring arrives and the danger of frost has passed, prune the stems 4 to 6 inches above the ground. This will help keep the plant compact and allow for new growth.

Take Your Pick

There are several cultivars of the popular garden variety of Russian sage.

Little Spire is a more compact variety that reaches only 30 inches tall. Filigran also is a smaller cultivar at 2 to 3 feet tall and has narrower fine-textured leaves. Longin has wider less dissected leaves and grows in a straight, upright form.

Finally, for a wider choice of bloom colors, try Blue Haze, which has lighter blue flowers with fewer lacy leaves, or Blue Spire for a deeper purple hue.

No matter what type of this dynamic perennial you select for your garden, it's sure to live up to its promises. After all, the plant already has received top honors.

READER TIP

Russian sage will complement many types of perennials. Some of the top picks include purple coneflowers, black-eyed Susans, daylilies, bee balm, garden phlox, coreopsis and aster.

Ray Packard

Alan and Linda Detrick

Ray Packard

DAZZLING DAHLIAS

These garden darlings provide beautiful bursts of color well into fall.

By Kathleen Zimmer-Anderson
Waukesha, Wisconsin

If variety is the spice of life, then this lush bloomer is one of the zestiest flowers around! With more than 20,000 different cultivars, dahlias come in all shapes, sizes and colors (except for blue), making them a favorite among gardeners across North America.

Dahlias have cast their spell on me. I've been a fan ever since I saw them growing at my younger brother Mike's new home. Once I'd gotten over the fact that he had a hidden green thumb, I caught sight of the full red and yellow blooms gracing his flower bed and couldn't look away.

Mike figured out pretty quickly what had captured my attention and promised he'd help me pick out a few for my garden. I've been growing dahlias ever since.

New-World Native

Appreciation for these members of the daisy family dates back to the Aztecs in Mexico, who used the indigenous plant they called *cocoxochitl* as a cure for epilepsy. Elsewhere in Central and South America, the fleshy, sugar-filled tubers were used for food. Later on, sugar extracted from the tubers served as a treatment for diabetes.

Spanish conquistadors admired the plant's beauty and brought the blooms to Spain in the 18th century. In 1789, the king of Spain bestowed the name "dahlia" on the plant. He chose the moniker in honor of Swedish botanist Anders Dahl, who'd created numerous hybrids.

Hundreds of years later, the flowers are more popular than ever before.

"Dahlias have as broad a range as you'd find in any flower group in terms of size, shape and color," says Alan Fisher of the American Dahlia Society, who raises hundreds of varieties at his home in Rockville, Maryland. "Many gardeners grow

Ray Packard

Alan and Linda Detrick

SHAPING UP. There are 11 different dahlia shapes, providing enough variety to satisfy any gardener. They pair well with other flowers, too, like the ball dahlias with cleome above left.

them to enjoy their beauty, while others like to cultivate show-quality blooms and compete in local dahlia shows.

"There's really something for everyone, from tiny specimens to huge tree dahlias that thrive on the West Coast. They can reach as high as 20 feet in a single season and produce flowers as late as November."

Take Your Pick

Because of this huge variety, dahlias are separated into six categories for size and 11 categories for bloom type. The flowers range from dainty 1-inch pompoms to 6- to 8-inch mid-size varieties and giant versions that can measure well over 15 inches wide.

Shape categories include decorative dahlias with full curving, multipetaled blossoms; ball-shaped dahlias with a full pompom of petals (top far left photo); cactus dahlias that sport spiky petals (center left); collarette varieties that have a ring of rounded petals topped by smaller ones; orchid dahlias that feature a pinwheel of inward-curling petals and single dahlias (bottom left) that look like daisies. And that's just the tip of the iceberg!

Most dahlias are on the tall side, standing anywhere from 2 to 5 feet high, with some soaring to 6 feet or more. The loftiest varieties need to be staked in order to prevent the wind from damaging them.

Even the dwarf varieties are sizable, measuring 1 to 2 feet

in height. They are ideal for filling the center of smaller flower beds or in containers.

Aside from catching attention, dahlias will attract hummingbirds and butterflies during summer, and provide a blaze of color until the first frost, much like chrysanthemums.

Friends and Foes

Dahlias pair up nicely with a variety of garden favorites. Try bunching together several short and medium-sized varieties in different spots in a garden that's filled with perennials or annuals.

You can also combine them with threadleaf coreopsis or ornamental grasses—the contrast between the finely textured plants and the bold and leafy dahlias works nicely.

Pests can be a problem on occasion. I've had trouble with slugs that savor my dahlias' meaty foliage, and my brother has battled mites and aphids.

Insecticidal soap will help control insects, and there are a number of commercial sprays and traps for slugs. I've found that sinking containers of yeast and water into the ground near my dahlias to capture slugs works well, too.

Don't forget that dahlias aren't hardy unless you live in an area that doesn't see frost. If your home is in a colder cli-

> ### READER TIP
>
> Dahlias are available in nearly every size, shape and color. Try tiny specimens for small areas, or if you live on the West Coast and have the space, plant a tree dahlia, which reach up to 20 feet.
>
> **—Alan Fisher, Rockville, Maryland**

DIGGIN' DAHLIAS. Although dahlias' tuberous roots (above) have to be stored indoors for winter in cold regions, the vibrant blooms that emerge in summer (below and left) are well worth the effort.

mate like mine, dig up each plant's tuberous roots after the first light frost in fall. Then dry them off and store in a cool, dark place, like a cellar, until planting them in spring.

Not only do these lovelies brighten sunny gardens, they also make outstanding cut flowers, thanks in large part to their sturdy stalks and ability to look fresh for a long time.

Early morning or early evening are the best times to snip the long-stemmed blossoms for a bouquet. Cut the stems at a 45-degree angle, then submerge them—flower and all—in a container of warm water. After a bit, move the flowers to a vase filled with cold water. Trim 1 inch off the stems before creating an arrangement.

A Little TLC

Some gardeners start their dahlias indoors each spring for earlier blooms, but I've never bothered with this. I just pop the tubers, with the "eyes" up, into 4-inch-deep holes once the threat of frost has passed. This method results in later blooming, but I don't mind.

Whether you plant dahlias indoors in early spring or head straight for the garden before summer begins, remember that these beauties like plenty of light. Plant them in a spot that receives 5 or more hours of sun each day.

Dahlias prefer rich, well-draining soil and regular watering. Add mulch to help retain moisture in the soil and apply fertilizer from time to time—these babies have a big appetite! If you don't fertilize regularly or if you water a bit too much, you'll notice because the leaves will turn yellow.

For short, bushy plants with an abundance of smaller blooms, pinch off the growing tips and deadhead spent blooms regularly.

READER TIP

Early mornings or early evenings are the best times to snip these long-stemmed blossoms for a bouquet. Cut at a 45-degree angle, submerge in a container of warm water and then move to a vase filled with cold water.

Dahlias will produce larger, more dramatic flowers if you confine the plant to a single major stem. Remove the side shoots as they grow, as well as any flower buds that develop along the stem, leaving one bud at the very top. The resulting blossom will be worth the effort!

Editor's Note: If you want to find out more about the flowers or meet other gardeners who share your enthusiasm for dahlias, contact the American Dahlia Society. Visit its Web site at *www.dahlia.org* to learn how. Or, send inquires to Richard Peters, 931 W. Wellington Ct., Muskegon MI 49441.

Plant Profile

Common Name: Dahlia.
Botanical Name: *Dahlia* species.
Bloom Time: Summer to first frost.
Hardiness: Zones 7 to 11; tubers must be dug up and stored indoors for winter in other areas.
Flower Colors: All colors except blue; many bicolored varieties are available.
Flower Shapes: There are 11 different basic shapes.
Height: 1 to 6 feet.
Spread: 1 to 3 feet.
Light Needs: Full sun.
Soil Type: Rich and well-draining.
Planting: Once the threat of frost has passed, plant tubers about 4 inches deep with an "eye" pointing up. Add mulch to help retain moisture.
Special Care: Stake taller varieties to protect from wind damage. After the first frost in northern areas, bring the tubers inside. Pack the roots in sand and store in a cool, dry place over winter.

GO FOR THE
GOLDENROD

Strike it rich with this autumn bloom.

It's not easy being gold.

If you point to a patch of goldenrod, the average gardener might tell you it's a weed. Show a friend a sprig of its beautiful yellow blooms, and she'll swear the plant is making her sneeze.

And as far as growing it in your garden...well, you've probably never even considered it.

You're in good company. Although most of goldenrod's 100 varieties are native to North America (you've probably seen them sprouting on the roadsides or near the woods), it took

Donna and Tom Krischan; inset, Richard Day/Daybreak Imagery

GOLDEN TOUCH. King Midas or not, anyone can turn a garden to gold by planting a patch of native goldenrod. You'll find that newer hybrids like Golden Baby (right) and Fireworks (left) are worth their weight in gold, especially when paired with other bright autumn blooms like asters or chrysanthemums. These nectar-filled flowers will also attract winged admirers, including monarch butterflies and bumblebees.

American gardeners until the 1980s to accept this golden treasure as a garden-worthy plant.

Twenty years later, many still shy from its sunny blooms, worried the tall stalks will take over their yards.

Their fears are not completely off base. Some goldenrod varieties are too aggressive, and are best suited for wild gardens. Others, however, are long-lived, trouble-free and will make anyone's backyard sparkle.

Goldenrod has an unusual beauty, captivating admirers with tall leafy stems that erupt into gold-petaled clusters of delicate blooms.

Still worried about hay fever? Ragweed—another tall yellow flower—is the real culprit behind those red eyes and runny noses. Both pollen-packed plants appear in late summer, but goldenrod pollen is too heavy to become airborne.

Tea Time

In fact, 18th-century physicians even believed goldenrod had healing powers. These doctors used its blossoms to mask the flavor of many medicines.

By the time of the American Revolution, dried goldenrod petals were being brewed to make a tasty tea. About 250 years later, the plant had moved on to another type of "tea"— the Model T. Thomas Edison cultivated goldenrod's natural latex to make a set of tires strong enough for the car.

Today, the beauty of this classic bloom is finally beginning to earn the recognition it deserves. In the past 5 years, after conducting in-depth studies of the plant, the Chicago Botanic Garden has put goldenrod on its list of the 19 top plants to grow in the Midwest.

Digging for Gold

Goldenrod, however, thrives as far north as Maine and as far south as Florida. This late-blooming golden perennial will make your garden gleam long after many summer blooms have faded.

Before you break ground for this backyard beauty, there are a few "golden" rules to keep this plant from growing out of control.

Although goldenrod thrives in full sun, it will spread less if you plant it in partial shade.

Goldenrod also grows too vigorously in rich soil. Instead, use it to add color to an area of moderate to poor soil.

> **READER TIP**
>
> If you want to attract butterflies, this is a great bloom for you. Try nectar-filled varieties such as zigzag, prairie or elm-leaf goldenrod.

And just like real gold, a little bit can go a long way. Keep it from overwhelming your garden by carefully selecting a few sites for this bloom. Large patches are more appropriate for a field or meadow.

With these tips in mind, you can choose from a whole band of varieties of this gorgeous gold.

For a showstopping display, plant a hybrid like Fireworks goldenrod (one of the *Chicago Botanic Garden's* top picks, pictured at far left), whose flowers seem to shoot out in every direction. Or try Golden Fleece (photo on page 155), a compact plant with arching clusters that will warm up any garden.

To attract butterflies, try nectar-filled varieties such as zigzag, prairie or elm-leaf goldenrod. Silverrod—the only type with cream-colored flowers—also has its charm.

A Winning Selection

Whatever type you select, it's sure to turn heads. Just ask Melody Rose of Benton, Kentucky, who has been growing Canada goldenrod in her backyard flower bed for the past 3 years.

"Pale-pink and pale-blue flowers are really nice, but that's not what you're going to notice in people's yards," she says. "Goldenrod is bright *and* beautiful—and those little blossoms are simply exquisite. It's just a wonderful plant."

Plant Profile

Common Name: Goldenrod.
Botanical Name: *Solidago.*
Bloom Time: Late summer to autumn.
Hardiness: Zones 3 to 9.
Flower Color: Most are gold.
Flower Shape: Clusters of small spiked blooms.
Height: 1 to 5 feet.
Spread: At least 2 feet.
Light Needs: Full sun to partial shade.
Soil Type: Poor soil helps control growth.
Planting: In spring and summer, plant goldenrod about 1 foot apart.
Prize Picks: Golden Fleece is a dwarf variety with arching clusters; Fireworks is known for its unique flowering stems that shoot out in every direction; Golden Baby is compact and blooms early; sweet goldenrod has showy flowers that emit an anise-like scent.

172

166

ALL ABOUT HUMMINGBIRDS

160

164

RUBY-THROATED HUMMINGBIRD

This beauty is one of nature's most intriguing birds.

By George Harrison, Contributing Editor

How does a 3-month-old ruby-throated hummingbird find its way to tropical wintering grounds, making the migration across thousands of miles all by itself?

How can hummingbirds flutter in midair, hovering so perfectly that they appear almost motionless, as if suspended by an unseen support?

How do males summon the tenacity to vigorously defend their territories—taking on intruders of any species and size?

It's true that hummingbirds are among the most fascinating birds in the world—they perform unbelievable feats like these every day. But it is the fall migration of ruby-throated juveniles that's one of the greatest mysteries in all of nature.

This flight to warmer climates in Central or South America includes a 500- to 600-mile nonstop journey across the Gulf of Mexico. And the youngsters go it alone, even though they've never made the trip before!

The parents of the recently hatched hummers leave their northern nesting grounds for the tropics weeks before their offspring do. Until late summer, the youngsters remain near the area where they hatched, busily feeding and preparing their bodies for the long flight ahead.

Then one day, the amount of daylight triggers a migration response, and the ruby-throated youngsters head south. No map...no bird to follow.

How they know when to leave, what direction to fly, how far to go and when they have reached their destinations is the great mystery. And the only plausible answer researchers have offered is genetic programming.

That this programming carries strong influence likely comes as no surprise to people who feed ruby-throated hummingbirds. Because the following spring, another miracle happens:

The secret to attracting ruby-throated hummingbirds is red...

LITTLE GEMS. Ruby-throated hummingbirds shimmer like jewels, especially the mature males (at far left) with their namesake red throats, called gorgets. Clockwise from above, a female tends to young...a birdbath dwarfs this female...a juvenile male starts to show a hint of its developing red throat.

Those same ruby-throats return to the exact locations in the North where they hatched the year before.

They remember precisely where they consumed sugar water the previous summer. Even after decades of admiring these birds, I'm still amazed when the first ruby-throat of spring returns to my Wisconsin backyard and hovers in the same spot where the sugar-water feeder hung last summer, though the feeder isn't there.

That's my signal to mix the first batch of sugar water, fill the hummingbird feeders and get them outside to the hungry ruby-throats, which are the only hummingbird that regularly nests in the East.

Can't Resist Red

The secret to attracting ruby-throated hummingbirds is red. Anything that is red in color will catch their eye. Just ask Alberta Hanson of Cushing, Wisconsin, whose husband was poked by two ruby-throats in his backyard when they probed their bills into the vent holes of his new red cap.

Mairiam Taylor of West Chester, Pennsylvania was shocked while reading a book in her garden when a ruby-throated hummingbird flew right up to her red lips. It obviously was looking for flower nectar, and Mairiam joked that her lips must have looked like red "two-lips."

Then there is the ruby-throated hummingbird's incredible power of flight. Not only long-distance flight, but hovering flight as well.

Hummingbirds can control their positions in midair as no other birds can. Because their shoulder joints are so flexi-

ble, they are able to rotate their wings with each of the 75 times they beat per second. This allows them to fly backward, sideways, up or down, and hover perfectly.

Defending Its Ground

I watch ruby-throated hummingbirds performing aerial acrobatics at the feeders in my yard, where a dominant male maintains his autocratic control over the food and habitat in my garden by chasing away other hummingbirds—all except "his" females.

The same bully male advertises his dominance over the area

FLY-IN DINING. Adding a sugar-water feeder in your favorite backyard spot is sure to be a hit with area hummingbirds. These ruby-throats (above) gather around this feeder for a meal.

Richard Day/Daybreak Imagery

with dramatic aerial displays of sweeping pendulum-patterned flights, 40 to 50 feet above the garden. The display impresses the females while warning off other males.

His control is effective, but I have found a way to offer sugar water to other hummingbirds despite the territorial bully. I place some additional feeders on the opposite side of the house—out of the alpha male's sight.

Proof of the male's effective strategy appears every July when green-backed hummingbirds with white bellies appear at the feeders. They are his offspring.

He allows them to feed, but he plays no part in rearing his young. The females do all the work, first by crafting tiny nesting cups of plant down, then attaching them to tree limbs with spider silk.

The nests are so well camouflaged that it took F. Dwain Phillips 20 years to find one in his Stillwater, Oklahoma yard.

"I finally understood why I hadn't been able to find a hummingbird nest before," Phillips explained. "They are only about 1-1/2 inches in diameter, and they blend so well with the tree bark that it looked like nothing more than a bump on the branch," he says.

The female incubates two tiny, pure-white eggs for 14 to 16 days until they hatch. For 3 more weeks, she feeds the youngsters in the nest by regurgitating nectar and tiny insects directly into their throats with her swordlike bill, a somewhat shocking sight to behold.

Another "Cool" Trick

Even short periods of cold weather, such as late-spring frosts, are not a problem for adult hummingbirds. They perform another amazing feat by placing themselves into a hibernation-like state called torpidity. This helps them save energy when temperatures are low.

Torpidity slows down their respiratory and metabolic systems, making them appear to be asleep or dead. People who find these "sick" hummingbirds hanging upside down from sugar-water feeders don't realize that the birds are just awaiting warmer weather and improved feeding conditions.

If you want to try feeding ruby-throats in your yard, start by reading the hummingbird feeding basics on pages 164-165. Soon, you will find yourself admiring the fascinating qualities of ruby-throats...and have some amazing stories of your own to share. ◄

Hummingbird Heaven

Southern hospitality attracts thousands of migrating jewels each year.

By Lola Autry, Hickory Flat, Mississippi

Let the celebration begin!

Each autumn, tiny ruby-throated hummingbirds prepare for their annual vacation to Mexico and beyond. Here in Mississippi, we give these glorious creatures a proper send-off with the annual Hummingbird Migration Celebration in Holly Springs.

The 2005 festival at the Strawberry Plains Audubon Center marked the sixth year of the event, held early each September. Every year, thousands of ruby-throated hummingbirds (like the one above) pass through the center's 2,500 acres of sanctuary. It's a weekend of celebration, education and bird banding.

CATCH AND RELEASE. During the celebration at Strawberry Plains Audubon Center in Mississippi, experts put tiny bands on hummingbirds, including rare finds like the calliope (above right), and then visitors to release them into flight (top right).

The Chosen Few

A couple of years ago, I was one of the lucky ones who got to release a hummingbird after it was banded. The experience was magical as I held the tiny bird in my hand and then set it free into the crisp, autumn air.

During my visit, I could almost sense the presence of the two sisters who had lived on the plantation years ago. Both nature lovers, they donated Strawberry Plains to the Mississippi Audubon Society. The organization now keeps up the gardens for both the public and the birds to enjoy.

It certainly doesn't go to waste, either. Thousands of people flock to the plantation every year for the festival to see the migrating hummingbirds. One day is even entirely dedicated to kids, who come by busloads for the chance to see a hummer up close and personal.

You can see the excitement in their eyes. Each child hopes to be one of the chosen few who will have the rare opportunity to embrace a hummingbird and then release it into flight.

Observation Deck

The birds flit around the gardens from flower to flower. To avoid disturbing them, onlookers like me watch in awe from a glassed-in solarium at the back of the elegant mansion. These miniature wonders drink up the sweetness from each bloom, storing up energy for their long trip south.

To me, it's no surprise this place has earned the nickname "Hummingbird Heaven." I feel fortunate to live nearby, so I can marvel at the birds every year. This is southern hospitality at its best.

How to Attract Hummingbirds

Use these five easy tips to make your backyard a hot spot.

By George Harrison, Contributing Editor

It's no wonder people are hooked on hummingbirds. With iridescent beauty and lightning-quick speed, there's a lot of spunk packed in their diminutive bodies.

At least 15 species of hummingbirds nest in the U.S. and Canada. Most species—including the broad-tailed, rufous, Anna's and black-chinned (like the one above right)—are found in the West. Only one, the ruby-throated, spends summers in the East (see pages 160-162).

All hummingbirds have a seemingly insatiable appetite for sugar water, which means many backyard bird-watchers attract hummingbirds by setting out a sugar-water feeder (below right) in their gardens.

Unfortunately, it is not always that simple, and I get a lot of questions from readers wondering how to coax hummingbirds to visit their yards.

That's why I've come up with these five basic tips that should help almost anyone successfully attract hummingbirds, and deal with some of the problems that can occur along the way.

1. GET THEIR ATTENTION. If you're just starting out, the best way to get hummingbirds to notice your sugar-water feeder is to plant red flowers. Then place the sugar-water feeder among those flowers.

The red blooms will attract the birds, and they will quickly find the feeder. As soon as they are comfortable eating from the feeder, you can move it a few feet a day so it's closer to your viewing window, or wherever you'd like to watch them feed.

As far as the proper placement for your feeder, it's best to keep it out of the sun so the sugar-water mixture does not spoil.

But don't worry about nearby human activity. Reader Evelyn Cook of Springfield, Oregon was concerned that traffic and children playing in the area could discourage hummingbirds from the feeder on her porch. Once hummingbirds find a feeder, they tend to be very tame, and no amount of activity will keep them away.

2. THE RIGHT RECIPE. Mix 4 parts tap water to 1 part sugar. Bring the mixture to a boil, then allow it to cool be-fore placing it in the feeder. This is the most widely accepted sugar-water recipe. It produces a mixture that is neither too light nor too heavy and resists quick spoiling. Do not use sugar substitutes or honey, which can actually harm the birds.

You can store leftovers in the refrigerator for up to a week. Change the sugar water every 3 to 5 days. It's not necessary to add red coloring because hummingbird feeders usually have red on them. If not, you can try attaching something red—like a gift bow or an artificial flower—to the feeder.

Karin and Walter Mullaney of Arden, North Carolina wondered if they should fortify their sugar-water mixture. There is no need to add other nutrients to the mixture. The birds get any additional nutrients they need from other sources, such as flower nectar and tiny insects.

George Harrison

SWEET TREATS. Hummingbirds aren't the only ones who like sugar water. To keep bees away from your feeders, use bee guards. To keep ants out, hang a water-filled moat (like the one above), which was made from a plastic bottle cap.

3. INSECT-PROOF FEEDERS. Since the sugar-water mixture is so sweet, bees, flies and ants are often attracted to the feeder spouts. This was a problem for Jerry and Lita Fish in Tucson, Arizona, who wrote in looking for a way to stop bees and ants from invading their hummingbird feeders.

Because ants don't fly, you simply need to block their walking pathway to the feeder ports. Deter them with a water-filled moat that hangs between the hook and the feeder. Moats are available at birding supply stores, or you can fashion your own using a deep, plastic bottle cap (see photo above right).

Discourage bees by inserting bee guards, also available at birding supply stores, in the feeder spouts. Some feeders even come with these guards already attached. In addition, you can hang a bee trap near the hummingbird feeder, using the same sugar water as bait. This will eliminate many of the invading insects.

4. OUTWIT BULLY MALES. It's common for a dominant male to chase other hummingbirds away from a feeder. This is one way the male protects his nesting territory. In fact, these males spend most of their time guarding feeders, and will allow only their mates and offspring to feed.

The simple solution is to place other feeders out of sight of the feeder the bully is guarding. He can guard only one feeder at a time, freeing up the others to entertain additional hummingbirds.

5. KEEP FEEDERS CLEAN. When sugar water ferments, it clogs feeder spouts and reservoirs. In hot weather, feeders should be cleaned at least once a week. Sometimes, hummingbirds will let you know when the feeder needs cleaning—they'll stop coming by to eat.

The easiest way to clean the feeders is to wash with a solution of hot water and a little vinegar, and use a pipe cleaner in the tubes. Give the feeder a thorough rinse, and it should look like new.

With these five tips, you're ready to welcome hummingbirds to your backyard this summer!

READER TIP

To get a close-up view of hummingbirds, start your feeders at a distance among red flowers. Then move the feeder a few feet each day until it's at the desired location near your house.

BLACK-CHINNED HUMMINGBIRD

The black-chinned hummingbird is the western counterpart to the ruby-throated hummingbird. It's the most widespread of all western species, with a breeding range spanning from Mexico to southern Canada.

At one time, these hummingbirds resided strictly near canyons and in the foothill forests of western mountains. However, because of the popularity of sugar-water feeders and hummingbird gardens, these birds are now frequent residents in urban and suburban backyards. And they're very comfortable with their human neighbors.

Like many other hummingbirds, the black-chinned is named for the male's most distinctive feature—its prominent black throat. In the right light, you'll also see a spectacular flash of bright, iridescent violet just above the white bib on its breast. Females are plainer than the male, and have no distinctive markings on their drab gray chins.

Black-chinned hummers almost always pump and wag their tails while in flight. And the males create a dull buzzing sound while in the air.

Besides nectar, these birds also drink tree sap from sapsucker wells and will catch insects by perching on a branch and dashing out to ambush their prey, much like flycatchers do.

READE

Look for b
hummers
ter feeder
bird gard
trees as
for sweet
sucker we

BLACK-CHINNED HUMMERS find plenty of room to roam. They are the most widespread of all western hummingbird species. Although most hummingbirds lay two eggs, black-chins can lay one to three.

Photo: Anthony Mercieca/Dembinsky Photo Assoc.

HUMMER HAPPENINGS

Encounters with these jewels are truly magical.

Hanging Around

A RUBY-THROATED hummingbird built these tiny nests (left) on either side of the decorative wind spinner on our porch. As you can see, the eggs were no bigger than my fingernail. The nestlings hatched a few weeks later.

As the babies grew, they hung precariously on the edge of the nest while they strengthened their wings. At last, one flew off, and the other followed the next day.

My whole family enjoyed the wonderful experience of watching the baby ruby-throats grow, and we were sorry to see them leave. —*Brenda Edwards, White Plains, Georgia*

Bring on the Food!

PEOPLE often wonder if hummingbirds return to the same feeding grounds each year. From our experience, we can say they certainly do!

In fact, if we miscalculate the return of our hummingbird friends, they let us know about it.

One May, we still had snow, so I hadn't yet hung the feeders in our yard. While washing dishes, I looked up and saw a hummingbird hovering outside my kitchen window, looking at me. It stayed there until I filled the feeders.

Another year, when we were late putting out feeders, the hummers came around to the living room window, hovering and peering inside.

They let us know when they run out of nectar, too. One summer day, the feeders ran dry while I was at work. When I got home, I stopped in the front yard for a moment to talk to my husband. A hummer suddenly buzzed me in the face, then flew to the backyard. I got the message and quickly refilled the feeders. —*Kathie McIntosh, Rathdrum, Idaho*

Aerial Acrobat

ONE JUNE morning, we saw two ruby-throated hummingbirds buzzing around the feeder. We thought they were competing for territory, until we realized they were flying in small loops around each other. We were witnessing a courtship ritual!

The female then landed on a crabapple, and the male flew out in front of her to show off his flying skills. He darted from side to side in short, quick bursts, always facing her. It reminded me of football players practicing their dodging skills, except this little guy was much faster.

At sunset, we saw another courtship flight. The female sat in the tree while her suitor made big arcs above her. He flew up about 10 feet, then out to the side about 7 feet, then back up and out to the other side. He repeated this precise, quick pattern several times.

I don't know whether the female was impressed with his flying, but we certainly were! —*Linda Rearick, Milford, Ohio*

A Lucky Shot

HUMMERS aren't the easiest birds to photograph because they're constantly in motion. I snapped this one (below) at a sugar-water feeder while in San Diego, California. It still arrived and left fairly quickly, however.

We didn't even have a chance to get a good look at it to determine what kind of hummingbird it was.

When we processed the photos, we were even more puzzled. This little beauty had a small red ruffle on its neck rather than the red throat we expected.

After doing some investigating, we learned it was a juvenile male Anna's hummingbird. It had yet to fully develop its red throat and hood. What an interesting discovery! —*D.J. Armstrong, Maple Glen, Pennsylvania*

She Wouldn't Be Bullied

EVERYONE who feeds hummingbirds knows that there's often a male "bully" in the crowd that'll chase other birds away from the feeder.

We had one hummer like that, and one day while he was doing his bullying, a female, probably his mate, decided she was going to eat at the sugar-water feeder no matter what. She landed on the perch and put her bill into the opening as far as she could.

The male hovered over her, jabbing at her back and tail, trying to get her attention. But the female didn't budge until she'd had her fill at the feeder.
—*Frances Felder*
Rodney, Ontario

Deep Sleep

ONE COOL summer morning, my husband called me over to see a "surprise guest." I was wondering who would be visiting so early, when he pointed to a tiny hummingbird hanging upside down from a feeder on our back deck (right).

As it dangled there, other hummingbirds kept coming to the feeder for their early morning breakfasts as if nothing were out of the ordinary.

Concerned that there was something wrong, we took a closer look at the bird. It was breathing normally and appeared to be sleeping soundly. About 5 minutes later, the hummer woke up and flew to the protection of the nearby trees.

The only explanation we could think of is that the night was a bit cool, and this bird hibernated until it warmed in the morning sun. —*Lorrain Chien, Floyds Knobs, Indiana*

Editor's Note: Lorrain is absolutely correct. When temperatures drop, hummingbirds often go into a temporary hibernation-like state called "torpor" to conserve energy.

Hook, Line and Hummer

MY HUSBAND and I enjoy fishing on a lake near our home, and some curious hummingbirds often join us when we are out on the boat!

The canopy and rim on our boat is a maroon color, and we have a red tackle box and red life jackets. When we're trolling near the shore, the hummers are often attracted by the red color and come check out the canopy. Sometimes they even get brave and fly around the tackle box and jackets. A hummer once perched on the back of the seat right beside my husband.

We enjoy our fishing trips, even when we don't catch any fish. Close encounters with these amazing birds are just as fun! —*Karen Lee, La Pine, Oregon*

Beautiful Breeze

AFTER MOWING the lawn one hot day, I laid down near a clump of tall tiger lilies for a short rest. A few minutes later, I was roused by a strong breeze cooling my face.

I opened my eyes and saw a hummingbird about 3 feet above me, feeding on the lily blooms. I was astonished its wings could create such a breeze—but I certainly enjoyed it!
—*Paul Williams, Belmont, California*

Handy Feeders

LAST FALL, we had 10 to 15 female hummers and their young all trying to eat from our feeders at one time. Sometimes they'd even perch on top of one another to feed from the same opening.

I had to replenish the sugar water daily, and when I took each feeder down, the hummers would buzz around my head until I'd filled it and put it back up.

Eventually, they began to land on the feeder while I was still holding it. And after about a week, they started landing on my fingers! My husband and grandson had fun watching and taking pictures of these unforgettable "hand-feeding" sessions (right).
—*Linda Gilson, Lamont, Iowa*

Beat the Heat

ON A DAY when the heat index was near 100°, I noticed a ruby-throated hummingbird cooling off in a sprinkler we had going in the front yard.

My son and I watched and laughed as the hummer hovered above the sprinkler, waiting for its shower. Then it began to follow the path of the sprinkler back and forth to get a better drenching.

When it got tired, it would perch in a nearby tree before returning to the sprinkler for another dousing. That hummingbird sure had the right idea to beat the heat!
—*Mick Kurowski, Spring Grove, Illinois*

Summer Fun

WITH OUR grandson George staying with us for a 2-week  visit, we were looking for something fun to do on a particularly hot day. So we thought we'd try hand-feeding hummingbirds while sitting in the shade (left).

After holding a small sugar-water feeder for a while, George was rewarded for his patience when a hummingbird flew up and started to eat right in front of him. The delight is obvious in his expression.

Afterward, George told us that feeding the hummingbirds was even more fun than fishing!

—*Laura Thompson*
Prescott, Arizona

A Perfect Pose

LAST SUMMER, I was pleased when my zinnias attracted this female ruby-throated hummingbird (left) to my backyard. It visited several times, and one day, I had my camera ready.

I was busy taking a close-up of a monarch butterfly among my zinnias, when the hummingbird zoomed in for some nectar. After flitting from flower to flower, it decided to rest for a few seconds right in front of the camera.

I couldn't believe my luck. It was like she was posing for a photo!

I now plant zinnias every year and would recommend the same to other readers who want to attract hummingbirds.

—*Emily Howald, Kankakee, Illinois*

A Bright Surprise

THIS albino hummingbird (below) visited my sugar-water feeders late last summer. The little white wonder stayed for 2 weeks, stocking up on liquid energy before its journey to the tropics for winter.

I'm sure one reason this pale marvel stayed around so long was the abundant supply of food. My two neighbors and I maintain a total of six feeders in our yards.

I hope our buffet provided the hummer with sufficient nourishment for at least one leg of its long trip.

—*Donna Wolfe, Hebron, Kentucky*

Thirst-Quencher

I WAS watering a blooming hosta in my backyard, when a hummingbird flew within a foot of where I was standing. I figured the bird wanted to get near the bloom, so I slowly began backing away. Much to my surprise, the hummingbird followed!

Turns out, the bird must have been thirsty. I watched in awe as the hummingbird took a drink off a leaf that held a droplet of water. Even more surprising, the hummer returned the next morning and watched while I watered a hydrangea. Perhaps it was hoping for another drink of water!

—*Kathy Dolge, Silver Spring, Maryland*

Cold Drink on a Hot Day

IT WAS a steamy 100° afternoon when I decided to change the sugar water in my hummingbird feeder. I added the new nectar, which I store in the refrigerator, then sat back to watch my little friends.

Soon, a male ruby-throated hummingbird arrived. It took a sip of the cold liquid and jumped back, as if startled by the icy drink. It almost fell off the perch. But then it took another sip and sat there for a while, drinking.

Normally, after about 10 to 15 seconds, the hummers fly off, but this one did not. When he did finally leave, he flew quite slowly, almost wobbling. Perhaps he had overindulged a bit on the cool refreshment.

—*JoAnn Ennis*
Yardley, Pennsylvania

Granddaughter Knows Best

WHILE visiting our son in Iowa, a hummingbird flew into the

house and up to the high cathedral windows near the ceiling. The tiny flier would not come down and ended up staying through the entire night.

The next day, our son Eric got an extension pole and tried, unsuccessfully, to guide the bird out the door. Meanwhile, our granddaughter Kali made a "nest" from a plastic cup. She chose a red one because she said hummingbirds like red, and she put dry grass in the bottom.

Kali then asked her dad to attach it to the pole and hold it up for the frightened bird. He did, and within 30 seconds, the bird flew into the cup.

Feeling proud about her role in the rescue, Kali took a moment to say good-bye to her new feathered friend (above), and then released it safely outside.

—*Jerry and Sally Groves, Tucson, Arizona*

On Guard

THE MALE anna's hummingbird who guards the feeders on my patio has earned its nickname, "Bull," short for Bully. As soon as I put this decorative hummingbird stake (right) in my garden, the hummer immediately took ownership of it. It now serves as its perch for it to keep watch over the nearby feeders.

—*LaVerne Otis, Bellflower, California*

No Storm Stops 'Em

LAST YEAR, my area in Florida was hit by several hurricanes. But, despite the 40- to 50-mph winds, the hummingbird that frequents my fire bush and salvia made its appointed rounds like clockwork every day. I was totally amazed it could navigate, since it's difficult even to walk in those conditions.

I guess those little hummers have the postal carriers beat, since the hurricanes did stop the mail! —*Karen Lawrence*
Altoona, Florida

Wait Your Turn

NOT A single feeder port went unused as these juvenile hummingbirds prepared for their migration (below). And they weren't the only hungry ones. At least 14 others were waiting nearby for their turn at the feeder. It was amazing to see so many hummingbirds in one place! —*Myrtle Stauffacher*
Englewood, Colorado

Splish Splash

I WAS helping some vacationing neighbors by filling their bird feeders when I ended up helping out a little hummingbird—big time! One day, I found a hummer spread-eagle on the bottom of a small pan of nectar, stuck and caked with sugar and syrup.

Thinking it was dead, I started to remove it. Suddenly, I heard a feeble chirp. The little guy was alive!

I held it under a faucet to remove all the sugar I could, but it was still covered in the sticky stuff. Not knowing what to do, I put it in a square plastic jar and gingerly drove the 3 miles home. The whole time, I could only think one thing: How do you bathe a hummingbird?

Once home, I put the jar on its side and slowly poured in about a 1/2 inch of water. The hummer started to beat its wings and splashed around, dissolving the crusted sugar on its belly. I picked it up and carried it outside. Eventually, it took off and landed on a limb near my kitchen window.

I spent the next hour watching the bird. I was thrilled when it lifted off, flew directly toward my window and landed on a feeder about 3 feet from my nose. Now that's what I call a day well spent. —*Glen Keith, Junction, Texas*

A Balanced Home

WHEN A bold Anna's hummingbird made a nest on

their clothesline, my friends in Wilton, California invited me over to take some pictures. Sure enough, the hummer had built its happy home on a wooden clothespin! I set up my Nikon camera on a tripod, went into the house and watched through the kitchen window. When the bird returned to its nest, I used a remote to snap this picture (above). —*Boyd Jensen*
Rancho Cordova, California

A Top-Notch Meal

A FEW years ago, I read about someone using a small plastic ladle as a temporary feeder for hummingbirds. Intrigued, I tried a version of that experiment, instead using the red plastic top from a mayonnaise jar.

The birds immediately took to it. In fact, they consumed more sugar water from the jar lid than from the regular feeder in my yard, which was completely full.

To fancy up the impromptu porch-rail dining room I had created, I made a tiny roost out of twigs. This little "stool" seemed to suit them perfectly, as you can see in this picture (below) of a female ruby-throated hummingbird.

—*Lois Ament, Dillard, Georgia*

After admiring the stunning hummingbirds in *Birds & Blooms*, Dale Harmer of Sequim, Washington decided to write about his favorite "humdinger."

"I'd like to add the rufous hummingbird to your list of these amazing and beautiful creatures," Dale says.

"We look forward to the arrival of this little gem each spring and make sure to put up sugar-water feeders as soon as the first one appears."

You're right, Dale. Rufous hummingbirds are pretty remarkable.

The male rufous is the only North American hummingbird with reddish-brown feathers covering its entire back and much of its head and tail (thus the name "rufous," which means reddish).

It also sports green wings and an orange-red iridescent throat that sparkles like burnished gold in the right light. The female has little of the namesake rufous coloring, however. Instead, it has green feathers on its back, head and tail with a bright, orange-red spot on its throat.

The rufous inhabits a summer range that's farther north than any other hummingbird. It nests from Oregon and Idaho to southern areas of Alaska and the Yukon.

READER TIP

The rufous travels farther north during the summer than any other hummingbird, from Oregon and Idaho to southern areas of Alaska and the Yukon.

But you don't have to live in the Northwest to spot one of these brilliant birds. Rufous hummingbirds migrate through most western states. They follow a coastal route northward in spring, then fly over the Rocky Mountains in fall.

They're also one of the most common vagrants, sometimes drifting off course during southern migration. They've showed up in just about every state and province, even spending winter in some southern states.

Most hummingbirds are aggressive, but the rufous becomes especially territorial when defending temporary feeding areas during migration "pit stops" or when nesting. No creature is safe from attack, whether it's larger birds like blackbirds and thrushes, or critters like chipmunks.

THE RUFOUS HUMMINGBIRD boasts many distinctive characteristics, including reddish-brown feathers and a northern summer range. They will also nest in loose "colonies" of up to 20 pairs in a small area.

Francois Gohier

RUFOUS HUMMINGBIRD

FLOWER POWER FOR HUMMINGBIRDS

Put out the welcome mat for these tiny miracles with a nectar-filled garden.

By Jeff Nowak, Executive Editor

I'll never forget the look of amazement on our friends' faces when a hummingbird buzzed over the patio, past our picnic table right to the bright-red bee balm just a few feet away.

Their jaws dropped in amazement. They had never seen a hummingbird that close before. In fact, they'd never even seen a hummingbird!

That's when my chest swelled. "Oh, yeah," I said. "They come every day at this time."

"The hummingbirds zip from flower to flower," I boasted. "It's part of our dinner routine—to see who spots one from the kitchen window first."

Judging by the roll of my wife's eyes, I knew what she was thinking…if they only knew my "lazy-man's approach" to attracting these iridescent wonders.

My secret is simple—plant nectar-filled flowers hummingbirds can't resist, and kick back and enjoy the show.

Sid and Shirley Rucker

Richard Day/Daybreak Imagery

DIGGING FOR NECTAR. There are many sweet flowers that will attract hummingbirds (like the ones at left) to your backyard. For the best results, plant bright-red varieties that have tube-shaped blooms.

these blooms with their long bills and tongues to lap up the energy drink that keeps their high-revving motors humming.

What do the flowers get in return?

"Hummingbirds play a large role in pollination," explains backyard bird expert George Harrison of Hubertus, Wisconsin. "As hummingbirds dip their bills down into each flower, pollen clings to their bills and feathers (see photo at left), so they transfer it from plant to plant."

The pollen fertilizes the flowers, which produce seeds that ensure their survival.

Hummingbird Gardens

Reader Marie Harrison of Valparaiso, Florida started her hummingbird garden, admittedly, by accident.

"It was a little bit of luck," she says. "The first flowers that attracted hummers to my garden were planted simply because I love flowers. When I started noticing the hummingbirds coming to certain flowers, I wanted to attract more of them. So, I started planting the flowers they liked best."

Among her favorites are red pentas, Turk's cap lilies, butterfly weed and honeysuckle.

Over the years, Marie has learned what many hummingbird lovers have discovered—if you know exactly what flowers hummingbirds are looking for, you're almost guaranteed regular visits.

Ready to set out the welcome mat for hummingbirds in your backyard? Here are some tips to get started:

■ **Seeing red.** A patch of red flowers to hummingbirds is like a neon "EAT" sign along a lonely highway. These birds search out nectar from many different colored flowers, but it's the red ones that really have magnetic drawing power.

Scientists believe hummingbirds are attracted to red flowers because they've learned through experience that red tubular flowers contain the most nectar. So anything red—be it a flower, baseball hat or tricycle—triggers their instincts to investigate. That's why hummingbird feeders usually have red feeding ports.

■ **Tube-shaped blooms.** Many plants on hummingbirds' hit list are tube-shaped flowers that provide large amounts of nectar deep at the base of their blooms. Hummingbirds can easily reach this sugar water, while bees and most other nectar-loving insects are left out.

Trumpet vine is an excellent example of tube-shaped nectar producers. It offers hummingbirds 10 times more sugar water than other plants!

■ **Less fragrant, more filling.** Many flowers hummingbirds flock to surprisingly have little to no scent. And, as nature would have it, there's a good reason.

Sweet-smelling flowers attract bees and other insects. Hummingbirds, like most birds, have a poor sense of smell. They rely on sight to find food. So, by remaining odor-free, these flowers cater largely to hummingbirds.

■ **Cascading blooms.** Hummingbirds are in a flying class of their own, with the ability to fly forward, backward, hover and even upside down!

Some nectar flowers, like fuchsia, have adapted specifical-

Hummingbird Buffet

Hummingbird gardening is something anyone can try in most parts of the country and, yes, expect success.

You don't need a huge manicured garden to get started. A simple hanging basket, container or window box packed with mostly red nectar-producing flowers does the trick. And once you see an iridescent hummingbird flitting from flower to flower, I guarantee you'll want to expand your plantings next year to bring in more of these unbelievable birds.

What Is Nectar?

Nectar is nothing more than sugar water produced naturally by all kinds of flowers. Some, like Queen-Anne's lace and zinnias, produce nectar on their shallow clusters of flowers. These attract bees, butterflies and other insects, along with hummingbirds.

The real surefire plants designed to appeal to hummingbirds are deep, tube-shaped flowers. Hummingbirds probe

ly to accommodate hummingbirds. Their blooms hang downward, so only agile hummingbirds can reach their sweet treat.

Planting Your Hummer Garden

Planting a hummingbird garden is no different than creating a perennial border, mixed container or any other garden. The basics are the same—soil rich in organic matter that drains well will keep the flowers healthy. And healthy nectar plants produce loads of the sweet stuff.

There are hundreds of sweet blooming plants—annuals, perennials, trees, vines and shrubs—that hummingbirds will feed from. Which ones should you choose? How should you plant them? It's easier than you think:

■ **Mix plenty of annuals.** Annuals ensure long-blooming flowers that immediately produce nectar, from the time the migratory hummingbirds return north from their tropical winter grounds, until they leave in fall.

■ **Aim for continuous blossoms.** Perennials, flowering trees and shrubs are excellent additions to a hummingbird garden, but plan carefully before you plant. Seek a mix of nectar producers that bloom in succession, from early spring to fall.

■ **Plant in clusters.** Again, red is a sure bet for attracting hummingbirds. To get their attention, cluster red blooms together so they shout out, "Dinnertime!"

But that doesn't mean your garden has to be monochromatic. These sweet-toothed birds will gladly feed from any color nectar flower, but use red to draw them in.

■ **Plant low to high.** Consider your hummingbird garden as a stadium, placing shorter plants in front of taller ones. This gives the birds a chance to easily get to all the blooms, without plant stems and leaves interfering with their whirring wings. As a bonus, you get to see them better from your patio or window.

■ **Add to existing gardens.** You don't have to start from scratch. Many hummingbird plants blend in beautifully with existing flower gardens.

■ **Deadhead for more blooms.** The longer your nectar-producing plants produce flowers, the more hummingbirds you'll attract.

Even though many hummingbird plants are low-maintenance annuals and perennials, take time to deadhead blooms before they go to seed.

This keeps the plants pouring energy into flower production…a sure way to convince hummingbirds to stay near your backyard, and come back year after year.

Sweet Results at Hummingbird Feeders!

"I believe the ultimate goal for a hummingbird garden is to attract hummingbirds to eat at sugar-water feeders," says George Harrison. "In spring, I place my feeders right among red flowers, then move them a few feet each day until

Mark and Sue Werner/The Image Finders

DUAL ACTION. Once hummingbirds are accustomed to visiting your garden's blooms, put out a sugar-water feeder to attract even more visitors (like the one above). You won't be disappointed!

they're close to the windows where we can see them."

Here are more feeder tips…

■ **Make your own nectar.** Mix 4 parts water to 1 part sugar, boil and cool before filling feeders. It's that easy!

Change the solution every 3 days or so, keeping leftovers in the fridge for up to a week.

■ **Red accents help.** While most feeders are red plastic, try this clever trick so your hummers see the feeder: Place a bright-red bow on it to draw attention.

■ **Hang feeders in shady areas.** This keeps the nectar solution from fermenting and algae from messing up your feeders.

■ **Protect from pests.** Sugar water is sure to attract the attention of ants and bees. A small ant guard above the feeder's hanger keeps ants from reaching your feeder. Buy one for a few bucks from a birder's store, or make one from an inverted spray paint can cap.

The most effective way to keep bees and yellow jackets from the feeders is by using a feeder with plastic "bee guards." These mesh covers allow only the hummingbirds to reach the nectar.

'GLAD YOU ASKED!'

Expert answers your hummingbird questions.

By George Harrison, Contributing Editor

What's on the Menu?

I'm wondering how hummingbirds feed their young. My neighbor thinks they hold nectar or sugar water in their mouths and feed it to their babies, but I think their bills are too narrow to do this. Can you solve the mystery? —Millie Howard
Little Rock, Arkansas

George: I'd be happy to settle this discussion. Hummingbirds usually feed tiny insects and spiders to their young. They insert them right into the mouths of their babies.

They'll also feed nectar and pollen to the young birds. They do this by holding it in their throats and then squirting it into the mouths of the nestlings. Sometimes this will cause the youngster's throat to swell temporarily, resembling a goiter.

MOUTHS TO FEED. This female hummingbird tends to hungry nestlings.

comes from flower blooms into which the birds thrust their long bills to draw out nectar.

Water Color

I've heard you're not supposed to add red food coloring to the sugar-water mixture for hummingbirds. Is this true? —Florence Neilson
Duchesne, Utah

George: One of the older red food colorings was found to be toxic to birds, but with the new formulations, I don't believe that's still true.

However, it isn't necessary to dye sugar water for hummingbirds under most circumstances. The feeders usually have red or orange parts, which provide enough color to attract hummingbirds or orioles.

Clear sugar water (one part sugar to four parts water) will work just fine.

Have a Drink

I've heard pigeons and doves are the only birds that drink by suction. But what about hummingbirds? I've never seen a hummingbird tip its head back to swallow. —Calvin Wheeler
Auburn, Washington

George: You're right, hummingbirds can be included in this select group. They are one of the few species of birds that swallow liquid without throwing their head back to allow gravity to help them swallow.

This is true of hummingbirds because most of their food

Aggressive Behavior

Why do the hummingbirds around our sugar-water feeders act so aggressive? There's plenty of room for several to feed at once, but one often chases the others away. —Matthew Welch, Hyrum, Utah

George:There's usually a dominant male hummingbird that controls which birds feed from sugar-water feeders and flower beds in its territory. Females that are sociable with the dominant male usually are allowed to feed, while other males and females are sent packing.

194

190

200

180

PLAN A GREAT GARDEN

183

FULL OF APPEAL

Once an empty field, this colorful yard is now the apple of their eyes.

By Doris Witzgall, Bay City, Michigan

A jumble of dirt and weeds—that's what our yard looked like back in 1964. We'd just built our home on an acre of farmland, and things couldn't have been more barren. Little did I know that some 40 years later, we'd be surrounded by a garden paradise, complete with an apple orchard!

My husband, Wayne, and I weren't experts, but we were eager to brighten the scenery, so we dug right in and encountered our first major gardening challenge—clay soil. We decided then and there to create raised beds to deal with this problem. We also added a lot of organic matter to help break up the hard clay.

Vegetables and evergreens were the first items we cultivated. Next we fashioned a few flower beds and started adding annuals and perennials, from alyssum and columbine to lilies, petunias, hostas, roses, chrysanthemums, salvia, hollyhocks, phlox and more. Things just kept growing from there!

Weather Woes

It didn't take long to run into another stumbling block. The weather in our area is unpredictable, thanks to nearby Lake Huron, which can trigger unexpected changes in temperature and erratic conditions in general.

Some years we've had a severe frost as late as June and lost all our blooms. Since fall temperatures often start in September, we can wind up with a very short growing season. Other times, we've been lucky and had delightful weather from April to October.

Wayne and I quickly learned to roll with the punches. We know if one season is too short, too wet or too cool, the next one likely will be just perfect. We've also been careful to stay away from exotic plants and to pick hardy flowers, trees and shrubs.

Experimenting with different varieties in our garden beds is the secret to our success. After all, you never know what will work in your yard until you try it!

There certainly have been surprises over the years. In some instances, we've found flowers that were supposed to do well in sunny spots that performed better for us in shady areas, and other shade lovers that preferred brighter locations. And from time to time, we've tried species that just haven't worked in our yard at all.

Seed of an Idea

One addition that took off in a big way is Wayne's apple trees. He started with a few and kept adding more until we had 6 acres of orchard to the south of our yard and across the road.

I often describe our apple grove as a hobby that got out of hand. Honestly, though, the orchard is a real delight. We open it to the public each fall and sell apples and cider, along with the birdhouses and feeders Wayne crafts during winter. Anyone who stops in is welcome to wander through our gardens.

Friends and visitors alike often comment on all the work we've done...and all the rocks we've used to build our raised beds. By our calculations, we've hauled *150 tons* of stones over the years.

We also learned some important lessons about how to use the rocks. Proper placement is critical!

Position the stones from largest at the bottom to smallest along the top and off-set each row so it interlocks with the one below it. Then the formations will last for years. It's also a good idea to stack the

READER TIP

When creating rock borders in the garden, proper placement is critical. Position the stones from largest at the bottom to smallest at the top and off-set each row so it interlocks with the one below it. Then the formations will last for years.

It's also a good idea to stack the stones at a slight angle so they settle into the dirt.

—**Doris Witzgall, Bay City, Michigan**

NO STONE UNTURNED. Rocks encircle almost every flower bed in the Witzgalls' yard. They estimate they've used 150 tons of them in areas like this shady retreat (right). Their butterfly garden (above left) is packed with nectar-rich perennials, and even a decorative butterfly house (top).

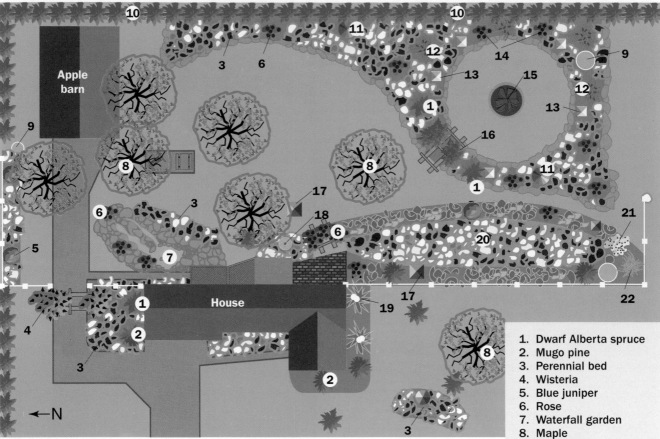

Apple barn

10 · 10 · 11 · 12 · 14 · 9 · 3 · 6 · 13 · 15 · 12 · 9 · 1 · 13 · 11 · 16 · 1 · 8 · 8 · 17 · 21 · 18 · 20 · 6 · 7 · 22 · 5 · 17 · 1 · 19 · 4 · 2 · 3 · 2 · 8 · 3

← N

House

1. Dwarf Alberta spruce
2. Mugo pine
3. Perennial bed
4. Wisteria
5. Blue juniper
6. Rose
7. Waterfall garden
8. Maple
9. Birdbath
10. White cedar
11. Birdhouse
12. Butterfly bush
13. Butterfly house
14. Rose of Sharon
15. Raised fire pit
16. Honeysuckle
17. Bird feeder
18. Fountain
19. Yucca
20. Angel garden
21. Spirea
22. Weigela

ROSE TO THE CHALLENGE. A variety of roses keep the Witzgalls' yard looking, and smelling, sweet. One of the most striking is a William Baffin climbing rose (above) next to the angel garden.

stones at a slight angle so they settle into the dirt.

Three Seasons

We've never really had an overall design in mind for the yard. We just wanted to make sure it was blossoming from spring to fall.

Wayne is very creative and likes to try new things, like the waterfall garden he completed last spring near our hosta-filled shade garden. I pitch in by "decorating" with flowers, birdhouses, lanterns and more.

In addition to the waterfall and pond, we've created a butterfly garden filled with bee balm and other nectar-rich perennials they love, plus butterfly houses and stone benches. Not far away is an angel garden with a rose arbor and a collection of angel accents. Shrubs like spirea, arborvitae and weigela outline many of the beds. Maples, spruce and other trees add interest all through the year.

We no longer grow vegetables, since our daughter, who lives nearby with her family, put in a patch for us at her house. Our son and his family live across the road from us (many of our apple trees are behind his house). We love being so close to the kids and grandkids—and they're happy, too, especially when Wayne works in their gardens.

There's still plenty of work to be done at our place. The backyard is full, but we have a whole front yard for more gardens. I doubt we'll ever finish—and that's just fine with us!

DIGGING COLORADO

This couple battled rocks, deer and a fickle climate to create a mountain oasis.

By Ramona Boone, Colorado Springs, Colorado

Living in Colorado has its advantages. My husband, Steve, and I enjoy breathtaking views of 14,000-foot mountains and fields of wildflowers. But as someone who grew up in Illinois, I couldn't stop dreaming of a lush, colorful garden filled with sweetly scented flowers.

Unfortunately, the deer that live near our home seemed to

share the same dream. They regularly came down from the mountains to forage. Apparently, our 1-acre property was a great place to nap and snack!

As a result, the landscaping around the house took on a very "native" look—just pine trees and rocks. For one small area of the yard, we brought in three truckloads of dirt, put mulch on top of that and laid flagstone paths. But I didn't plant anything there. I knew the deer and bears would munch it away.

A Blank Canvas

But there was hope. The previous owners had turned the large side yard into a dog run and surrounded it with a 6-foot-high fence. This space contained nothing but flat ugly dirt, plus a few trees. It was perfect for a deer-proof garden.

At least we *thought* it was perfect. Then we started trying to dig holes in the soil for planting.

Colorado clay doesn't even come close to the rich, black soil

WORTH THE WORK. Ramona and Steve Boone (above inset) had to clear out loads of rocky dirt and bring in new soil to create a fertile area for their thriving—and protected—garden (top).

of Illinois. There's a reason our neighborhood is called "Rockrimmon." With every shovelful, we unearthed nothing but rocks, from egg-sized lumps to small boulders. And what we dug up was unusable for planting, so we had to bring in new soil.

If we had it to do again, we would have skipped the digging and trucked in soil to make raised beds.

Still, we were fortunate. There were some natural assets within the enclosure, including a 40-foot pine tree, a shimmering aspen, a grove of small oak trees and a wonderful 4-foot by 2-foot boulder neatly located against the inside fence.

The first summer, we cleared weeds and laid out a design. Then Steve thought of a fish pond and decided to add a small water garden. Little did he know that after digging 6 inches down, he'd have to rent a jackhammer to punch through solid sandstone to finish the job.

Blossoming Landscape

We planted the basics that year—peonies, asters, rudbeckia and other hardy plants capable of withstanding the late snows and dry seasons of the High Plains. As a Midwestern native, I always thought abundant snow meant moisture. But in the Front Range of the Rocky Mountains, the snow often evaporates in the dry air instead of melting into the ground.

The next summer, I started trying the flowers I'd been dreaming about—roses, lilies and garden phlox. Although we're in Plant Hardiness Zone 5, there are pockets in the yard that are colder. And some years, it's like we're living in Zone 2! I spent a couple of years moving plants around and adding new ones to replace those flowers that froze in these cooler microclimates.

The existing oaks gave us an opportunity to try shade-loving plants like hostas that the deer would devour if planted outside the fence. Columbine loves the dappled shade, as do bleeding heart, rubrum lily, astilbe, hellebore and lamium.

Nature Takes Root

As the garden matured, we were thrilled to see volunteer plants emerge. Fragrant Hyperion daylilies appeared one summer, and a low-growing purple dome aster spread like crazy. One plant I mistook for a wayward oak—and almost yanked out—turned out to be a celandine poppy. It gives us lovely yellow flowers every spring.

Birds must have dropped some hollyhock seeds, because we never planted any, but have a nice array of them against the fence.

We turned an empty corner of the enclosure into a seating area by laying a flagstone patio. We loved it so much that the next year we tripled its size, adding an area for a hammock where we can relax while watching the hummingbirds and bees enjoy what the deer would love to eat.

Deer did manage to come in a few times when I forgot to close the gate, however. They sure enjoyed the tulips!

I put in a few annuals each year, like cosmos, but most of the plants in the garden are perennials.

To keep digging to a minimum, I use containers for anything that needs to be stored inside for winter, such as dahlias,

1. Boulder
2. Hollyhock
3. Daylily
4. Perennials
5. Butterfly bush
6. Hosta
7. Oak
8. Patio
9. Honeysuckle vine
10. Primrose
11. Lilac
12. Phlox
13. Rose
14. Lily
15. Clematis
16. Pond
17. Aspen
18. Blackberry bush
19. Peony
20. Porcelain vine
21. Pine

Deer fencing

House

FENCE THEM IN. Deer used to eat every single plant in sight. Then the Boones decided to transform an empty fenced-in spot into a sanctuary for their favorite flowers, including many *deer*-lectable varieties, such as (from top) lily, dahlia and rose.

angels' trumpets and gladiolas. That way, I just dump out the containers in fall, wrap up the tubers, and repot them the next year.

Lessons Learned

Now that I've figured out where everything should be, the perennials are doing well. The roses are thriving, thanks to the wood chips I place over them every fall for protection from the cold weather and the fish fertilizer I recycle from one of Steve's ponds.

To conserve moisture, we use lots of mulch, and we installed a drip irrigation system. This gives the roses a little extra moisture, and I water them by hand a couple times a month, too.

Now we have gravel paths dotted with flagstones that meander past two ponds. Our flower beds are bursting with scented charmers like phlox and sweet peas. And the entryway features a welcoming wrought-iron archway covered with Iceberg roses.

It's just like the garden in my dreams.

A Woodland
Wonder

This adventurous gardener turned mistakes into marvelous results.

By Sylvia Hoehns Wright
Glen Allen, Virginia

SHADY SANCTUARY. Colorful tulips and eye-popping azaleas light up Sylvia's lush wooded landscape with beautiful bursts of color (above). A pretty garden bench and path beckon visitors to pause and enjoy the natural scenery around them (near left).

Sometimes, a garden emerges through experimentation. The only drawback is that you never know what you'll get with trial and error as your guide. I learned that firsthand when I started landscaping the heavily wooded yard around my new home.

Somewhat overwhelmed by the space, I decided to begin my landscape overhaul by constructing a simple rectangular patio. Patio blocks, sand, a wheelbarrow and a carpenter's level provided me with the structure, while surplus azaleas from a nearby nursery offered instant hedging and privacy. A large shade arbor added later was the perfect finishing touch.

Right Plant, Right Place

With the patio complete, I moved on to developing the rest of the yard. It didn't take me long to realize, however, that the 100-year-old oak trees scattered throughout the property were going to be a formidable challenge.

Although the stately trees provided shelter from the glaring sun and occasional windstorm, the trees' dense canopies made it difficult for much of anything to grow beneath them.

In the beginning, I made the typical mistakes. I often considered my preference for showy flowers rather than soil requirements, plant endurance and practicality. I learned the hard way what would—and would not—thrive in my shady yard.

> *I learned the hard way what would, and would not, thrive in my shady yard.*

Eventually, I discovered it's as easy as choosing the right plant for the right place. That meant selecting shade-tolerant plants, like vinca, ivy and some evergreen shrubs.

Flowering bulbs, such as tulips and daffodils, provided a welcome punch of color in the wooded landscape. And in areas that couldn't support plants, I spread wood mulch to help

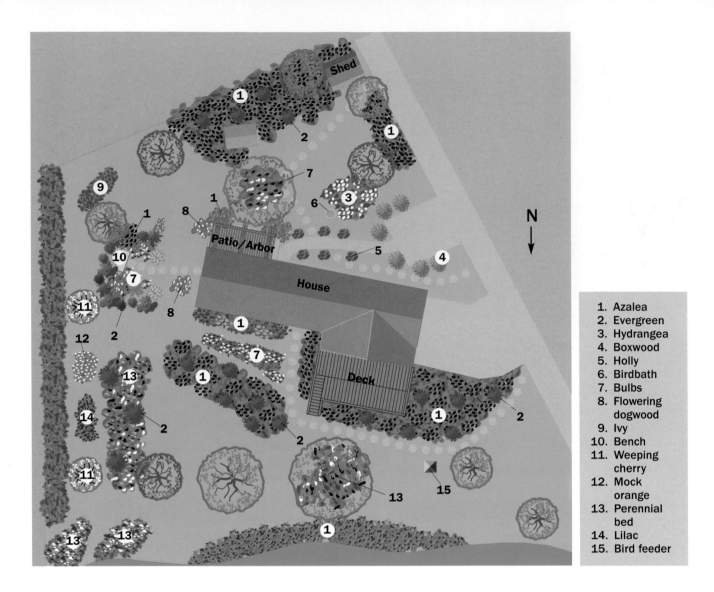

1. Azalea
2. Evergreen
3. Hydrangea
4. Boxwood
5. Holly
6. Birdbath
7. Bulbs
8. Flowering dogwood
9. Ivy
10. Bench
11. Weeping cherry
12. Mock orange
13. Perennial bed
14. Lilac
15. Bird feeder

naturalize the garden and protect the trees' vulnerable roots.

Clusters of trees provided the best planting sites. Tree drip lines became natural flower bed borders, and the sparse area beneath the trees' leaf canopies provided an empty palette on which to paint my woodland garden.

And because I began to work with the natural environment, something unexpected occurred. Volunteer seedlings of native plants, such as flowering dogwood, mountain laurel, lady's slipper and cardinal flower, began springing up.

After establishing the basic framework, I moved on to different challenges. The first was a relatively basic perennial and annual bed. Framing the area with colorful azaleas first, I planted the flower bed with a variety of hostas, ferns, lilies and iris. The addition of seasonal annuals kept the bed buzzing with continuous color all year.

READER TIP

In areas that won't support plants, spread wood mulch to help naturalize the garden and protect the trees' vulnerable roots.
—Sylvia Hoehns Wright
Glen Allen, Virginia

A Change of Plan

My next project, an herb garden, didn't quite turn out as I envisioned. The design included a bed of herbs around two large oak trees.

Yet, regardless of my dedication, the project remained plagued by problems as the fragile herbs competed for vital sunlight. I finally transferred the less shade-tolerant plants into some sunlit containers, where they thrived.

My birdhouse garden encountered a similar result. I designed the garden specifically for birds, including nest boxes and berry-producing shrubs, but it wooed no winged activity. Maybe the birds preferred the vast woodland sanctuary instead.

The project wasn't a total loss, however, as a flying squirrel finally moved into one of the birdhouses.

It was then that I made the choice to join the Virginia Master Gardener Program. After completing the course, my mistakes became less, and my successes grew.

Although it would be easy for me to second-guess my early gardening endeavors, I try not to be too hard on myself. After all, it was through those first efforts that I developed an awareness of nature's "big secret."

I learned I'm only a caretaker of the surrounding woodland environment—and working with it produces the best results.

THINK SPRING

With leaves to rake and mums to transplant in fall, spring flowers are probably the farthest thing from your mind. But by planting bulbs in autumn, you can set the stage for a showstopping, make-the-neighbors-green-with-envy color explosion next year.

Before you dig in, check out these common questions and answers to planting spring bulbs. If you're looking for more, simply log on to the Netherlands Flower Bulb Information Center's Web site at *www.bulb.com*.

Q: How soon after buying bulbs should I plant them?

A: Plant bulbs when you get them, but not before cooler fall temperatures arrive. Six weeks before the ground freezes is ideal.

If summer lingers, store your bulbs in the crisper of your refrigerator until cooler temperatures return. Just be sure to keep the bulbs away from fruits, which emit a gas as they ripen that's harmful to bulbs.

Q: How do I plant spring bulbs?

A: The easiest way is to dig a flat-bottomed hole about 12 to 18 inches wide and drop several bulbs into it. Plant large bulbs, such as tulips and daffodils, about 8 inches deep in well-draining soil, 6 inches in heavy. Smaller bulbs, like snowdrops, crocus and scilla, should sit about 5 inches deep.

Plant the bulb's pointy end up, and don't worry about fertilizing. Just give them a good soaking after planting. Mulching can be beneficial, but wait until the ground freezes lightly.

Q: How can I create the most impact with my bulbs?

A: Here are three simple planting rules you can use to get the most from your bulbs.

Plant in clusters. This concentrates the colors, making them look like bouquets.

Plant shorter bulbs in front. This is a good rule for bulbs that bloom at the same time, such as grape hyacinths and tulips. However, if the low-growing bulbs bloom early and the tall late, plant the taller-growing flowers in front. Their display will camouflage the dying foliage of the smaller bulbs.

Plant a double-decker. Plant small bulbs right on top of large bulbs. If they flower at the same time, it creates a colorful two-tone effect.

Q: What should I do after the flowers fade?

A: It's important to keep the leaves on the plants until they brown, or 6 weeks have passed since blooming. The leaves feed the bulb so it can flower next spring.

Clip tulip blooms after they fade so they don't go to seed, but leave daffodils alone.

READER TIP

Want to keep squirrels and other critters from digging up and raiding your newly planted bulbs?

■ Try planting daffodils and other Narcissi bulbs, because most animals don't like the way they taste.

■ Lay wire mesh, such as chicken wire, on top of bulb plantings. Squirrels can't dig through it, but flowers grow through the holes.

■ Use repellents or a variety of scare tactics—dog or cat hair spread around the flower bed, aluminum pie tins on twine or plastic scare owls and hawks—to fend off hungry critters. Be sure to vary your tactics, or the critters will catch on.

BEST GARDEN IDEAS

Readers share ways to make yards special.

Garden Dishes Out Smiles

WE HAVE LOTS of flower and vegetable beds scattered about our 1-acre yard. Most are outlined with stones or railroad ties—but there is one bed with an unusual border that catches everyone's eye.

To surround the blossoms I planted there, including butterfly bush and Texas sage, I turned to china plates and saucers (see photos above). Some of the dinnerware belonged to my grandmother and mother, and the entire design has become a real conversation piece!

That's not the only spot I've dressed up with unlikely supplies. I transformed an old iron bed frame into a zinnia patch,

and my husband and I built a bench using stones from his grandparents' fireplace.

But I have to say the focus is on whatever's growing—and since I plant everything from azaleas to zucchini, there's always something to feast your eyes on.

—*Karen Nettles, Groesbeck, Texas*

SERVING UP BLOOMS. Karen Nettles has many varied flower beds in her yard, but one is especially unique—it has a border of old china plates and saucers (above left). Purple brachyscome blooms (above right) accent the pretty platters.

Daffodils Spell Out Fun

RATHER THAN PLANT daffodils in typical flower beds, I like to play around with the bulbs—literally!

About 4 years ago, I used the bulbs to create a large tic-tac-toe board, complete with the X's and O's. Above the board, I added the date in Roman numerals, which I change each fall so it's current for the following spring (top left photo).

Then, a couple years ago, I added more bulbs in order to spell out "Ohio" in our yard (above right).

My "designer flowers" tend to catch everyone's attention when they stop in for a visit.　　—*Richard Balmer, Ironton, Ohio*

Everlasting Geraniums

THANKS TO my husband's green thumb, we haven't had to buy geraniums in a long, long time. The ones in this picture (below right) are at least 9 years old!

Each fall, Jim pulls up the plants, shakes off the dirt, then lays them in a large, covered cardboard box, which he tucks into a corner of the basement.

Throughout the winter, he sprays water on the plants once a month. In spring, he replants them and they come back bigger than ever, with even more red blooms.

If you want to try this yourself, it helps to be patient. The plants look dry and dead when they're replanted, but if you keep them in their pots and water them as you normally would, they eventually bounce back.

To help keep plants shorter and more compact, try cutting them back to 4 to 6 inches above the soil line. It will take several weeks to see the new growth, so don't give up!　　—*Kathie Speas*
Marshalltown, Iowa

Geraniums That Last

I HAD TO SHARE my husband's own money-saving method for overwintering his bright geraniums to plant again the following year.

Every fall, he cuts the stems off our geraniums and places them in canning jars with water so they'll root. Then he puts the plants in our sunroom, where there's plenty of natural light. The geraniums bloom all winter long. When spring comes, the plants go back outside and into the soil to add color to our window boxes, planters and garden.

This method has really saved us money. My husband has been growing the same geraniums for years. And we no longer have to buy them each spring from the garden center.

　　—*Marilyn Redden, Columbus, Ohio*

Scent of the Times

LAVENDER often is associated with old-fashioned sachets, but this fragrant flower isn't just for grandmas.

It's true that as far back as Victorian times, lavender was used to scent sachets, linens, furniture polish and cosmetics. People even dried their bedding on top of lavender plants so the cloth could soak up the soothing aroma.

Dried blossoms were brewed as a tea to treat insomnia, added to face creams to clear blemishes and speed healing, and used as edible garnish for pastries. Who knew this little garden herb was so useful?

Lavender isn't as common in modern gardens, but I love bringing this plant's lovely scent from my yard into my home. I fill muslin bags with dried blossoms and toss them into the dryer and clothes hamper. I use them to make herbal pillows for the couch and my bed, and add them to candles for a relaxing aroma.

Adding just one lavender plant to your garden can provide a lifetime of sweetly scented pleasures. So maybe Grandma was on to something with those old-fashioned sachets!

—*Jennifer Ziegler, Sullivan, Missouri*

Garden Strikes a Graceful Note

I'M A MUSIC teacher, so a garden with a musical theme is right in tune with my style.

My husband, sons and I poured this concrete pond (above) and painted on the keys after measuring my piano to get the correct proportions. The keys need a touch-up of paint each summer, but it's not too tough.

At the corner of the pond, we included an old French horn. My husband ran tubing to it from the fountain to create a miniature waterfall.

The wind chimes on the treble clef sign behind the pond were a gift from a gardening friend who sang in my church choir. She's since passed away, so they're very special to me.

Off to one side, although not visible in the photo, are wooden chimes my nephew brought from Chile, and a garden bench a friend made from old piano parts.

This summer, I plan to add a brick path through the nearby flower bed and paint the bricks to look like piano keys. And when my niece is married in our yard in July, we'll all have something to sing about!

—*Teresa Rotert, Sutherland, Nebraska*

A New Twist for Faded Bulbs

WHAT CAN YOU do with those unsightly leftover leaves after your spring bulbs have bloomed?

You can't cut them off until they turn yellow or brown, or the bulbs won't get the food they need to flower the following year.

But not everyone can live with 6 weeks worth of straggly leaves. To hide the not-so-green greenery, some gardeners fold the leaves over and tie them. And then there's the approach Lois Smith takes.

This Duncansville, Pennsylvania gardener braids bulb leaves and tucks them under once the blooms are spent (see the photo at left). Her method works with most bulbs except for tulips, whose leaves are too sparse and broad.

The braided leaves add extra dimension to a garden —and have even prompted people to ask her what kind of new plant she's put in the beds because the twists look so unusual.

This spring, don't be afraid to give your bulbs a brave new "do." Then wait to see if your neighbors take notice!

—*Barbara Dunn, Field Editor*
Hollidaysburg, Pennsylvania

Bumper Crop of Cukes

MY METHOD for growing cucumbers produces a prolific crop in record time. Last year, I planted six hills on May 15. I picked my first cucumber a little more than a month later, on June 24.

And the bounty continued throughout summer. I stopped counting the harvest when I got to 700!

My secret for quick maturation and extended productivity is feeding and watering through a tube. I put a 12-inch section of 4-inch pipe in the center of each cucumber hill and plant five seedlings around it.

To water, I fill the pipe to overflowing every other day. Once a week, I mix in a dose of vegetable or flowering plant fertilizer and fill the pipe again.

This slow-watering method encourages the plants' roots to grow deep. I've raised cucumbers this way for 10 years and have never harvested fewer than 450 cucumbers in a season.

I've found the technique works on other vine plants as well. Give it a try with pumpkins, zucchini, squash and melons.

—*Ken Sohl*
Richmond Heights, Ohio

A Wall with a View

HERE'S a suggestion for readers who have a large outdoor wall that they'd like to decorate: Hang an old window on it!

Larry and Sue Lapp of Ozark, Alabama found some old window frames and put mirrors where the glass would normally be. Then they placed the frames in a prominent spot to reflect their flower beds.

"We hung these frames on the back of the garage to reflect the beautiful view of our backyard," write Larry and Sue. "They blend in perfectly because they're from the original windows of our 100-year-old house.

"It's a nice effect, and the 'view' is different each time we look at it."

Believe it or not, the garden in the photo above is the *reflection* of their flowers!

Get the Message?

HAVE YOU ever had the feeling your plants were trying to tell you something? Faith McDowell certainly did when she spotted this interesting scene.

"These Oriental poppies looked like they were illustrating the saying, 'See no evil, hear no evil, speak no evil,' " says Faith, who snapped this series of photos in her Mt. Sidney, Virginia yard.

It just proves that you never know what garden surprises await...if you take the time to look.

ABUNDANT BEAUTY. Well-manicured plants line the curving pathways (right) that Sumiko and Doyal Holmon (above) created in their yard.

This couple transformed an overgrown yard into a green-thumb showcase.

By Sumiko Holmon
Escondido, California

PARADISE FOUND

When I look at our yard today, with its lovely islands of flowers and trees amid winding stone paths, it's hard to believe it wasn't always this way. A mere 6 years ago, the property wasn't so picturesque.

We bought this 1/2-acre property because the spacious lot seemed perfect for gardening and provided room for a workshop for my handy husband, Doyal. We knew the lawn—consisting of scraggly patches of Bermuda grass interspersed with weeds—needed work, but we were unprepared for the huge number of gopher holes we discovered after moving in that summer. The size of the project mushroomed.

It wouldn't do any good to complain, however, so we both dug in and started cleaning things up.

194

READY FOR A WALK? The Holmons' yard is a lush retreat packed with plants that thrive in southern California's heat. They edged pathways (above and below left) with trees, shrubs and flowers, and fashioned small sanctuaries (like the one far lower left) with evergreens, a homemade lantern and river rocks. At left, dusty miller and rosemary surround a lemon tree.

First, we had to cut down several overgrown berry and eucalyptus trees along the side of the house. Then we addressed the gopher problem by hiring a professional pest remover. It took the better part of a year, but it was worth it!

Digging up the front yard was next on our list. We eliminated the grass and weeds and decided to install rock gardens and plant trees to add shade. This plan seemed so perfect, we adapted it for rest of the property.

On the Rocks

Finding interesting shade trees became a regular activity on the weekends. We first chose peppermint willows (*Agonis flexuosa*) and carrot woods (*Cupaniopsis*)—and that's when we hit another snag.

Planting those pretty specimens turned out to be a much bigger task than either of us thought, thanks to bone-dry soil that was hard as a rock. We had to water the dirt just to soften it, then dig it up a bit and water some more. It was quite a process!

Finally, we were able to dig big enough holes and finish planting the trees. As a precaution, Doyal covered the softened soil with chicken wire to keep any nosy gophers from returning.

In addition to the willows and carrot woods in front, we added a variety of other trees along one side and in the

back, including a Japanese black pine and juniper that we surrounded with river rocks. A Japanese lantern Doyal crafted from concrete was the perfect Zen touch for that peaceful nook (see photo bottom far left).

The next challenge we faced was choosing flowers to plant around the trees. I wondered what varieties would thrive in the poor soil. Finally, I decided to try whatever caught my eye and settled on begonias, asters, salvia, vinca, anemones and dianthus, which all thrived.

Since we have no grass, our last task was to cover the bare areas of dirt by placing permeable weed barrier on the ground and covering it with granite chips. I could hardly believe we were finished! The 6 months of hard work truly paid off, though, when a neighbor stopped by and asked, "Do you do this for a living?" I couldn't stop smiling.

Separate Paths

Up until that point, Doyal and I had been working side by side, but we headed in different directions once the front was finished.

I tackled the side yard. Day after day, I hacked away thick, tough weeds and dried-up old bushes. After everything was cleared, I filled in the sloping area with durable geraniums, ornamental grasses, daisies and ice plants.

In the meantime, Doyal busied himself out back, building a shed, an arbor, a wooden arch, a covered bench, a gazebo

---

READER TIP

To keep gophers from returning to our yard, we covered the soft soil around our newly planted trees with chicken wire.

—**Sumiko Holmon, Escondido, California**

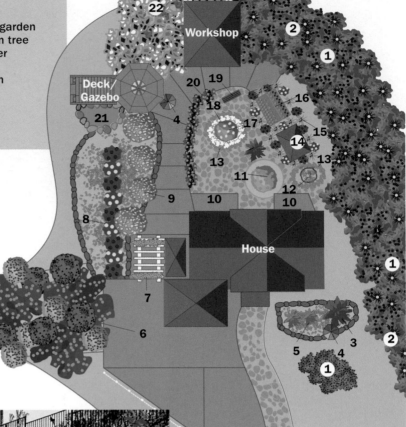

1. Ivy geranium
2. Ice plant
3. Japanese black pine
4. Japanese lantern
5. Juniper
6. Orchard
7. Arbor
8. Rose
9. Carrot wood tree
10. Patio
11. Orange tree
12. Peppermint willow
13. Rosemary hedge
14. Shed
15. Iris
16. Vegetable garden
17. Pink lemon tree
18. Dusty miller
19. Bench
20. Pink Indian hawthorn
21. Pond
22. Perennials

THERE'S BEAUTY AT EVERY TURN in the Holmons' yard, whether it's a colorful slope of ivy geraniums and ice plants (below) or a lantern-accented nook next to their gazebo (above).

and a deck, and putting in a vegetable patch and a koi pond.

His next job involved fashioning concrete rocks and using them to form meandering paths around the trees and rock gardens in the backyard, turning them into instant islands.

Just as we'd done in the front, we filled in any remaining bare areas with granite chips.

The whole process of shaping the yards took about 2 years. But that doesn't mean we've stopped working in the yard. We regularly try new shrubs, fruit trees and flowers, replacing varieties that haven't worked out, or planting new ones that appeal to us.

Oasis Out Back

While the front yard is lovely, everyone agrees that the backyard is the showstopper. As soon as visitors pass through the side gate and walk under the arbor, they're greeted by fragrant roses and a view of our small fruit orchard, filled with tangerine, kumquat, plum, nectarine, apple and avocado trees.

The path runs past the patio and a cluster of rock gardens that feature junipers, yuccas, a tangerine tree, a pink lemon tree and flowers galore. We've also tucked in silver garlic grass, rosemary and various ornamental specimens among the trees and blooms, along with several graceful pieces of driftwood.

Farther down the path sits the bench Doyal made, nestled among pink Indian hawthorns, roses and irises. The gazebo is stationed nearby, connected to the deck by a small Japanese bridge called a *taikobushi*. This is the best spot to enjoy the water garden with its colorful koi, cattails, waterfall and water lilies.

Whether we choose to walk along the path, rest in the gazebo or entertain on the patio, this plant-filled space offers so much. I love to relax and enjoy the flowers and the sight of butterflies and birds among the blooms, and appreciate all the wonderful things my husband and I created. ◀

SOMETHING FROM NOTHING

Starting from scratch, this gardener built a blooming paradise.

By Lena Jascur
Flora, Indiana

W hen we moved into our home 9 years ago, the yard was pretty much flower free, with the exception of a lone peony. But that plant didn't stay around for long—the former owner had a sentimental attachment to it and asked if she could take it with her!

After I dug up the plant, I surveyed the landscape, which consisted mostly of grass and weeds. Still, I could see plenty of potential.

What encouraged

me most was a beautiful willow shading the front of the house, and the stately pines that outlined the lot. I knew that hard work and perseverance would pay off in the end.

One Garden That Grew

I started with a simple bed of irises, positioned so I could see the blossoms from the kitchen window. That garden turned out so nice, I decided to make it bigger by adding more flowers—and I have yet to stop!

Putting in a new patch or two of flowers or enlarging an existing bed is my springtime ritual. I've also gotten into the habit of choosing plants for each new flower bed that will bloom at the same time. This way, different spots in our yard burst into color well into fall.

I've also developed a routine of planting bulbs each autumn after the current year's flowers have faded. Over the years, I figure I've planted more than 1,000 tulips, hyacinths and daffodils, and seeing them come up each spring is a real treat.

I haven't focused solely on flowers to brighten our yard, however. I've also included pear and crabapple trees, lilacs and a number of eye-catching shrubs, including barberry, weigela, viburnum and rhododendron.

Share and Share Alike

In the beginning, I used cuttings of various perennials to fill new flower beds. Annuals came in handy when I needed to cover up empty spots, and I quickly learned how to save the seeds to use the following year.

Now my gardens burst forth with everything from azaleas to hydrangeas, purple coneflowers, assorted lilies, zinnias and more. I always make sure to share the bounty by giving cuttings of my plants to family and friends, as well as seeds gathered from the annuals.

I have encountered challenges as I've expanded my gardening efforts. The biggest test has been finding out how to get around the many shady areas on our property. Packing the spots that receive the least amount of sun with different kinds of hostas and ivy has proven to be the perfect solution.

Getting my husband, Mike, and our two children involved hasn't been any trouble, however. They're eager to dig in beside me.

In fact, I think I have two budding green thumbs in daughter Hannah and son Cody (photos above). They like to help me put in annuals, including marigolds and morning glories, and we all enjoy watching them bloom.

Mike likes to tackle heftier jobs, whether it involves hauling tons of fieldstones to the beds or building garden structures.

Accent on Handmade

We have a number of beautiful arbors and a stately pergola gracing our gardens, all built by Mike. He also put together one item I can't do without—my potting bench. That bench sees plenty of activity as soon as spring arrives!

His can-do attitude has rubbed off on me, and I'm happy to say I've constructed the many birdhouses, bird feeders and benches that garnish these gardens. The two outhouses are projects of mine, too. One is purely decorative, the other holds my shovels.

Everything we have made has cost us nothing but time. Rather than invest in building supplies, we're constantly on the lookout for old barns and sheds that are being torn down, in the hopes we can salvage some wood to create more clever fixtures to use in our yard.

Old items like balusters, sections of fence, chairs and railings that other folks toss out find new life at our place. We even found a novel way to use a wooden ladder from an old outdoor play set. It now tops one of the arbors and provides a solid climbing surface for the vines planted at the arbor's

PERSONALITY APLENTY. A double-decker birdhouse became a mailbox (above), and a homemade potting bench is a useful accent in a shady nook (above).

base like morning glory and wisteria.

I've also planted rustic signs around our property and trimmed empty walls with simple grapevine wreaths. A wheelbarrow full of blossoms greets visitors near the path to the front door. Even our mailbox (above) is crafty—it was made from a two-story birdhouse.

Room for More

Gardening is definitely a passion of mine, and I'm constantly coming up with new ideas. That's a good thing, because I still have a lot of space to fill.

My goal is to eventually eliminate the grass (and the need to mow) and have a series of pretty pathways meandering among the many flower beds. Maybe someday I'll be done. But in the meantime, I'm happy to keep my garden growing. 🐦

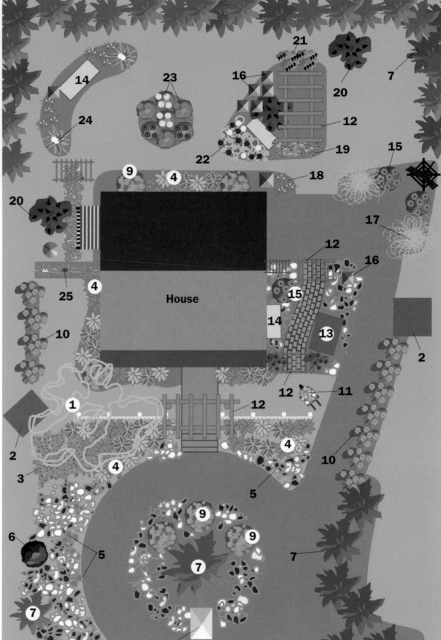

READER TIP

Hostas and ivy are the perfect solution for shady areas around your yard.

—Lena Jascur, Flora, Indiana

1. Willow	8. Birdhouse mailbox
2. Outhouse	9. Azalea
3. Ivy	10. Rose of Sharon
4. Hosta	11. Wheelbarrow
5. Annuals/perennials	12. Arbor
6. Barberry	13. Potting bench
7. Pine	14. Bench
	15. Purple coneflower
	16. Birdhouse
	17. Zebra grass
	18. Daylily
	19. Morning glory
	20. Lilac
	21. Wisteria
	22. Moss rose
	23. Zinnia
	24. Yucca
	25. Iris

Audrey Gibson/The Image Finders

3 STEPS TO A BEAUTIFUL BACKYARD

FINISHING TOUCH. After planting, add a layer of mulch (like the gardeners at left and below) to keep weeds down and conserve moisture. Pull weeds (above) when they appear.

A former nursery owner shares her simple system for a thriving and healthy garden.

By Nancy Herman, Montague, New Jersey

When I owned a nursery and garden center, I heard a lot of questions from novice gardeners, but they all seemed to boil down to one thing: "Why did my plants die?"

I understood their frustration. It's discouraging to spend time and money on new plants, only to have them die over the winter—or survive, but fail to flower.

No wonder these gardeners thought they had "brown thumbs."

I knew from experience that skipping the basics could be a recipe for disaster, and I wanted to do whatever I could to

Karen Bussolini/Positive Images

Alan and Linda Detrick

ALL BUNDLED UP. Some shrubs benefit from the winter protection of burlap (above). Another important garden duty is regular watering at the plant's base (left) to avoid evaporation.

help these newcomers flourish. So I developed this easy-to-understand three-step system for gardening success.

1. Prepare the Soil

This is the most important step. Skip this one, and I can almost guarantee that your garden won't live up to its full potential.

First, you need to determine what kind of soil you have. One test is to squeeze a handful of your garden soil and then rub it between your fingers.

If the soil feels gritty, you have sandy soil. If it sticks together or feels slippery, it's clay.

This will tell you something about how your garden uses water and nutrients. Sandy soil dries out quickly, so your plants' roots dry out faster, too. In hard clay, the soil stays wet, but it's difficult for the roots to absorb the water, as well as nutrients and oxygen.

For most plants, loam is ideal. It contains clay, sand and silt, plus organic material—decaying plant matter—which encourages the growth of microorganisms and bacteria, providing food for plants.

Adding compost is the single best thing you can do for your soil. It adds heft to sandy soil and helps it hold moisture, while making dense clay soil lighter and fluffier. And it provides nutrients in any type of soil.

You can buy a bag at the local garden center if you don't have your own compost pile.

To apply compost to an entire garden, spread about 2 inches over the soil, then till or turn it under to a depth of 6 inches or more, and plant as usual. Top-dress the garden every year with 1 inch of compost.

2. Proper Upkeep

Once your plants are in the ground, you need to pay attention to three duties during the growing season: watering, fertilizing and keeping your garden tidy.

I prefer to water my garden by hand—I think it's the only way to ensure all plants get the moisture they need. Lawn sprinklers lose

water through evaporation, and can overwater some plants while missing others.

Water only in the morning, and when the soil is dry down to a depth of 2 inches. Use a nozzle that produces a gentle flow, watering each plant at its base for about 30 seconds before moving to the next one. When you've watered all the plants, return to the first plant and water everything again.

Check the top 6 inches of soil. When that's moist, you've watered enough.

Fertilizer can be another necessary component—but don't overdo it. Nature has its own feeding process, and if you planted with good compost, you probably do not need extra fertilizer.

When in doubt, take a soil sample to your county Extension office. For a small fee, the soil lab will test it and tell you what type of nutrients your soil might need.

Keeping a clean garden also is important. Pull out weeds, prune dead and unwanted branches and remove spent flowers. One thing that helps reduce weeds is a 2-inch layer of bark mulch. This keeps the soil cool and retains moisture, which means less watering, too.

3. Get Ready for Winter

Your work doesn't end because it gets cold outside. Rake leaves and put them in your compost pile, and protect tender shrubs by surrounding them with burlap.

After the ground freezes, put mulch around your dormant plants. This keeps soil temperatures even, protecting roots from frequent freezing and thawing in colder climates. Later, as the mulch breaks down, it will add beneficial organic material to your soil.

And before you settle in for the winter, clean and oil your garden tools (WD-40 works well), and store them so they'll be ready to use in spring.

That's all there is to it. I have recommended this three-step method hundreds of times over the years…and it's a delight to see beginners turn into budding gardeners.

If you're new to gardening, try them yourself. Start enjoying your own beautiful, healthy garden—and stop wondering if you have a brown thumb!

> ## READER TIP
>
> Adding compost is the single best thing you can do for your soil. It adds heft to sandy soil and makes dense clay soil lighter and fluffier.
>
> **—Nancy Herman**
> **Montague, New Jersey**

Chapter 7

FROM WILDERNESS TO WONDERFUL

Couple carves out a delightful hillside garden retreat.

By Fran Parr, Field Editor, Eldon, Missouri

The house sat in a wasteland of weeds and unkempt trees. Just 2 years old, the building had not been cared for or even inhabited. Still, when Wayne and Eva Studley saw the place, they fell in love with it.

From its spacious interior to the deck that overlooked a wooded lot, this home on the outskirts of Jefferson City, Missouri was the private haven the couple had been looking for. The only drawback—and it was a big one—was the sloping lot.

Not only was it overgrown, but from the street to the rear property line it pitched downward at a steep 25% grade, ending in a deep ravine. It was so extreme that erosion threat-

ened the rear deck, as well as the foundation of the house.

But after 27 years of farming, Wayne was accustomed to terracing and longed to work the soil again, enriching it and bringing beauty and utility to neglected land. Eva, a retired teacher, loved working in the yard and tending flowers. So, despite the visible shortcomings, these two experienced gardeners bought the home.

The first order of business after the Studleys moved in was to

---

SHADY RETREAT. Wayne and Eva Studley (above inset) transformed the overgrown ravine in their backyard by planting hostas and ferns to create a secluded low-light landscape (top).

DARKNESS AND LIGHT. Shade garden favorites like goatsbeard (above left) and spiderwort (above right) thrive in the backyard. In front, sun-lovers brighten the landscape, including dwarf zinnias lining the flower beds (below) and a stunning rose of Sharon (bottom) towering over artemisia, perennial salvia and iris.

landscape the backyard and stabilize the exposed foundation.

Sudden downpours and flash floods are common springtime occurrences in their area, so Wayne installed drainage pipes from the upper to the lower levels to prevent further erosion. He also added terraces and berms and cleared the underbrush in the ravine, leaving many large native trees for shade, including several kinds of oak, hickory, cedar, sassafras and dogwood.

Hauling in loads of mulch was the next step—and an important one, Wayne says.

"I prefer to use shredded mulch instead of the chipped kind," he says. "It decomposes faster, strengthening the soil and feeding the roots of the plants."

Although he lost track of how many pickup-truck loads he brought in, when the project was done, they'd applied a 6-inch layer of mulch over much of the area.

Then the couple designed various flower beds, walkways and peaceful retreats. The plans included a stepping-stone path encircling a sunken garden. Wayne made the "stones" himself, using forms and concrete.

Picking the Right Plants

Finally, it was time to plant...but what would work best? To find out, Wayne and Eva turned to experts at a local nursery for advice on plants, particularly those that tolerate shade and others that could handle the steep situation of their backyard.

Today, many plants known for foliage rather than flowers flourish in the Studleys' yard, including eight varieties of hostas and five different kinds of ferns that fill the sunken garden.

"A plant doesn't need to bloom for me to think it's beautiful," Eva explains.

That's not to say their place isn't blooming. The gardens burst with color, thanks to the bleeding hearts, quince, hydrangea, lilies, astilbe, columbine and moneywort.

"I really enjoy the pink and white bleeding heart blossoms that are the first to bloom each spring," says Eva.

"The moneywort is nice, too," adds Wayne, "but it tends to 'crawl' down the hill. I think I'll replace it with something else once it travels on."

Fun in the Sun

The backyard might be shady, but that's not the case out front. Eva took full advantage of the rays that area receives by filling curving beds with sun-loving plants.

"While we planned on having 95% perennials in front, we simply cannot resist adding a selection of annuals each year," she says.

Both Wayne and Eva are particularly fond of dwarf zinnias, which they use to line the beds. Pink Wave petunias are another favorite and look especially pretty spilling out of a sunken old oak bucket near the front door.

"Honestly, my favorite is whatever's blooming at the moment." Wayne says.

Looking to the future, this green-thumb twosome want to improve a wildflower garden they created. They originally bought a large can of mixed wildflower seeds, scattered them on a hillside and then watched as Queen Anne's lace took over.

"We don't mind that plant at all, but we'd like more variety and color in the bed," Wayne says.

Also waiting in the wings is a playground for their grandchildren. They'll construct it on the two vacant—and flat—lots next door.

Sage Advice

"The most important thing I'd share with others is to learn as much as you can about what you want to plant," Wayne says.

They've learned the hard way that some varieties can be too aggressive, like Missouri primrose. The couple loved the pink flowers it produced...but weren't pleased when the plant sent runners underground that popped up in their lawn. They've learned that such plants should be confined to pots buried in the soil...or avoided.

And others, like wisteria, wouldn't produce flowers in shade, no matter how much they pampered the plant.

"We fed that baby, urging it to grow up a 20-foot pole Wayne had secured in cement so it would stay on that hillside," Eva says. "It thrived and threw out 10- to 15-foot suckers, latching onto neighboring trees and shrubs, without one hint of a flower."

Aside from those few experiences, the Studleys believe in blooming where you're planted.

"We feel very lucky to have happened upon the house nobody wanted," they say. "It was a wilderness, but now it's a wonderful place to call home."

READER TIP

I prefer to use shredded mulch instead of the chipped kind. It decomposes faster, strengthening the soil and feeding the roots of the plants.

—Wayne Studley, Jefferson City, Missouri

1. Artemisia
2. Rose of Sharon
3. Zinnia
4. Salvia
5. Iris
6. Holly
7. Barberry
8. Rose
9. Cherry
10. Cedar
11. Birdbath
12. Ajuga
13. Periwinkle
14. Bleeding heart
15. Honeylocust
16. Hosta
17. Redbud
18. Fern
19. Moneywort
20. Astilbe
21. Bench
22. Hydrangea
23. Sassafras

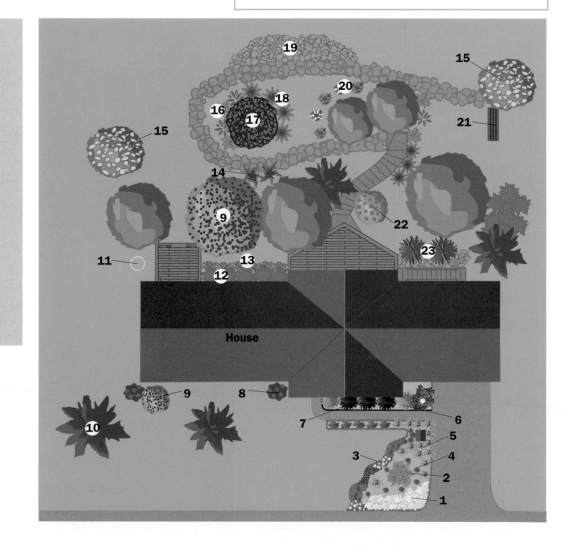

'GLAD YOU ASKED!'

Expert answers your garden questions.

By Melinda Myers, Contributing Editor

A Clue About Blue

Do blue spruces bloom? This one (below) is about 40 years old, and I'd never seen anything but plain pinecones grow on it until these bright-pink blooms emerged. —Donald Schweyer, Hudson, Indiana

Melinda: Although your tree's bright-pink display is impossible to miss, the blooms of spruce trees are often much more subtle.

Spruce trees produce separate male and female flowers on the same tree. The pollen-bearing male flowers can be quite colorful, like the ones on your tree. These will release pollen to the female flowers, resulting in the development of seed-filled cones. The cones are actually the fruit that forms once fertilization occurs.

After they've done their job, the male flowers dry up and drop off the tree. Though it happens every year, it often goes unnoticed.

Pretty Surprise

Last spring, this lovely flower (left) appeared in my mother's garden. Do you know what it is? Will we see it again this spring?
—Pat Pietras
Weeki Wachee, Florida

Melinda: This beautiful bloom is commonly known as rose turmeric (botanically it's *Curcuma elata*). It is one of a group of 40 plants that are native to the rain forests of Asia and Australia.

Since it's hardy in Zones 7 to 11, you should see it next season. This adaptable plant grows best in partial shade, but will tolerate full shade through full sun as long as the soil is moist.

Ready for the Holidays

I'd like to bring my potted red and green caladiums inside as holiday decorations. However, I've heard they must rest in winter to return in spring. Is this true? —Amanda Henry, Wimberly, Texas

Melinda: The shorter, cooler days of autumn usually send this plant into its resting stage. But all you need to extend its show of colorful leaves is a little extra warmth and some added light.

Caladiums are tropical plants that can be grown as perennials outdoors in Zones 10 and 11 or as annuals in colder climates. To maintain them indoors, grow the plants in a warm area with 16 hours of light. Use artificial lights to extend the natural daylight.

For added humidity, place the plants on a saucer of pebbles that's filled with water. The pot should sit on the pebbles, not directly in the water.

Then allow them to rest for several months after the holidays by placing them in a cooler and darker location.

When the weather warms in the spring, set your plants outdoors and get ready for another spectacular display of striking foliage.

Weeds Gone Wild

How can I get rid of the wild strawberries (like the ones below) that are invading my backyard? They are growing into my lawn.

—Jean Kline
Reading, Pennsylvania

Melinda: Pulling is the only nonchemical solution. Or you can spot treat these unwanted plants with Roundup or Finale. These total vegetation killers will destroy the tops, roots and runners of these weeds. Just be careful not to get any of these chemicals on nearby grass or flowers—it will kill them, too.

Try painting the weed killer directly on the strawberry plant to avoid damaging the surrounding plants. Or create a makeshift shield to contain the herbicide.

To do this, remove the bottom of a plastic milk jug or carton. Place it over the weed, keeping grass and other desirable plants outside the container. Spray the weed through the top and wait for the dripping to stop. Carefully move the jug to the next weed.

As always, read and follow the manufacturer's label directions and wear the recommended protective gear when applying any herbicide.

Going Nuts

About 6 years ago, I planted two self-pollinating pecan trees. Though the trees are growing well, they have yet to bloom or produce any pecans. What's wrong? —Chuck Himebauch, Port Byron, Illinois

Melinda: Patience is the answer to your problem. All plants must reach a mature state before they produce flowers and fruit. For nut trees, that waiting period can be as long as 10 to 20 years.

Mulch the soil around the trees and water thoroughly when needed. By taking proper care of your trees over the next few years, you'll ensure a future full of bountiful and tasty pecan harvests.

Unknown Beauty

This beautiful wildflower (at left) shows up in the woods behind my house every June. Can you tell me what it is?

—Karen Britton Tamaroa, Illinois

Melinda: Known as Indian pink or Maryland pinkroot (its botanical name is *Spigelia marilandica*), this beauty is native to moist woodlands. You can find Indian pink from Maryland south to Florida and west to Texas, Missouri and Oklahoma. Watch closely, and you'll notice the colorful flowers open from the bottom up during spring and summer.

If you'd like to extend its display, remove the spent flowers. They thrive in fertile well-draining soil and partial shade.

Mysterious Beauty

I planted this perennial (below) 20 years ago, but I don't know what it is. It's hardy, drought tolerant and blooms in May. Can you solve this mystery?

—June Lake, Cayce, South Carolina

Melinda: A quick look may remind you of a cornflower. But the bloom time, foliage and growth habit reveal it's a Stokes' aster (*Stokesia laevis*). This native of the southern United States is hardy in Zones 5 to 9, and blooms from late spring through most of summer. Northern gardeners, however, have to wait for summer to enjoy its show.

This lavender beauty grows 12 to 24 inches tall with a mounded growth habit. Plant it in full sun with well-draining soil for best results. Add mulch in winter to increase its hardiness in northern gardens.

Dogwood Is a Dud

I have a dogwood tree that never blooms. How can I coax spring flowers out of my reluctant tree?

—Hattie Wiant, Weston, West Virginia

Melinda: Age, fertilization, pruning and sunlight all affect flowering.

Young trees will often bloom in the containers when you buy them, but expend their energy developing a root system when transplanted into a landscape. Once established, however, the blooms should return.

The second most common problem is overfertilization. Too much nitrogen can produce large plants with few or no flowers. Make sure your dogwood isn't getting extra fertilizer from a nearby garden or lawn area.

Though shade tolerant, dogwoods need sufficient light to flower. Those growing in excess shade have sparse growth and very few blossoms.

Lastly, save all pruning chores until after the tree blooms or should have bloomed. Flowering dogwoods set their flower buds the previous season, so winter pruning might eliminate the spring show.

Family Flower

My grandmother gave me the seeds to this pretty plant (at left). What is it?
—Shari Lemke
Waterloo, Wisconsin

Melinda: Known as Texas plume or scarlet gilia (*Ipomopsis rubra*), this biennial makes a nice addition to a naturalized planting area or perennial garden.

During its first year, the plant grows only 3 inches tall and produces no flowers. The next year, however, it stretches toward the sky and can reach heights of 6 feet. The long, orange-red flower spikes provide color throughout summer.

Grow it in full sun and well-drained soil for the best results. Because it's a biennial—flowering only in its second year—sow seeds several years in a row to ensure colorful blooming plants each summer.

Mosquito Control

I'd like to discourage mosquitoes from breeding in my backyard pond. Is there anything I can add to the water?
—Gwyn Pollard, Ontario, Canada

Melinda: Water gardens that contain fish or have moving water usually are not the cause of overabundant backyard mosquitoes. Standing water in trash cans, discarded tires and birdbaths is more often the culprit.

Still, you can use a larvacide to kill any mosquito larvae that might be in your pond.

Use ones that contain Bacillus thuringiensis israelensis (also known as Bti), a bacterium that kills the larvae without harming fish, people or wildlife. It's available in doughnut-shaped blocks, called dunks, which you can place into the water to control these pests.

A Vine to Share

I'd like to share my honeysuckle vine with friends. Can I start it from a cutting? If so, how?
—Sue Shepherd, Greenfield, Indiana

Melinda: Woody plants, such as shrubs and perennial vines, are tricky to start from cuttings.

To do this, take several 4- to 6-inch cuttings from the tips of the new growth in spring or early summer, and dip them in a rooting hormone. Place the treated cuttings in moist sand, vermiculite or perlite, and set them in a shaded location.

Once rooted, plant the cuttings in a container filled with a well-draining potting mix. Move the established plants to the garden in fall, or keep them in a protected location and bury the pot over winter, then plant them the following spring.

Layering is another way to propagate vines. To use this method, bend a stem to the ground or to a container of potting mix, and nick it 9 inches below the tip. Bury this portion of the stem, leaving the tip above the ground and the stem attached to the parent plant. Roots will form on the buried portion. Once rooted, disconnect the stem from the parent plant and move to a permanent location.

Strange Sight

Several years after we planted this evergreen, it grew a section at the top that looks like a ball (below). We've never seen anything like it. Can you explain how this happened?
—Lucille Adams
Reynolds, North Dakota

Melinda: The tree's bizarre growth is called a broom. Brooms can be caused by insects, disease, environmental stresses or plant mutation.

A single broom on a healthy tree is usually a harmless mutation. In fact, cuttings and seeds from cones produced on these growths are sometimes used to propagate many of the uniquely shaped or dwarf evergreens that are available in the market today.

Bird's Nest spruce is one popular plant that had its start from a broom that grew on a Norway spruce.

You may want to contact a local nursery to see if their propagator is interested in trying to develop a new variety using cones from the broom on your tree. Otherwise, just continue enjoying this unique feature and the attention it brings from passersby.

Not What You Think

I watched this lovely cactus bloom (below) over the course of a month, but haven't had any luck identifying it. Can you help?
—Dieter Hain
Walla Walla, Washington

Melinda: This plant has the look of a cactus, but it's really a bromeliad. This particular bromeliad is known as urn or vase plant (the botanical name is *Aechema fasciata*) and is one of over 200 bromeliad species.

Most are native to rain forests and are a type of epiphyte, meaning they anchor onto trees or shrubs with their roots, and use their leaves to gather water and nutrients from the environment. Once the flower fades, the plant will start to decline.

But don't worry. New plants called offsets or pups will soon appear. These can be divided and planted in individual containers.

Mystery Growths

These weird growths (below) showed up in my front lawn last summer. They lasted 1 day, and then withered away and disappeared. They came up about 2 feet from where I had cut down a plum tree. Do you know what they are? *—Ken Buchholz, New Hope, Pennsylvania*

Melinda: These strange growths are mushrooms, the fruiting bodies of fungus that usually grow underground.

A type of fungus that feeds on rotting wood in the soil is like-ly feeding on the decaying roots of your plum tree, helping speed up decomposition. When it's wet, the fungus sprouts mushrooms. These are not harmful to your lawn, they just look bad. When dry weather returns, the mushrooms shrivel and disappear, while the fungus continues its work underground.

As soon as the plum roots have fully decomposed and there is no food for the fungus, it—along with the mushrooms—will disappear. In the meantime, you may want to rake and destroy any mushrooms that pop up to prevent kids and pets from eating them.

A Pox on Phlox

How can I eliminate white mold from my garden phlox? The plants continue to bloom, but they don't look very nice. *—Mary Boocher, Tipp City, Ohio*

Melinda: It sounds like powdery mildew has infected your plants. Gardeners growing other flowers, including bee balm, lilacs and zinnia, may know this disease as well.

Avoid the problem by using resistant cultivars of garden phlox, such as David, Kathryn and the Flame Series, or try its look-alike cousin, *Phlox maculata*.

You can reduce the problem on susceptible plants with proper management of the growing conditions. Garden phlox should be in full sun with good air circulation. Accomplish this by allowing plenty of room between plants, or by thinning individual plants in spring—removing about one-quarter of the stems as they emerge.

Fungicides can also reduce the symptoms. You'll need to treat the plants weekly once the disease appears. Remember to always follow the manufacturer's directions when selecting or using fungicides and other chemicals.

A Name for Lily

I love these beautiful blooms (below), but I have no idea what they are. Can you identify them and let me know if it's okay to leave them outside over winter? *—Marge Moffitt, Armstrong, Iowa*

Melinda: A relative of the amaryllis, this plant is commonly called zephyr lily, rain lily or rocket lily (botanically known as *Zephyranthes grandiflora*). It is hardy only in a few southern areas—Zones 10 and 11—so all other gardeners must winter it indoors.

This is a fairly easy plant to grow. Those who'd like to try can purchase and pot rain lily bulbs in spring. Then water the plant often enough to keep the soil moist, and use a dilute flowering houseplant fertilizer once the flowers appear.

In late August, begin to nudge the plant into dormancy, so it will stop actively growing. Cut back on watering so leaves begin to wither. Once the leaves are dried, store the plant in a cool, dark location.

Bring your rain lily out of hiding in February to start the growing season again. Place it in a sunny window in your home, and keep the soil slightly moist—leaves and blossoms will soon follow.

BACKYARD SHOWPIECE

221

218

Steve Terrill; inset: Skip Moody/Dembinsky Photo Assoc.

FLOWERING DOGWOOD

When it comes to four-season appeal, this showy tree is "top dog."

By Rachael Liska, Associate Editor

As the days grow longer and warmer, the flowering dogwood readies itself for an unrivaled spring show. That's when its elegant flowers burst forth, lighting up forests, orchards and country roads with a lovely wash of white or pink.

So reliable is this harbinger of warmer weather that some gardeners decide when it's safe to plant by watching for the flowering dogwood's emerging blooms.

"The wooded area on my grandparents' Ohio farm was home to many dogwoods, so this tree holds special memories for me," shares *Birds & Blooms* Contributing Editor Melinda Myers. "Their early blooms brightened the landscape and signaled the start of spring. When I see them now, it reminds me of good times on the family farm."

It's easy to understand why this ornamental tree has also captured the fancy of home owners everywhere. But as striking as it is in spring, the flowering dogwood wins praise all year with its four-season appeal.

Legendary Pedigree

The flowering dogwood has a long and colorful history.

According to legend, it once equaled the mighty oak in size…until its wood was used for Jesus' cross. This saddened the dogwood, and it never grew so large again. As a reminder, its four petals form the shape of a cross and each is marked with a nail print. In the center is a crown of thorns.

History also tells of American Indians using the aromatic

bark and roots as a remedy for malaria.

Today, the tight grains of dogwood make it ideal for golf club heads, knitting needles and tool handles.

Found in natural woodlands from New England south to Florida and west to Texas, flowering dogwoods evolved as so-called "understory trees."

Understory trees fill a unique niche since they grow in the shade of taller mature trees. In this microclimate, dogwoods receive filtered sunlight, high humidity and protection from drying winds—three conditions to keep in mind when adding a dogwood to the home landscape.

Best in Show

When properly cared for, flowering dogwoods will reward their owners with year-round pageantry in almost any landscape setting.

In spring, the blossoms appear before the leaves. But while this showy display is unmistakable, these "flowers" are actually modified leaves known as bracts, just like a poinsettia.

The true flower is insignificant and yellowish green, located in the center of the four "petals." White is the common color found in the wild, but some cultivars boast pink bracts.

Once the blossoms fade, green leaves unfurl. Their smooth, bright-green surface contrasts with the muted, silver-green underside. The small flowers then transform into dense clumps of green berries by early summer.

Autumn paints the leaves and twigs rich scarlet, while the fruits ripen to a glossy red. Various birds and other wildlife soon arrive to pick off the nutritious berries before the chill of winter sets in.

Sometimes said to resemble alligator skin, the flowering dogwood's rough, gray-brown bark makes it a standout in winter, too. This, combined with tiered branches and button-shaped buds at the tips of the twigs, makes for an attractive silhouette against a snow-covered yard.

Unleash the Beauty

The flowering dogwood's versatility has made it a popular choice for home landscapes. Slow growing, it does extremely well as a specimen plant or accenting a patio. And because it's a woodland native, flowering dogwoods are ideal for planting at the edge of a woods or in naturalized areas. Try pairing it with rhododendrons and azaleas for an informal yet pretty landscape feature with a lot of spring interest.

Flowering dogwood is a beautiful landscape plant, but is susceptible to many insects and disease if not kept healthy. Minimize the risk by purchasing healthy, pest-free plants from a reliable nursery.

Container-grown dogwoods may be transplanted any time of the year. Northern gardeners, however, might want to consider planting from late winter to early spring, so the tree has time to establish itself before the next winter. Southern gardeners should plant in fall to late winter, well be-

GARDENER'S BEST FRIEND. With its white (right) or showy pink (opposite page) blooms and attractive shape, flowering dogwood complements any backyard landscape. The eye-catching bracts (above left inset) are modified leaves, but are often mistaken for petals. The true flowers are at the center.

Backyard Showpiece

fore the heat of summer arrives.

Grow in a partially shaded location with moist, well-draining soil. Add a 3-inch layer of mulch around the tree, being careful not to pile it against the trunk. Water thoroughly during dry, stressful periods and as needed the first few years after transplanting.

Follow these few simple steps, and you're on your way to enjoying the grace of this sensational showstopper.

Plant Profile

Common Name: Flowering dogwood.
Botanical Name: *Cornus florida*.
Height: 20 to 30 feet.
Spread: 20 to 30 feet.
Leaves: Oval-shaped with prominent veins. Ranging from 3 to 6 inches long, they are medium green in summer and crimson in fall.
Flowers: Small, yellow-green flowers surrounded by four, 2-inch-long white or pink bracts.
Hardiness: Zones 5 to 9.
Light Needs: Full sun to full shade. Best in partial shade.
Soil Type: Prefers moist, well-draining, humus-rich and acidic soil.
Planting: Northern gardeners should plant from late winter to early spring. Southern gardeners should plant in fall to late winter. Avoid planting in compacted or shallow soils.
Prize Picks: Cherokee Chief is a popular pink flowering dogwood, though it doesn't tolerate extreme cold.

A heavy white bloomer, Cloud Nine is slow growing and more compact than most other varieties, making it ideal for smaller gardens.

With pink and yellow variegated foliage, Cherokee Sunset boasts red flowers and is disease-resistant.

Alan and Linda Detrick

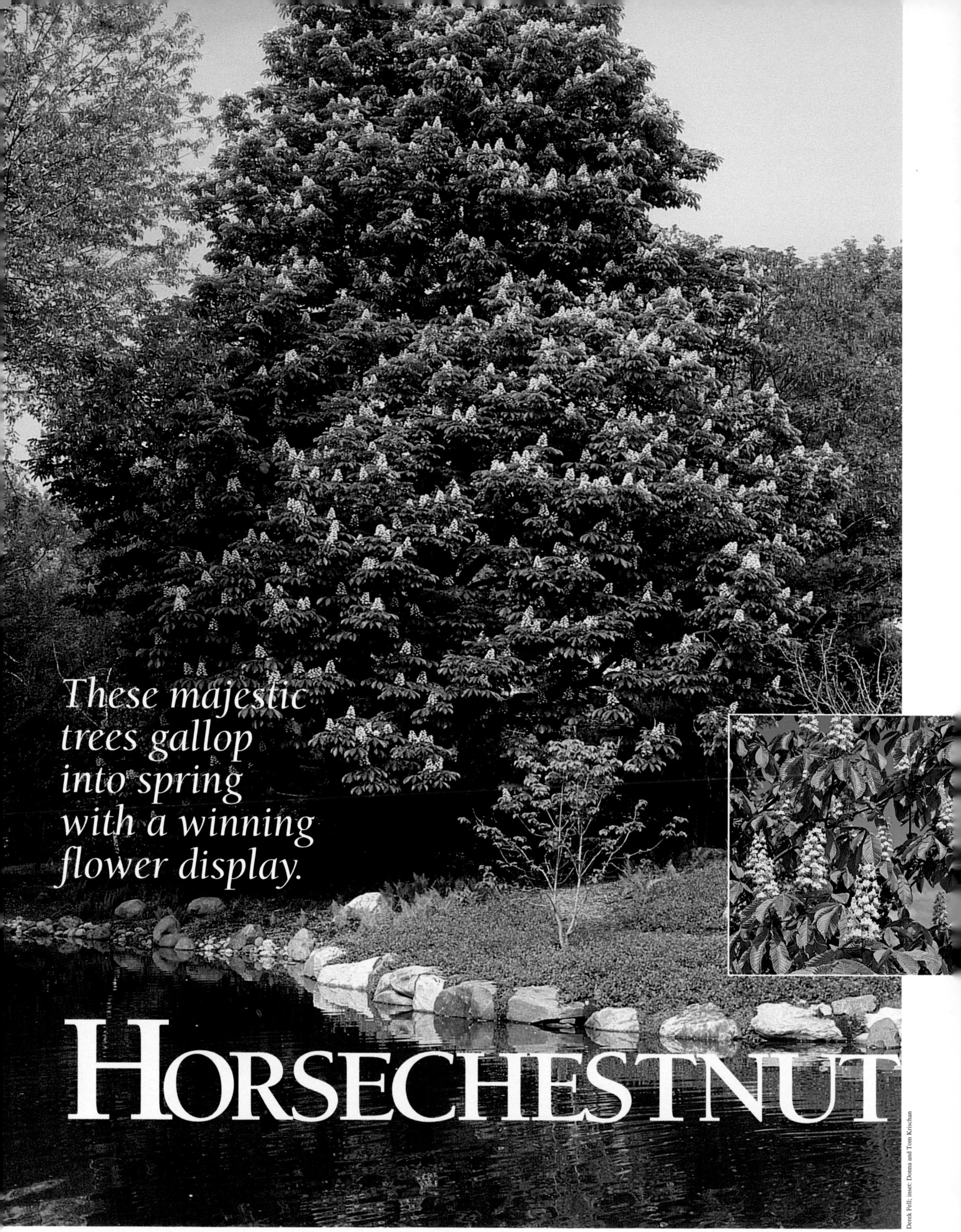

These majestic trees gallop into spring with a winning flower display.

HORSECHESTNUT

Derek Fell; inset: Donna and Tom Krischan

For sheer showstopping spring beauty, few ornamental trees can compete with the horsechestnut. This magnificent shade tree is one of the first to leaf out, setting the stage for sensational flower plumes in May.

Except for a handful of shrubby or smaller species, such as the bottlebrush buckeye, horsechestnuts grow to impressive heights, making their springtime performance even more magnificent. The most familiar tree, the common horsechestnut, tops out at 75 feet, with a spread of up to 70 feet.

White flowers appear in early to mid-May, forming upright clusters 2 to 5 inches wide and 5 inches to 1 foot or more in length. The blossoms are white with yellow markings and have a pink blotch at the throat of each flower.

Known botanically as *Aesculus hippocastanum*, this plant is native to the mountains of Greece and Albania. The palm-like leaves have pointed lobes, giving the foliage a graceful look. The color of its bark ranges from dark gray to brown, with attractive, platelike scales similar to that of apple trees.

With its imposing size and pretty spring show, the horsechestnut is a popular landscape choice for parks, college campuses, golf courses and other expansive settings with room to showcase its charms. It's particularly popular in the eastern U.S., where, as one tree expert notes, "Virtually every campus has a horsechestnut."

While prevalent in North America, the horsechestnut is truly prized in Europe. France's Palace of Versailles boasts extensive horsechestnut plantings, and the trees line many Paris boulevards, including the famed Champs-Elysees.

Going Nuts

Horsechestnuts are landscape mainstays in the United Kingdom, where their smooth shiny nuts are used for a popular game called "conkers."

These nuts are known as "buckeyes" in parts of North America because they resemble that of the Ohio buckeye tree, a cousin of the horsechestnut. The tennis ball-sized spiny fruits contain one or two nuts, and attract deer and squirrels when they begin to fall in September.

Where wildlife visits or fruit clean-up causes problems, Baumannii horsechestnut (*Aesculus hippocastanum* 'Baumannii') is a good alternative. This cultivar produces no fruit and has an especially long blooming period with double flowers.

The Right Fit

Because of its size, common horsechestnut is a good fit for only the largest home landscapes. However, the red horsechestnut (top right), *Aesculus* x *carnea*, is sized right for suburban lawns. At maturity, it's 30 to 40 feet tall, about half the height of a common horsechestnut, and has rose-red flowers.

This smaller variety also is more resistant to leaf blotch and powdery mildew. Both diseases can make horsechestnut leaves discolor and drop, but cause no permanent damage in otherwise healthy plants. Prompt raking and disposal of diseased leaves helps reduce the risk of future outbreaks.

Horsechestnuts don't grow true from seed, so it's best to purchase a tree from a nursery and plant it in spring. Choose a site with full sun to partial shade, moist soil and good drainage. Keep soil moist throughout the growing season, and give the tree room to spread. In time, you'll have a horsechestnut worthy of the backyard triple crown.

UNBRIDLED BEAUTY. The horsechestnut puts on a showy spring floral display, whether it's the statuesque common horsechestnut (opposite page) or the smaller red horsechestnut (above). Although known for its unique flowers (opposite page inset), you can't miss its spiny hulls as they mature (left).

Plant Profile

Common Name: Horsechestnut.
Botanical Name: *Aesculus hippocastanum*.
Height: 50 to 75 feet.
Spread: 40 to 70 feet.
Leaves: Large five- to seven-pointed leaflets that are greenish-yellow in spring, dark-green at maturity and yellow or brown in autumn.
Flowers: White panicles up to 5 inches wide and 1 foot long.
Hardiness: Zones 3 to 7.
Light Needs: Full sun to light shade.
Soil Type: Moist and well draining.
Planting: Plant balled-and-burlapped trees in spring; container-grown plants anytime during the growing season. Dig a hole as deep as the root system and 2 to 4 times the width of the root ball. Root flare should be at or slightly above soil. Do not amend soil in planting hole.
Fruit: Shiny, light-brown nuts inside spiny hulls.
Prize Picks: *Aesculus hippocastanum* 'Baumannii' produces long-lasting double white flowers and no fruits. Red horsechestnut (*Aesculus* x *carnea*) grows 30 to 40 feet tall and boasts rose-red flowers.
Backyard Benefits: Its flowers attract butterflies.
Caution: Plant parts are poisonous if ingested.

While all ornamental cherry trees are striking, this hardy variety outranks the rest.

A Salute to the Sargent

There's no question that ornamental cherry trees are nature's showstoppers. These beauties produce a truly breathtaking cloud of blossoms to greet each spring.

In fact, the fragrant display is so amazing that many communities across the country host celebrations to honor them, including the National Cherry Blossom Festival, held each spring in Washington, D.C.

But ornamental cherries aren't reserved for arboretums and parks, the flowering specimens make appealing additions to home gardens as well. The problem is that many types are susceptible to disease or pests like borers. Luckily, the Sargent cherry is the exception to that rule.

BLOSSOMS AND MORE. When it comes to ornamental trees, it's hard to top the beauty of Sargent cherry. This colorful tree is a good choice for home landscapes—it's relatively carefree and offers year-round interest, producing pink flowers in spring as well as brightly colored leaves in fall. Even its marked mahogany bark (right inset) is attractive.

Mark Turner; inset: R. Todd Davis

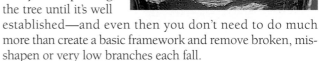

Tough Enough

First brought to the U.S. from Japan in the 1890s by its namesake, noted arborist Charles Sprague Sargent, this variety has long demonstrated its hardiness, as well as its ability to withstand insects and disease.

What's more, the tree thrives in Zones 4 to 9, making it an ideal addition to gardens in most parts of North America. Plus, the Sargent cherry will live for 30 to 50 years.

Best of all, this ornamental beauty puts on a show all year long. In spring, it produces clusters of graceful, pink blossoms that cover every branch. But the show doesn't stop there.

Shortly after the flowers appear, new red-tinged leaves emerge. When fully unfurled, the tree's oval leaves deepen to an attractive, dark-green hue and measure about 3 to 5 inches long.

By summer, pea-sized cherries appear, starting out reddish and ripening to a purplish black. Because of their diminutive nature, the fruits are rather inconspicuous, but they attract plenty of birds that will devour most of the cherries before they can hit the ground, keeping mess to a minimum.

Come fall, the Sargent is ready to shine again. As the days shorten and nights cool off, the leaves turn a brilliant, flaming orange-red before dropping in late September.

Then, during winter, the bare branches and multiple upright trunks are visible—and even that's a treat. Satiny bark the color of rich mahogany covers the tree and features extended horizontal markings called lenticels (right inset), which add interest to the otherwise dull landscape.

Most Sargent cherries grow 20 to 40 feet tall and wide with a rounded shape that works in varied settings.

A Place in the Sun

As with most ornamental fruit trees, spring is the preferred time to transplant a Sargent cherry. And the best place to put one is in a very sunny spot, although the tree will tolerate a little shade. Avoid low spots or areas subject to late-spring frost, however.

It isn't terribly fussy about soil and will do well in almost any conditions as long as the drainage is good. You'll need to dig a hole that's the same depth as the roots but wider to give the roots room to spread out. Then gently position the tree in the hole, fill it with soil, water thoroughly and apply mulch.

The tree grows fairly quickly, though it may take 5 to 6 years to flower.

You don't need to worry about pruning the tree until it's well established—and even then you don't need to do much more than create a basic framework and remove broken, misshapen or very low branches each fall.

Other than that, all you have to do is sit back and watch this tree parade its beauty in your yard throughout the year. And that's something worth celebrating!

Plant Profile

Common Name: Sargent cherry.
Botanical Name: *Prunus sargentii*.
Hardiness: Zones 4 to 9.
Height: 20 to 40 feet (can grow up to 70 feet in the wild).
Spread: 20 to 40 feet; 10 to 15 feet for the Columnare variety.
Flowers: Bowl-shaped, 1- to 1-1/2-inch pink flowers in clusters in spring.
Leaves: Oval or rounded leaves 3 to 5 inches long with serrated edges. Leaves are reddish tinged in spring, deepening to dark green in summer. By fall, they turn bright orange-red.
Fruit: In summer, inconspicuous, glossy 1/2-inch round cherries that start out reddish and ripen to purplish black; are readily consumed by birds.
Light Needs: Full sun.
Soil Type: Moist, well-draining and moderately fertile.
Planting: Plant trees in spring. Add mulch and water well to encourage strong root development.

TOWERING
SYMBOLS OF STATE

Mark E. Gibson/Unicorn Stock Photos

Official trees have roots in each region's history and character.

By Karen Sutherland, Downers Grove, Illinois

For centuries, trees have been an important natural resource to Native Americans, pioneers, farmers and city dwellers alike.

They've offered shelter, fuel and building materials for everything from transportation to toys. And wood continues to be invaluable today.

All 50 U.S. states have recognized the role of these woodland beauties by selecting official state trees.

Varieties selected for this honor include the tallest (California redwood, at top), the largest (giant sequoia), the

HISTORIC ROOTS. All 50 states have acknowledged the importance of trees by selecting one as an official state symbol. At left, California redwoods are just one of the lofty emblems of The Golden State. They also recognize the giant sequoia as one of their state trees. New Hampshire claims the distinctive peeling bark of the white birch (above). Also known as a paper and canoe birch, this tree produces decorative, dangling catkins in spring. These long clusters of seeds resemble a cat's bushy tail.

Find Your State Tree

State	Tree
Alabama	Longleaf pine
Alaska	Sitka spruce
Arizona	Palo verde
Arkansas	Loblolly pine
California	California redwood, Giant sequoia
Colorado	Colorado blue spruce
Connecticut	White oak
Delaware	American holly
Florida	Cabbage palmetto
Georgia	Live oak
Hawaii	Kukui/candlenut
Idaho	Western white pine
Illinois	White oak
Indiana	Tulip tree
Iowa	Oak
Kansas	Cottonwood
Kentucky	Tulip poplar
Louisiana	Bald cypress
Maine	Eastern white pine
Maryland	White oak
Massachusetts	American elm
Michigan	Eastern white pine
Minnesota	Red pine
Mississippi	Magnolia
Missouri	Flowering dogwood
Montana	Ponderosa pine
Nebraska	Cottonwood
Nevada	Single-leaf pinyon, Bristlecone pine
New Hampshire	White birch
New Jersey	Northern red oak
New Mexico	Pinyon
New York	Sugar maple
North Carolina	Pine
North Dakota	American elm
Ohio	Buckeye
Oklahoma	Redbud
Oregon	Douglas fir
Pennsylvania	Eastern hemlock
Rhode Island	Red maple
South Carolina	Palmetto
South Dakota	Black Hills spruce
Tennessee	Tulip poplar
Texas	Pecan
Utah	Blue spruce
Vermont	Sugar maple
Virginia	Flowering dogwood
Washington	Western hemlock
West Virginia	Sugar maple
Wisconsin	Sugar maple
Wyoming	Plains cottonwood

Canada's Provincial Trees

Province	Tree
Alberta	Lodgepole pine
British Columbia	Western red cedar
Manitoba	White spruce
New Brunswick	Balsam fir
Newfoundland	Black spruce
Northwest Territories	Jack pine
Nova Scotia	Red spruce
Ontario	Eastern white pine
Prince Edward Island	Northern red oak
Quebec	Yellow birch
Saskatchewan	Paper birch
Yukon Territory	Quaking aspen

oldest (bristlecone pine) and some of the showiest (the redbud and the flowering dogwood).

All told, 38 different tree varieties are state symbols, with a number of states picking the same tree.

For example, the flowering dogwood is the state tree of both Missouri and Virginia; the white oak represents Connecticut, Illinois and Maryland; and the sugar maple is the tree that has been selected by four states—New York, Vermont, West Virginia and Wisconsin.

A pair of states even adopted more than one tree to share the top honor. California recognizes the prominence of the redwood *and* the giant sequoia, while Nevada designated the single-leaf pinyon and the bristlecone pine, both common in its desert countryside.

Began with Arbor Day

The state tree movement dates back to the inauguration of Arbor Day in 1872.

Settlers in Nebraska were encouraged to plant trees to

Redbud, flowering dogwoods

Joseph Kayne/Dembinsky Photo Assoc.

Sugar maple

Ann Trulove/Unicorn Stock Photos; top photo: Adam Jones/Dembinsky Photo Assoc.

Bristlecone pine

help celebrate the new holiday. One of the most popular varieties used to seed the vast prairies was the cottonwood, which later became Nebraska's woody mascot.

The first state to choose a tree officially, however, was Texas. In 1919, the Lone Star State picked the pecan in memory of a much-loved former governor who passed away in 1906.

His last request was that a pecan be planted on his grave, and the nuts from that tree shared so people could plant more.

Other states followed suit for a variety of reasons. Minnesota, Montana, Oregon and Maine all recognized coniferous trees that were important to their lumber or ship-building industries.

History Lessons

History played a role in the selection of Massachusetts' state tree. The legislature selected the American elm, in honor of the "Liberty Elm," under whose branches the colonists made plans for gaining America's independence from Britain.

Connecticut singled out the white oak to commemorate the important role of its famous "Charter Oak." In 1687, England's King James II sent representatives to retrieve a charter he'd granted the colony, so colonists hid it in a hollow section of the white oak's trunk.

More modern events have had an impact on state tree selection, too. Charles Lindbergh's famous airplane, the *Spirit of St. Louis*, had wings made of Alaska's Sitka spruce, prompting

the Union's largest state to grant honorary status to the towering evergreen.

Child's Play

Children played a role choosing trees in three states, where they voted for their favorite species. Mississippi youngsters elected the magnolia, and kids in West Virginia and Wisconsin gave the nod to the sugar maple.

All but one state—Hawaii—picked trees native to their particular regions. People there decided to acknowledge the kukui or candlenut, a variety imported from Malaysia. This tree's small, white blossoms often appear in leis, the floral necklaces associated with the Aloha State.

Only a handful of the hundreds of tree species growing in this country are honored as official emblems. But that doesn't mean they're hard to find. Take a good look at the trees near your home, and you're sure to spot a few with stately roots.

READER TIP

Hawaii is the only state that didn't pick a tree native to their region. The people there chose the kukui or candlenut, imported from Malaysia, because the tree's white blossoms often appear in the state's signature leis.

—**Karen Sutherland, Downers Grove, Illinois**

ENJOY THE SHOW

Our resident plant expert explains the "mystery" of fall color.

By Melinda Myers, Contributing Editor

As summer turns to fall, the leaves on many trees start changing from shades of green into yellow, red and orange hues. The transformation is spectacular, so it's not surprising that I hear two common questions each autumn:

First, how does the magnificent process work? And second, why do some leaves change color while others that should don't?

Back to Basics

Let's start with a little basic biology. Plant leaves actually contain a variety of colors, but the green pigment in the chlorophyll found in leaves is the most dominant. Because of this, it masks the other colors, and we see brilliant greens throughout most of the season.

The green chlorophyll is critical to the life of the plant. It captures energy from the sun, and then through the process of photosynthesis, combines it with carbon dioxide and water to produce the plant's nourishment in the form of sugars.

During the process, the chlorophyll slowly breaks down, but the cycle doesn't stop. The plant continues to produce new chlorophyll to maintain the vivid-green leaves we know and love in summer.

Transformation Explanation

But as fall takes over with its shorter days, the cycle changes. Plants must begin to get ready for winter.

To do this, the leaves develop a layer of corky cells between the leaf stem and branch to prepare for fall leaf drop. This layer slows the production of chlorophyll, and the green leaf color begins to fade. As it does, it exposes other color pigments (called carotenoid pigments), unveiling the pleasant hues of yellow, brown and orange.

These pigments are responsible for the gorgeous yellow leaves of ginkgo, redbud, witchhazel, larch and birch trees. The warm browns and tans often found on oaks are due to the accumulation of tannins in the leaves as the green chlorophyll disappears.

Now add in the effects of cool fall nights. If temperatures drop below 45° while the days are still sunny and warm, the plant is unable to use all the sugars produced in the leaves during the day. To avoid a toxic buildup of these sugars, the plants use the excess to produce a chemical called anthocyanin. These pigments are what give us the red and purple leaves of red maple, burning bush, black gum, flowering dogwood and sweet gum.

Delayed Display

Magnificent yellows, oranges and reds help give autumn its vibrant identity, but not every season sparkles like we want it to. A poor fall color display, like so many gardening woes, can be blamed on the weather.

Gray days and warm nights will dim the display, and early frost may damage leaf tissue, causing it to turn black before it has a chance to show off its rich colors. Cool, wet springs or warm, humid summers also can cause leaf spot and early leaf drop, eliminating the canvas on which nature paints its colorful season finale.

Gardeners can influence the intensity of the fall show as well. Too much nitrogen fertilizer may dim the color, preventing the beautiful red hue from developing on red maples, burning bush and others. Sun-loving plants placed in shade also can lose their fall luster.

Although you can do your part to ensure a great fall show by monitoring the environment of your plants, the rest is up to nature. So as the crisp autumn weather takes over, just sit back and enjoy the transformation.

READER TIP

Be careful using nitrogen fertilizer. Too much may prevent the beautiful autumn hue from developing on red maples, burning bush and others.

WHITE ASH

These trees provide a dazzling autumn show.

By Kathleen Zimmer-Anderson, Waukesha, Wisconsin

Each fall, I pat myself on the back when I look at our yard. Why? Because I had the bright idea to add a white ash to the garden several years ago, and now we're blessed with a glowing autumn display when shorter days and cooler temperatures prompt the tree's leaves to change color.

The only downside is that the leaves turn in September, and the ash is bare well before winter—but that smoldering purple hue is worth it in my book. And besides, those ash-gray branches add texture and interest to our yard until spring coaxes pretty new leaves to emerge.

There's much more to like about the white ash besides autumn color, however. For one thing, they can grow as much as 2 feet a year, so gardeners don't have to wait long for their trees to be tall enough to provide shade.

White ash is the largest of the ash trees, rising anywhere from 50 to more than 100 feet when mature. Branches can spread about 50 feet wide, making this deciduous specimen ideal for larger yards, where a lush crop of leaves will cool down sunny decks and patios or provide an oasis in the middle of an open space.

Well-Rounded Selection

Another key quality is the tree's ability to tolerate a wide range of soil conditions. Moist, well-draining loam is preferred, but the white ash can handle clay and sand, too.

It thrives in a variety of climates as well. This North American native can be found throughout eastern Canada and the eastern half of the U.S., from Nova Scotia to Minnesota and as far south as Florida and Texas. It is a common sight in forests and parks from north to south.

Although flowers do bloom in spring, the red or purple clusters lack petals and don't attract much attention. Winged

Michael P. Gadomski/Dembinsky Photo Assoc.

seeds develop later in summer and can be a bit of a nuisance. Seedless varieties such as Autumn Purple are a clean alternative. Other seedless options to try include Autumn Applause and Rosehill, both of which turn a rich, bronze red in fall.

What a Sport

The wood of the white ash is light yet strong and nicely pliable, allowing it to endure storms and high winds better than many other types of trees. These characteristics also make it a top pick for crafting sports equipment like tennis rackets and oars, although it's probably best known as the preferred lumber used to make baseball bats.

Well before becoming an important resource for our national pastime, the white ash was regularly used by Native Americans to shape bows and arrows for hunting. And woodworkers have long relied on the timber to make furniture and cabinets.

Of course, gardeners prefer to enjoy living trees, not lumber. And from its handsome bark to its pleasingly symmetrical crown, the white ash is an asset in any setting.

There aren't any special planting requirements for the white ash, which handles transplanting quite well. Simply select a sunny spot with room for the tree to grow. Once it's in the ground, cover the roots with moistened soil and then top with mulch to help retain moisture.

Continue to water regularly, and don't fertilize until the ash has been in the ground for a year. Once it's fully grown, the tree shouldn't require any fertilizer.

Unfortunately, the white ash is susceptible to several pests and diseases, including various borers, ash plant bug, cankers, leaf rust and anthracnose. One pest of recent concern is the emerald ash borer, which was first discovered in Michigan and has been found in nearby states. Gardeners in these areas should monitor their ash trees, and contact their county Extension service for more information if a problem arises.

It's important to remember that most vigorous specimens don't succumb to these culprits, but it still pays to keep an eye out for any trouble.

Chances are good, though, that your experience with the white ash will be nothing but positive, just like mine has been. And your reward will be year after year of beauty, with a brilliant "fashion show" each fall!

READER TIP

Monitor your white ash, keeping an eye out for pests and diseases. If you suspect a problem, contact your county Extension service for additional information.

Plant Profile

Common Name: White ash.
Botanical Name: *Fraxinus americana*.
Height: 50 or more feet.
Spread: Up to 50 feet.
Leaves: Usually 8 to 12 inches long and composed of five to nine leaflets that are 2 to 6 inches long. Leaflets are oval or spear shaped and finely toothed along the edges. They are dark green on top and lighter underneath, turning purple or yellow in autumn.
Bark: Ashy brown or gray, divided by narrow, interlaced ridges when mature.
Flowers: Inconspicuous, dark-red or purple clusters that appear before leaves in the spring.
Seeds: 1- to 2-inch-long, winged, light-brown seeds that hang in clusters.
Hardiness: Zones 3 to 9.
Light Needs: Full sun.
Soil Type: Prefers moist, well-draining soil, but will tolerate less hospitable conditions as long as water is plentiful.
Planting: Plant balled-and-burlapped trees as soon as possible; container-grown trees can be transplanted throughout the growing season. Dig a hole that is as deep as the tree's roots but three to five times wider. Remove container, burlap, wire or twine and place tree in hole. Fill with existing soil, water and add mulch.

Michael Wendt

PURPLE REIGNS. The white ash has many admirable characteristics, but its typically reddish-purple autumn leaves attract the most attention. Varieties like Autumn Purple (above and opposite page, left) are especially eye-catching. These trees are handsome in other seasons as well with their attractive leaflets (above left) and graceful branching habit (opposite page, right).

Derek Fell; inset: Bill Marchel

ELDERBERRY

Put out the welcome mat for birds with this fruity favorite.

By Deb Mulvey, Associate Editor

Want to turn your backyard into a bird buffet? Planting an elderberry is an easy way to do it. These native plants produce a bounty of berries that birds absolutely love.

Elderberries, or elder, grow wild in woodland borders and thickets in much of North America, providing birds with food, habitat and cover. And they can perform the same function in your home landscape.

There are about 25 species of elderberry, but the type known as American elder (*Sambucus canadensis*) is the best for attracting birds. This species blooms profusely in June and July, producing flat-topped white flower clusters that resemble Queen-Anne's lace.

Beauty, Then Buffet

These clusters, known as cymes, attract butterflies—another backyard bonus. The cymes are so dense that they sometimes cover the plant completely, obscuring the bright-green foliage. As the blossoms fade, they begin forming glossy purplish-black fruits, which ripen in August and September.

Once the fruits appear, keep your binoculars and bird guide handy, because they attract a multitude of species (see the list in "Plant Profile" at right).

Don't worry about running out of berries, though—a single plant is enough to feed a hungry crowd. An American elder produces so much fruit that branches may bend to the ground under the weight of the berries.

Bill Marchel

Derek Fell

BEAUTIFUL BENEFITS. What elderberry lacks in looks, it makes up for with an ability to attract a bounty of interesting birds (like the cedar waxwing left inset). Photos, from left: white flower clusters emerge in spring…berry bunches droop from the branches…unique cultivars like Aurea offer bright-golden foliage.

Growth Spurt

As you might expect with a native plant, the elderberry is fairly easy to grow. Started from seed or suckers (these are shoots that grow from the roots), it can quickly reach 12 feet in height and width.

For home landscapes, the big issue is the American elder's unkempt appearance. The branches arch and sprawl, and suckers pop up constantly. If your goal is to keep this plant looking tidy, you're in for a never-ending task.

While aggressive pruning will keep it in bounds, a more suitable solution is to use it in spots where its "untamed" look won't be an issue.

Naturalized gardens, property lines and fencerows are good choices. A woodland border is even better. This creates a "transitional zone" for birds, luring more of them to nest and feed close to your yard.

Many Choices

If a manicured landscape is your first priority, however, you might be happier with another type of elderberry that offers a more shrublike appearance.

Some varieties of *Sambucus nigra*—also known as black elder or European elder—have a neater, more upright growth habit. The cultivar Gerda, also sold as Black Beauty, produces pink, lemon-scented flowers and purplish-black leaves, and reaches heights of 10 to 12 feet. A type called Black Lace has similar features, but is even more compact at 6 feet.

Another species, *Sambucus racemosa*, known as European red elder, has cone-shaped yellow flower clusters and shiny red fruit. One of the best cultivars, Sutherland Gold, has leaves that are copper colored in spring but turn gold in summer.

These plants won't produce the same bumper crop of berries as American elders, and may need to be cut back in winter or early spring. But they'll still attract birds and butterflies to your yard—and look good doing it.

Plant Profile

Common Names: Elderberry, elder.
Botanical Name: *Sambucus* species.
Height: 5 to 12 feet.
Spread: Up to 12 feet.
Leaves: Bright-green and toothed; some varieties have yellow or purple leaves.
Flowers: Clusters of small white, pink or yellow blooms.
Fruit: Shiny, purplish-black fruits 1/4 inch in diameter appear in August and September. Some cultivars produce red fruit.
Hardiness: Zones 3 to 9.
Light Needs: Full to partial sun. Colored-leaf varieties produce the best color in dappled shade.
Soil Type: Prefers fertile, moist and well draining.
Planting: Plant in spring or fall, or propagate by seeds or suckers.
Prize Picks: American elder Aurea is one of the most attractive cultivars, with golden foliage and cherry-red fruit.
Backyard Benefits: Attracts birds and butterflies. The bird species that eat its berries include: American robin, Baltimore oriole, blue jay, brown thrasher, Carolina wren, cedar waxwing, common grackle, eastern bluebird, eastern towhee, gray catbird, hermit thrush, indigo bunting, mourning dove, northern cardinal, northern flicker, northern mockingbird, red-bellied woodpecker, ring-necked pheasant, rose-breasted grosbeak, ruffed grouse, scarlet tanager, song sparrow, summer tanager, Swainson's thrush, tufted titmouse, wild turkey, wood thrush and yellow-bellied sapsucker.
Warning: All plant parts can cause digestive discomfort if ingested raw, but the fruits are safe to eat if cooked. Contact with leaves can cause skin irritation.

Mark Turner

SHRUBS ADD WINTER 'WOW'

Try these plantings for color that doesn't cool off with the weather.

By Melinda Myers, Contributing Editor

When winter arrives, the beauty of your garden doesn't have to be locked away in cold storage. You can keep your yard bright and interesting by adding a few shrubs with eye-catching seasonal appeal.

The first step is to tour your winter landscape. There's no need to throw on a coat yet—we're starting indoors.

Examine your yard through the windows you use the most during winter. For instance, I always start my day with a cup of coffee in the kitchen. So the view outside that window is important to me.

Now grab your coat and go for a walk through the yard. Look for spots with room to plant shrubs or for flower beds that can be expanded. Note the light and soil conditions of each area so you can match new plants to the growing conditions.

With the chosen spaces in mind, you're now ready to make a list of specific shrubs for your backyard.

Color is a good place to start. The holiday lights and decorations that adorn many homes this time of year are clues that we all crave a little more brilliance in winter. Planting a few shrubs can fill that need.

Bark Is a Pretty Sight

Red twig dogwood, also known as redosier dogwood, is a longtime favorite. It has unique red stems that make a nice backdrop to overwintering perennials or an accent plant for evergreens.

Regular pruning keeps the color vibrant year-round (though in spring and summer, the leaves disguise it). Simply

A FLURRY OF CHOICES. From berries to evergreen leaves, winter shrubs offer plenty of variety. Clockwise from top left: winterberry features vibrant fruit…evergreen holly paints a pretty holiday picture…witch hazel unfurls cold-weather flowers…clusters of purplish berries make beautyberry a unique sight…the crooked branches of Harry Lauder's walking stick stand out once the leaves fall.

remove older brown stems at ground level in late winter. This encourages new growth, which is the most vivid.

The yellow twig variety, Flaviramea, adds a different look to the garden. Just a few of these yellow-stemmed beauties pack a punch in the landscape.

Another shrub with colorful stems is Japanese kerria. Its glossy, bright-green stems are sure to catch a second look. The slender stems stand upright and provide welcome contrast.

But it's not just about color. The texture of the bark can add interest, too. Burning bush, also known as winged euonymus, has stems with corky ridges that look especially pretty after a snowfall. However, gardeners in parts of the Northeast and Midwest, where this plant is invading native woodlands, should avoid using it. Instead, consider its native coun-

terpart, eastern wahoo. Although it lacks the corky bark, it produces small pink and orange fruit.

The oakleaf hydrangea has several attractive features for winter. The coarse textured older stems are covered with peeling, cinnamon-brown bark. This, combined with the dried flowers, creates cold-weather charm.

Another way to increase appeal is with uniquely shaped shrubs. Harry Lauder's walking stick is the first to come to mind. Its curled and twisted stems, which become more apparent after the leaves have fallen, make this a nice focal point in a patio garden, mixed border or foundation planting. Remove any straight stems that sprout from the roots beneath the graft.

Serving Up Fruit

One of the most common ways to create a bright spot amid the snow is with fruit-bearing shrubs. You'll appreciate the color—birds will appreciate the food.

Holly is the traditional berry for the holidays, and these shrubs (and trees) come in many evergreen varieties that also produce colorful fruit.

Southern gardeners have a wider selection of evergreen types that work in warmer climates. Northern gardeners need to look for hardier cultivars of the Meserve hollies, such as China Boy, China Girl, Blue Boy, Blue Girl, Blue Prince and Blue Princess. As the names imply, there are both male and female plants. I suggest at least one male for every five females to help guarantee fruit.

A hardier alternative is the deciduous holly, known as winterberry. The lack of leaves in winter is not a problem, since red fruit covers the upright stems.

And take a second look at the off-season potential of a longtime garden staple—the rose. Not only are the rose hips colorful, but you can also gather some of the hip-covered stems

These 19 Shrubs Shine in Winter

Name	Hardiness/Zone	Size	Light Needs
Beautyberry (*Callicarpa*)	5 to 8	4 to 10 ft. tall; 4 to 6 feet wide	Full sun to partial shade
Burning bush (*Euonymous alatus*)	4 to 8	Up to 15 to 20 ft. tall and wide	Full sun to partial shade
Chokeberry (*Aronia*)	3 to 9	6 to 10 ft. tall; 3 to 5 ft. wide	Full sun to partial shade
Eastern wahoo (*Euonymus atropurpureus*)	4 to 9	12 to 24 ft. tall; half as wide	Full sun to partial shade
Harry Lauder's walking stick (*Corylus avellana* 'Contorta')	4 to 8	8 to 10 ft. tall and wide	Full sun to light shade
Meserve hollies (*Ilex* x *meserve*)	5 to 9	Up to 12 ft. tall and wide	Full sun to partial shade
Hydrangea, oakleaf (*Hydrangea quercifolia*)	5 to 9	4 to 6 ft. tall and wide	Full sun to partial shade
Hydrangea, panicle (*Hydrangea paniculata*)	3 to 8	Up to 15 to 20 ft. tall; 10 to 20 ft. wide	Full sun to partial shade
Hydrangea, snowball (*Hydrangea arborescens*)	3 to 9	3 to 5 ft. tall and wide	Partial shade to full sun
Kerria (*Kerria japonica*)	4 to 9	3 to 6 ft. tall; 6 to 9 ft. wide	Full sun to full shade
Northern bayberry (*Myrica pennsylvanica*)	3 to 6	5 to 12 ft. tall and wide	Full sun to half shade
Red twig dogwood (*Cornus sericea*)	4 to 8	Up to 10 to 15 ft. tall and wide	Full shade or sun
Running serviceberry (*Amelanchier stolonifera*)	4 to 8	4 to 6 ft. tall and wide	Full sun to partial shade
Shrub roses (*Rosa* species)	2 to 9*	Up to 10 ft. tall	Full sun
Southern wax myrtle (*Myrica cerifera*)	8 to 9	10 to 15 ft. tall and wide	Full sun to partial shade
Viburnums (*Viburnum* species)	3 to 9*	Up to 15 ft. tall and 12 ft. wide	Full sun to partial shade
Winterberry (*Ilex verticillata*)	3 to 9	6 to 10 ft. tall and wide	Full sun to partial shade
Witch hazel, common (*Hamamelis virginiana*)	3 to 8	15 to 20 ft. tall and wide	Full sun or shade
Witch hazel, vernal (*Hamamelis vernalis*)	4 to 8	6 to 10 ft. tall and wide	Full sun or shade

*size and hardiness varies with species

for unique indoor arrangements.

The colorful fruit of beautyberry adds a seldom-seen pinkish-purple hue to the winterscape. For the best fruit display, prune regularly and avoid excess fertilizing.

When selecting this plant, look for the American beautyberry, which puts on a good show of berries. But if you like a challenge, search for the purple beautybush (*Callicarpa dichotoma*). It's more difficult to find, but its graceful appearance and impressive fruit display will make the effort worthwhile.

Cool Flowers

Hydrangeas, a shade-garden favorite, take on new character in winter. Both the snowball and panicle types produce flowers that dry on the plant. These brown blooms and tiny, capsule-like fruit provide a nice contrast to the fine texture of nearby overwintering ornamental grasses or perennials.

And let's not forget about flowers. No, I'm not just speaking for southern landscapes. Most gardeners can enjoy the fall and winter blooms of witch hazel. Common witch hazel unfurls fragrant, strap-like flowers for about a month between October and December.

For those who like an early start to the growing season, plant vernal witch hazel. These long bloomers start flowering as early as January in the South, to late February or March in the North. The blooms last for 3 to 4 weeks, providing a much-needed winter flower fix.

Ever-Popular Evergreens

We can't discuss winter shrubs without at least mentioning evergreen conifers. They've long been the backbone of a winter garden, providing a green ray of hope in otherwise barren landscapes.

Although thousands of varieties provide virtually endless possibilities, there are a few basic pointers for selecting the right conifers for your yard.

Look for dwarf pines, spruces or junipers for hot sunny locations. Arborvitae and false cypress add texture with their somewhat lacy appearances. And hemlocks and boxwood provide a bit of year-round greenery in sunny or shady locations.

These shrubs also form great backdrops to the other colorful and interesting shrubs we've discussed. For a winter yard that really stands out, consider planting mixed borders of evergreens, deciduous shrubs and perennials.

Each will lend its own form of beauty to awaken your slumbering yard. ◂

READER TIP

Create a bright spot in your yard during the winter with fruit-bearing shrubs. You'll love the color, and the birds will appreciate the food.

Chapter 8

HSP Photo

TREE TRIMMING KNOW-HOW

With the right tools and techniques, a professional-quality tree trimming job is a snap.

By Jean Bartholome, Durango, Colorado

Trees are an important part of any yard. And as any tree owner knows, they need occasional trimming. Properly done, trimming controls the shape of the tree, keeps the tree healthy, and eliminates branches that endanger property or could potentially interfere with overhead wires or nearby structures.

Rather than using the haphazard hacking approach, with the right equipment and a little patience, you can trim your own trees and save a bundle over hiring a professional tree trimmer.

A word of advice: The most common mistake is to over-trim a long-neglected tree. If you haven't had the pruning saw out for a long time, take it easy! Your tree will thank you.

The Anatomy of a Tree

In trimming, the most important parts of the tree are the buds (Fig. A and inset). The direction the tree will grow is determined by the buds. When trimming, spare the buds that are pointed in the direction you want the tree to grow.

The terminal (end) buds continue the outward or upward growth. The removal of a terminal bud causes the growth of side branches, making the tree bushier.

Buds that lie dormant for many years are called latent buds. They may only start to grow after the tree has sustained damage to other branches.

Proper Trimming Technique

The photo on page 231 (far right)) shows the best way to trim a branch larger than 2 inches. The initial undercut is important, as it prevents the weight of a branch from pulling a strip of bark off the tree. Your goal is a cut that's close to the trunk, angled up and flush with the branch collar (Fig. B).

When to Cut

The best time to trim living branches (dead branches can be trimmed any time) is late winter, when the tree is dormant, or very early in the spring prior to new growth. Technically, most trees can be trimmed any time, but some trees are more susceptible to disease and infestation if trimmed in the summer. Elms and oaks should be trimmed in dormant season to reduce the chance of developing Dutch elm disease or oak wilt.

What to Cut

When you're ready to trim, you'll have to decide what to cut and what to leave alone. You should look for:

■ **Dead or dying branches.** Cut them back to another healthy branch or back to the main trunk. If trimming a diseased tree, be sure to disinfect tools between each cut.

■ **Branch stubs.** Remove all too-long stubs back to the nearest healthy branch or trunk.

■ **Chances to correct the tree's shape.** Familiarize yourself with how the tree should look naturally. An ideal tree has a strong central trunk and scaffold limbs that are spaced along the trunk with no two of them directly above and shading the other branches.

■ **Branches growing too close together.** The process of removing excess branches is called thinning. It opens up the tree to let in air and light for the leaves on the inside and lower portions of the tree, improving fruit and flower production.

■ **Rubbing branches.** Remove any branches that rub against each other or might in the future. These branches often develop open wounds where insects can enter and disease can start.

■ **Suckers and water sprouts** (see Fig. A). Remove any suckers growing at the base and trunk of the tree, as well as water sprouts that grow on branches vertical to the trunk.

■ **Weak crotches.** Remove branches that have weak or narrow-angle (less than 30 degrees) crotches. These branches are the most likely to tear away in storms, damaging the bark and nearby branches.

Fig. A
Tree Terminology

TERMINAL BUDS

NEW WOOD

RUBBING BRANCHES

STUB

WATER SPROUTS

SCAFFOLD BRANCH

WEAK CROTCH

MAIN BRANCH, LEADER, OR TRUNK

SUCKERS

TERMINAL BUD

LATENT (DORMANT) BUD

LATERAL BUDS

Illustrations: Ron Chamberlain/Lisa Pahl-Knecht

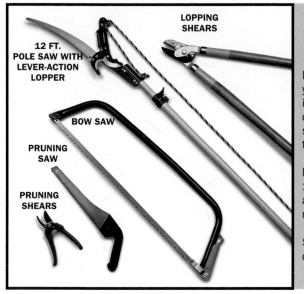

12 FT. POLE SAW WITH LEVER-ACTION LOPPER

LOPPING SHEARS

BOW SAW

PRUNING SAW

PRUNING SHEARS

The Right Tools Make All the Difference

If you buy a few moderately priced tools and rent others as needed, you'll be able to properly maintain your trees for years. With good pruning shears (around $20), you'll be able to cut flush with the branch collar. Position the thin blade on the trunk side to keep the resulting stub as short as you want it to be. Use the shears for branches up to a 1/2 inch thick.

If you have to struggle with the shears, you should move up to the lopping shears (around $45). You'll be able to cut branches around 1-inch thick with loppers. For larger branches, use a pruning saw or a bow saw. Never use a regular shop saw because it will require much more effort and it won't do a good job.

For really high branches, you can rent ($25 per day) or buy (around $48) a pole saw. Some have a small curved saw on the end and others have a cord- or rod-operated lever-action pruning shear.

What About Safety?

First off, always wear eye protection and gloves when trimming trees. Second, stay away from all utility wires.

If you must remove a large limb over a patio or close to your house or garage, take steps to reduce the risk of damage as it drops. One good way to control the drop is to tie a rope around the limb to be cut and throw the other end of the rope over a higher limb. Have a helper keep just enough tension on the rope to control the limb without binding the saw blade. Caution: Watch for the thick end of the limb as it falls. If the job just seems too dangerous to tackle yourself, don't hesitate to call a certified arborist.

Fig. B Cutting Technique

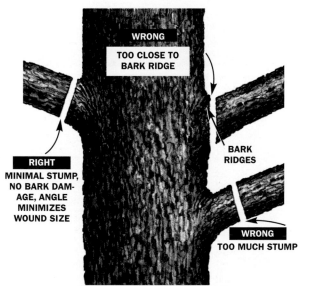

WRONG
TOO CLOSE TO BARK RIDGE

RIGHT
MINIMAL STUMP, NO BARK DAMAGE, ANGLE MINIMIZES WOUND SIZE

BARK RIDGES

WRONG
TOO MUCH STUMP

RIGHT AND WRONG. Correct cutting technique prevents damage to the bark and bark ridges, leaving a clean, slightly angled cut that produces the smallest wound, and avoids long stumps, which are avenues for insect infestation and rot. For the best results, always use sharp tools for the cleanest cuts.

SECOND CUT

FIRST CUT

THIRD CUT

BRANCH COLLAR

EASY AS 1-2-3. Remove a limb using the three-cut method. Make the first cut (an undercut) from below, about 12 inches from the trunk and approximately one-third of the limb's thickness. Make the second cut from above, about 1 inch out from the undercut, going completely through the limb. Then the third cut removes the small remaining piece of limb.

READER TIP

If you are trimming a diseased tree, be sure to disinfect your tools between each cut.

—**Jean Bartholome, Durango, Colorado**

234

246

244

RDA, INC.; top photo, Mike Grandmaison

240

237

Terry Wild

THE BEST OF BIRDS & BLOOMS

SECRETS TO COLORFUL CONTAINERS

The splash of a container garden adds brilliance where you least expect it. Here's how to help yours steal the show.

By Melinda Myers, Contributing Editor

I've been growing plants in containers for as long as I've been gardening. My first container garden started on the balcony of my apartment.

Now that I have my own backyard, modest as it may be, I still rely on containers.

To me, they're the perfect way to brighten up your front entrance, expand a vegetable garden or soften your deck, porch or patio. Often, I'll use containers to add color and interest to areas that need instant color. One of my favorite tricks is placing pots of annuals among ground cover or in flower beds to add additional color and a new dimension.

If you haven't tried container gardening, you're missing out on the fun. And I'll let you in on a secret…it's easy!

Location, Location, Location

Before starting, I recommend taking a simple walk around your house. Are there entrances you want to highlight? Views you want to block or spots that need a bit more color? If the answer is yes to any of these, then containers are the perfect answer.

But remember, just like selling a home or planting a garden, there's no doubt location is the most important factor to success.

Container gardens can be grown in sun or shade. Just match the plants to the light, and you already have put yourself in position for quick success.

And, I'll save you some frustration—avoid windy locations that can break tall plants, increase water needs and even knock over and crack the pots. I know because I learned the hard way.

Everything…Plus the Kitchen Sink

Once you've determined where you're going to use containers, it's time to think about what kinds of pots will work the best.

Plain pots, even black nursery pots, make the plants the star. Decorative pots complement your decor, so look for plants that mix with their style, too. And don't forget to check out neighborhood yard sales. Old boots, coffeepots, weathered barrels, an old kitchen sink and other recycled items can have new life as garden containers.

Here are a few tips for selecting the right container for your plants:

Always provide drainage holes. This prevents water from collecting in the bottom, which could lead to root rot and the early death of your plant. If your pot doesn't have drainage holes, drill a couple in the bottom yourself using a cordless drill.

Complement your garden. Select pots that blend well with your gardens. Unglazed clay pots are heavy and dry out faster than other materials. Plastic, fiberglass, metal and other materials reduce watering chores because they cut down on evaporation and help hold the moisture in the soil longer.

Select lightweight pots. This way, you can move them around in your backyard. This is also important if you're going to display them on a balcony, where you'll want to keep weight to a minimum.

Bigger is better. Select a container large enough to fill the space and hold the plants you select. Small containers require frequent watering and often get lost or look out of place in the landscape.

Fill It Up

Even more important than selecting the right container, is

WELCOMING ENTRYWAY. Numerous pots of brilliant annuals can liven up even a modest front entrance. The containers are easy to maintain and the payoff is instant curb appeal.

WHAT IS INSIDE COUNTS. Potting mix that drains well, not garden or topsoil, is the most important ingredient to healthy container plantings.

TAME THE BULLIES. Aggressive plants can take over a container. Trimming back the overgrown coleus (above) created a more balanced container in about 2 weeks.

what goes inside. Don't take a shovel of garden soil and toss it in a pot. The drainage, water-holding ability and growing conditions in a pot are drastically different from your regular garden. Containers require a special mix. You can make your own potting mix or purchase a container mix at the garden center. Most ready-to-use potting mixes contain basically the same ingredients: perlite and/or vermiculite mixed with peat moss. Some have fertilizer added and many have water-holding polymers, a great addition that helps reduce watering needs.

Planting mix with good drainage and water-holding ability will minimize your work. Unfortunately, all the bags look basically the same, so experience, yours or others', may be your best guide.

If you prefer to blend your own potting mix, follow this basic step-by-step recipe:

1. Combine 1/3 peat moss, 1/3 perlite or vermiculite and 1/3 garden soil. If you have some already, you may substitute compost for peat moss.
2. Mix it well in a wheel barrow, on a potting table or in another large container.
3. Add more peat moss or vermiculite, if needed, to help increase drainage.
4. Mix in water-holding crystals to keep soil from drying out quickly.

Time for Design

To me, this is when the real fun begins. Just about any plant will do well in a container if it receives the light it needs and the proper amount of water. With a little planning, container gardens will look their best and require less work.

Here are the basics you should think about before you start planting:

Look for perfect matches. Combine plants that have the same light and water needs, making sure they are the right choice for the light, wind and temperatures of the location you've selected.

Save water…and chores. Drought-tolerant plants are perfect for beginning container gardeners. Moss roses, zinnias and gazania are more tolerant if you need a forgiving watering schedule.

No bullies. Use plants that are equally assertive. Otherwise, fast-growing plants take over and hide their more timid neighbors.

Maintaining Good Looks

Because they dry out fast, containers should be checked daily to see if they need watering. Use your fingers as a moisture meter. If the top few inches of soil feel crumbly yet slightly damp, it is time to water.

Water thoroughly until excess water runs out the bottom drain holes. Here are some more tips for outstanding container gardens with less work:

Group near water. Be sure containers are close to a water source. Try my favorite shortcut—empty your dehumidifier water into a watering can and use that to water containers. Two chores, one step!

Give them a boost. Poor growth, lack of flowers and pale leaves may indicate your plants need a nutrient boost.

To save time, guesswork and the mess of mixing and applying fertilizer, mix slow-release fertilizer into the soil at planting time.

If you missed this opportunity, just sprinkle some on the soil surface even after it's planted.

If you like to mix and apply the fertilizer yourself, check out one of many fertilizers at your garden center. You can either apply a small amount often, or use a stronger concentration less frequently. Let your plants and the fertilizer label be your guide.

Routine chores. Deadhead, trim back and control weeds in your containers just like other gardens. Because container gardens can be moved, soilless mixes are weed free and the smaller size makes the chores manageable, they work for even for the busiest schedules.

Now you're armed with all you need to know to get a container garden off to a great start. Look through the garage, check out a few yard sales or pick up a few pots at your area garden center. Then fill 'em up and watch a beautiful container garden bloom.

Secret Ingredients for Container Combos

Container gardening may not be a perfect science, but there are three basic ingredients—vertical, filler and trailing plants. Mix those together in one container and you're virtually guaranteed a perfect combination.

Vertical accents. Look for tall, narrow plants, or consider growing a vine on a small trellis for your vertical accent.

Keep in mind that tall plants may need support. To keep them from tipping, try adding some extra weight, such as a rock, for ballast.

Trailing plants. These plants anchor a container and soften the look. Like your vertical accent, it's important to remember to pick something that doesn't take over the container.

Filler plants. The remaining space between vertical and trailing plants should be packed with fillers. These are medium-sized plants that round out the container.

Fillers give containers personality. Color echoing, repeating the color or foliage of the vertical or cascading plant, is a great way to tie it all together. You can also select contrasting colors for a visual punch or mellow it out with plants in complementary colors. The options are endless.

Here are my favorite surefire container picks that can be mixed and matched. It's that easy!

Vertical Plants	Trailing Plants	Filler Plants
Bronze fennel	Dichondra	Coleus
Dwarf papyrus	Lamium	Geranium
Ornamental grasses	Licorice vine	Impatiens
Purple Majesty millet	Petunia	Penta
Spike (Dracaena)	Sweet potato vine	Verbena

BEAT THE HEAT

Blazing sun and drought wilting your garden? Don't worry...here are answers for an always refreshing summer garden.

By Julie Drysdale, Aptos, California

It's hot out there! Whether you garden in a naturally arid climate, or a dry spell moves in and overstays its welcome, heat is supremely stressful on backyard plants across the country.

Surely, you feel the effects of heat, too. When outdoors without the protection of shade and sufficient water, our bodies begin to feel weak and woozy. We begin to wilt.

The same fate befalls our garden plants. And if there is no relief, once-vibrant flowers drop, leaves droop, and the plants eventually collapse and perish.

If this discouraging scenario takes a toll on your garden in summer, you might be tempted to do the obvious—pour on the moisture with frequent waterings. That is, if your area doesn't have water-use restrictions, or if your water bill isn't already sky-high.

There's good news...plan ahead, and you won't have to douse your thirsty plants. A much better solution is to grow flowers that stand up to the heat. With the right selections, you'll have plants that put on a terrific show even through the blazing, dog days of summer.

That leaves you with only one worry—keeping *yourself* well-hydrated. And don't forget the hat and sunscreen when you go outdoors to enjoy your vibrant heat-resistant garden.

Pick the Right Plants

Contrary to what most people think, you don't need cactus and a desert landscape to have a heat-tolerant garden. Though cacti and succulents are well suited for these conditions, and even occasionally produce bright flowers, they may not be your first choice. Or, your area's climate may be too humid or cold for them to survive. Luckily, there are plenty of other flowering plants that can beautify your yard in a hot summer season. (See our top 12 picks on page 239.)

If heat is a yearly problem in your garden, begin by choosing plants that are known to stand up to hot and dry conditions. There are many, and they share certain key qualities:

Smaller flowers and leaves. Smaller flowers mean smaller petals, and narrow leaves mean less surface area for evaporation. Ideally, look for plants that produce lots of small flowers, so the show is bountiful and their color makes an impressive impression, even from across the yard.

Strong root systems. Another quality that helps plants tol-

erate heat is below the soil line. It's in the roots of the plant.

Root systems of drought- and heat-tolerant plants tend to be stockier and to grow deeper and wider. This makes sense when you imagine the stress that dried-out soil can cause. Thin and wispy roots, or shallow ones, simply won't survive these tough conditions.

So seek out plants that are clearly labeled as adapted to

A LITTLE BREAK. Even the hardiest plants that survive hot dry conditions need a little relief from the blazing sun. A fence (below), lattice or a trellis offer a bit of welcome shade in sunny areas.

Terry Wild

Starve 'Em When It's Hot!

Hot, dry weather is the worst possible time to fertilize your flower garden. This is because plant roots respond to the difficult conditions by slowing or shutting down, and the nitrates in plant foods will only injure them in this state.

You could try fertilizing earlier in the year, before the blazing weather arrives, but that may only produce a flush of tender growth that is much more easily scorched or killed than hardened older plant tissues. It is better not to feed at all...or, if you feel you must, use a slow-release fertilizer early in the season.

dry climates, including desert natives, dry-meadow natives, prairie natives and plants that survive at high altitudes.

Incidentally, if you purchase seeds or plants of wildlings from the local native-plant nursery, don't worry about them looking as weedy as they might in nature. Garden conditions are always less stressful, and you will be pleasantly surprised at how beautiful they turn out to be when treated to a better life. This is especially true of garden-grown penstemons and coreopsis.

Also, it pays to seek out cultivars (cultivated varieties) of suitable native plants. These have been selected or bred to be better looking, with more compact growth habits, showier flowers, longer bloom periods—or all of the above. A perfect candidate is the prairie coneflower, which has seen a flurry of pretty new introductions in nurseries and mail-order catalogs in recent years.

A Fighting Chance

The best part of heat-resistant gardens is that extra effort on your part is not a requirement. Here's all you need to do:

Choose the right site. Even plants billed as sun-lovers need a little relief, especially at midday. So the number one rule is to avoid growing them in a full sun, especially on south-facing exposures. Part-day shade minimizes stress and also preserves flower color longer. So choose a spot where your house, garden shed, or even a tree or shrub, casts some shade at some point during the day. You may want to build a fence, lattice or trellis to help.

Improve the soil. Few plants actually enjoy dry, dusty nutrient-poor soil and hot conditions.

While you can't change the heat, you can change the growing medium. Work in plenty of organic matter prior to planting. This not only improves the soil texture, fertility and its ability to retain any moisture, it also helps the soil stay cooler. This should be an annual task.

Protect the vulnerable. Just-planted flowers are very susceptible to damage from a heat wave. It's important to give them a little extra shelter for their first few weeks. Temporary shelter works just fine, such as lawn chairs or boxes that create a bit of shade and shield them from drying winds.

Mulch! You may think of mulch for mainly fall or winter plant protection, but it's just as important to plant survival in very hot summer weather. Mulch keeps resource-stealing weeds at bay and retains whatever moisture there may be for your plants.

An inch or two can make a world of difference. If you can't cover the entire garden bed, at least sprinkle mulch over the root area of each plant. Use natural mulch, from bark chips to herbi-

Ben Phillips/Positive Images

238

cide-free grass clippings, but avoid pebbles and stone because they tend to soak up and reflect heat.

Water Works

Scientists studying the effects of heat and drought on plants have made an interesting discovery. Only about 10 percent of water supplied is actually retained by a plant in the best of circumstances. The remaining 90 percent is lost through evaporation and transpiration. This is not wasted water, however—it is used to cool the plant.

While 10 percent seems like a small amount of water to retain, the plants, especially flowering ones, need that small amount to survive and thrive. They drink it from the soil, with the roots moving the moisture upward into the leaves.

A plant naturally gives priority to feeding its leaves before developing buds or open flowers. This is why you see heat-stressed plants jettisoning buds and flower petals first.

If heat stress is bad enough, the next thing you'll see is damage to the leaves. Their edges and tips will appear scorched and brown, or entire leaves will wilt. In the final stage, the leaves will simply fall off the plant, dry and dead.

You don't want things to come to this point, of course. Proper, not indiscriminate, watering will help a lot. Instead of frequent, shallow watering sessions, soak your plants slowly over a few hours, with a trickle from the hose, soaker hose or a sprinkler set on low.

If your flower garden is large, consider investing in an in-ground irrigation system. These are regulated with a timer. (For containers, consider a drip-water system.)

In any event, always water at ground level so as much water as possible will soak into the root area. The watering area should be extended at least as far out as the plant's spread above the ground, and sometimes even a little farther so all the roots are moistened.

For the best floral display, remember to supply as much water as you are able to when you spot buds on your plants—this will allow them to plump up, develop properly, produce more color and finally, unfurl their very welcome beauty in your garden.

12 Tough-as-Nails, Drought-Tolerant Flowers

Annuals

1. California poppy. Though the deep-orange petals of this beautiful wildflower are silky and large compared to some heat-tolerant plants, they hold up very well. The ferny, somewhat succulent foliage is light blue to green.

2. Fan flower. These plants have a nice trailing habit, dense foliage of small, narrow leaves, and loads of small, fan-like flowers that are usually purple or blue. Some varieties have an accenting white dot. The plant is very durable.

3. Mexican sunflower. Forms a clump 3 or more feet wide and high, with somewhat coarse leaves. It's studded with bright-orange or red 4-inch daisies starting in late summer. Hummingbirds and butterflies flock to them!

4. Moss rose. Though the flowers are not large (no more than an inch across) and are carried on spreading, low stems of fleshy leaves, these plants are very charming. Flowers come in many bright hues, including yellow, orange, red, hot pink, purple and white.

5. Strawflower. Papery flower heads look great in the garden and in a vase, fresh or dried. They come in red, pink, white and yellow. Small, lance-shaped grayish leaves accompany them.

6. Zinnia. Bushy plants with tough, durable leaves and reliably perky flowers. The colors are always bright. Butterflies love them!

Perennials

7. Artemisia. Valued for their beautiful silver leaves on tall arching stems or low "cushion" mounds. These plants are reliably tough and trouble-free. Hardiness Zones 4-8.

8. Blanket flower. Perky daisies in yellow, red and orange. The stems are stiff, the leaves coarse and the plants bushy. Hardiness Zones 3-9.

9. Coreopsis. Scads of pretty little yellow daisies cover an airy mound of thin-needled foliage. Hardiness Zones 3-9.

10. Lavender. Stiff, gray-green leaves on mounding plants that are often taller than they are wide. The hauntingly fragrant flower spikes come in various shades of purple as well as plain white. Hardiness Zones 5-9.

11. Penstemon. Arching stems laden with showy, tubular flowers that attract hummingbirds. The plants can get tall (up to 4 feet) and rather shrubby in habit. Hardiness Zones 4-8.

12. Yarrow. Lacy, flat-topped flower clusters and thin, feathery sage-green foliage. Usually white or yellow, though other colors are available. Hardiness Zones 3-8.

'GLAD YOU ASKED!'

Our experts answer your most common questions.

By George Harrison and Melinda Myers,
Contributing Editors

Bald Bird

This strange looking cardinal (below) has visited my yard for the past two summers. Why does it look this way? —*T. Markman, Chagrin Falls, Ohio*

George: This male northern cardinal has a parasite problem that causes it to lose the feathers on its head, exposing the dark skin underneath. This is a very common condition that's most seen among cardinals, blue jays and other songbirds.

The feathers will eventually grow back, and the cardinal will survive. But during the several weeks that it takes for the new feathers to appear, the bird looks ill. I often remark that we have a "Frankenstein cardinal" when we see a bird with this condition in our yard.

Multitasking Tree

I'd like to plant a tall-growing deciduous tree near my deck. Can you recommend one that will flower and produce the kind of berries birds enjoy? —*Lottie Edwine, Rapid City, South Dakota*

Melinda: Look for a tree that's suitable to your growing conditions, hardy to your area and doesn't create a mess with its fruit.

Serviceberry (botanically known as *Amelanchier*) is tolerant of partial shade and hardy in Zones 2 to 9. It produces blueberry-like fruit that the birds will pick clean off the tree. The size varies with the cultivar selected.

European mountain ash (*Sorbus aucuparia*) grows 20 to 40 feet tall, prefers cool, moist soils in the summer and is hardy in Zones 3 to 7. Many birds, but especially cedar waxwings, enjoy its fruit.

A close relative that's more tolerant of hot, dry summers is the Korean mountain ash (*Sorbus alnifolia*). Hardy in Zones 4 to 7, it can reach heights of 40 feet. It has bright, pinkish-red fruit and beautiful fall color.

And don't forget about crabapples. Select cultivars bred for their disease resistance and persistent fruit. Some, like Birdland, are especially attractive to birds. Visit a reliable nursery to find the cultivar that best suits your needs.

Show Your True Colors

I know American goldfinches lose their bright-yellow feathers in winter. So why do some birds, like northern cardinals and blue jays, keep their bright plumage all year?
—Ethel Richards, Poland, Ohio

George: American goldfinches turn olive-brown in winter for protective coloration against predators. They're bright in the summer, when bolder colors abound, to attract mates and defend territories. Once breeding season is over, they don drabber feathers to match their surroundings.

Although appearing bright to our eyes, the feathers of northern cardinals and blue jays must provide whatever protection these birds need. Keep in mind that animals see color differently than humans.

Woodland Wonder

I found this wildflower (below) growing under a canopy of cedar trees. What is this beautiful plant?
—Marilyn Bilsbarro, Dryden, Ontario

Melinda: What a lucky find! This native fairy slipper orchid is primarily found in Canada and Alaska, with a few localized populations elsewhere in the United States. Its numbers are dwindling, especially in the southern parts of its range.

Watch for these natives to appear in cedar (*Thuja*) swamps or dry pine, fir and cedar woods. The fairy slipper (*Calypso bulbosa*) prefers cool soils and doesn't tolerate close contact with human activities. For more information about this and other native Canadian orchids, visit *www.osrbg.ca/orchid_native.html*.

Just Stopping By

Will you help us identify the hawk (above right) we spotted in our backyard? We were thrilled to see it until we realized it was hunting the birds at our feeder, so we took down the feeder until the hawk left. Is there anything else we should have done?
—Robert Keller, Scottsbluff, Nebraska

George: I believe that your large visitor was a juvenile northern goshawk, a bird that spends most of its life in the Rocky Mountains and northern regions into Canada and Alaska.

Occasionally, these raptors will move south in search of food, which includes songbirds, squirrels and rabbits.

Because the bird was just passing through, the most damage it could have done was to take a couple of mourning doves or juncos.

Witnessing a hawk hunt your favorite songbirds can be upsetting, but it's important to remember that they have to eat, too, and it is all part of the balance of nature.

If you'd like to help protect your songbirds against future hawk visitors, provide dense shrubs for cover near the feeders. Small birds can retreat into the branches for protection.

Backward Blooming

Every summer, I set my pots of bougainvillea outside, but never get more than a couple of the colorful bracts. In winter, however, they spring to life. How can I coax the plants to produce beautiful fuchsia-colored bracts outdoors?
—Kathy Phipps
Tulsa, Oklahoma

Melinda: Bougainvillea's beautiful bracts, what most gardeners call flowers, are a colorful addition to northern and southern gardens. These plants grow well in containers, but need to be moved indoors before the temperatures drop below 40°.

The plants require sun, warmth and regular fertilization to bloom. There are a few things you can try to encourage bracts to form in summer, rather than during winter.

Switch to a balanced or flowering plant fertilizer. This will avoid adding excess nitrogen, which can delay blooming.

Another suggestion is to keep the soil slightly dry. This

will often encourage blooming.

Also, try pruning the plant in spring. The pruning promotes new growth where the flowers will develop.

As evening temperatures increase to about 70°, the warmth initiates flowering, and blossoms (like the ones at left) appear in a couple of months. Make the needed adjustments, and you might be able to coax your plant to bloom earlier in the season.

Clean House

A family of wrens nested in my birdhouse several years ago, but I haven't seen any since. Do wren houses need to be cleaned out after nesting season? If so, how do I go about cleaning them?
—*Nancy Fields, Isanti, Minnesota*

George: You can clean out a wren house like any other birdhouse. Remove a panel, take out all the contents, wash out dirt or parasites and reassemble the house. Doing this after the nesting season gets rid of insects or other debris that might discourage birds from nesting in it next spring.

In the case of wrens, however, researchers have found that leaving a couple of sticks in the house improves the chances of a wren using it again for future nesting. Apparently, the wren believes that if the house was used in the past, it must be a good place to nest.

Reblooming Poinsettia

My poinsettia plant lost all its bright-red foliage. Should I trim it back so it will bloom for me again next Christmas?
—*Isaac Zook*
Gordonville, Pennsylvania

Melinda: Continue to grow your poinsettia in a sunny window, watering it thoroughly and often, enough to keep the soil slightly moist. Encourage fuller growth by cutting it back to 4 to 6 inches in mid-March.

Once the danger of frost has passed, you may move your plant outdoors. Just bring it inside before the first fall frost.

Then fertilize occasionally in spring and early summer with a flowering plant fertilizer.

Starting October 1, cover the plant or move it to a dark location where it can receive 14 hours of complete darkness each night. During the day, uncover and place the plant in a sunny window or under artificial lights.

Continue this process until the top bracts (the petal-like leaves) are fully colored. Keep the soil slightly dry and temperatures a bit cooler during the dark treatments for even greater success.

Every missed dark treatment delays the bloom by 1 day. But don't give up if you miss a couple of days. You can always go for a Valentine's Day poinsettia and start a new trend!

Two-Time Nesting

Last year, we had an eastern phoebe build two nests in the rafters over our deck. In one nest, we saw her caring for three fledglings. In the other nest, she incubated three eggs, sitting on them at night. Is it common for phoebes to make two nests?
—*Sharon Dennison, La Plata, Maryland*

George: Phoebes normally raise two broods each summer, but not at the same time. One possibility is that the pair you witnessed started on the second nest when the fledglings in the first nest were ready to fly.

In that case, the male would feed the youngsters, while the female incubated eggs in the new nest. Male and female phoebes look alike, so it would be impossible to tell the parents apart.

It is common, however, for phoebes to construct multiple nests. They are known for their lack of orientation, and often build several nests on one rafter before deciding which one to use.

In addition, sometimes the female will lay three eggs in one nest and one egg in another, but both nests will not be successful.

Out of the Zone

I harvested a few seed pods from a Japanese iris while visiting New York. So far, the resulting plants are doing well at my Florida home, but will they continue to grow in this climate?
—*Vito Derasmo*
Sebastian, Florida

Melinda: Japanese iris can grow as far south as Zones 9 and possibly 10. Many gardeners in mild climates will grow the iris in pots so they can keep them out of the wet, boggy soils in winter.

However, since your plant came from a northern garden, it may be a cultivar more suited for the north, or it could have difficulty adjusting to your warmer climate. This is just another gardening situation where you will have to wait and see what happens.

And be patient. It can take 4 to 5 years for iris to flower when grown from a seed pod. To increase your chance of success, keep the plants somewhat dry during the dormant period when they aren't actively growing.

Change of Appetite?

My mother always told me that bluebirds won't visit feeders because they don't eat seeds. So I was really surprised to see several eastern bluebirds lined up on my feeder one fall day (above). Do you have any idea what would draw them there?
—*Debbie Nagle, Dimock, Pennsylvania*

George: Your mother was right—it is rare to see these birds at seed feeders. Bluebirds mostly eat insects and fruits. The visitors at your feeder that day were probably searching for worms, grubs or larvae in the seed.

I suspect the seed got wet and attracted insects that laid eggs and hatched larvae. I'm sure it was a treat for those bluebirds, and you can be confident your mother was true to her word.

Look What Sprouted

To spice up our yard, we planted a wildflower seed mix. These purple flowers (below) came up, but we don't know what they are. Can you tell us?
—*Dave Clevenger, Laguna Beach, California*

Melinda: Your mystery plant is globe gilia, also known as blue or Queen Anne's thimbles (its botanical name is *Gilia capitata*).

This beauty tolerates hot and dry conditions, and is a native of western North America. A relative of phlox, it blooms from June through October and works well in native flower gardens, informal plantings and water-wise landscapes.

This annual will reseed itself in gardens where the soil is not disturbed. This allows the seedlings to sprout and develop into mature, flowering plants.

Back of the Book BONUS

Unwanted Alarm

My friend has a problem with a woodpecker that wakes her each morning by knocking its bill on her metal chimney. Do you have any suggestions to stop it?
—*Rosemary Brown, Dickson, Tennessee*

George: Although it may not seem like it at 5:30 a.m., think of the noise the woodpecker makes on the chimney as its song. It uses the sound to attract and court females and establish a breeding territory.

The noise will end when the breeding season ends, in mid- to late summer. In the meantime, try covering the chimney with a wire mesh that has small holes the woodpecker can't penetrate (like hardware cloth). This should stop the noise.

In fact, any kind of temporary enclosure around the chimney should keep the woodpecker—and your friend's mornings—quiet.

Orange Surprise

This bright-orange plant (below) appears in my garden every year. Can you tell me what it is?
—*Joan Langille, Truro, Nova Scotia*

Melinda: Your mystery plant is commonly called Maltese cross and goes by the scientific name *Lychnis chalcedonica*.

This perennial is relatively easy to grow in full sun and most soils. Avoid wet or poorly drained areas, since these conditions tend to shorten its lifespan.

Over the years, you should see more and more of this perennial. It readily self seeds, resulting in plenty of seedlings to grow and share. Avoid cultivating the soil early in the season, which tends to "weed out" such seedlings.

Letting nature do the work is the easiest way to propagate this plant. You also can dig and divide your existing plant in early spring or late summer to expand your planting.

Spring Pruning

What's the correct way to trim my forsythia?
—*Wendy Cloutier, Dover, New Hampshire*

Melinda: Forsythias are very tolerant of pruning. You can prune these and other spring-flowering shrubs right after they bloom. That way, you get to enjoy the flowers and still control the plant's size.

For the best results, remove one-third of your forsythia's older stems (they're the thickest) to ground level every year. If you'd like, reduce the height of the remaining stems by one-third as well.

Do this for 3 years, and you'll have a smaller and better-looking plant. Then remove a few older canes each year. This will keep new growth coming from the base and maintain the size you want.

BIRD GARDEN BASICS

W ant to know a secret? It's not hard to bring birds and butterflies to your backyard blooms. Really. You just have to know what to grow.

We've chosen a mix of flowers, trees and shrubs that will work for different climates, color schemes and garden layouts. Pick your favorites, pick a spot—and get planting!

BIRDS:

Seed

Attract seed-eating birds like chickadees, northern cardinals and American goldfinches by planting seed-bearing perennials and annuals. Some top choices:
Purple coneflower (Zones 3 to 9)
Liatris (Zones 3 to 9)
Black-eyed Susan (Zones 4 to 9)
Sunflower (Annual)

Berries

For our feathered friends who prefer to dine on berries (American robins, cedar waxwings, catbirds and more), try planting trees and shrubs like:
Juneberry (Zones 3 to 9)
Sea Green juniper (Zones 3 to 9)
Gray dogwood (Zones 4 to 8)
Mulberry (Zones 4 to 9)

Shelter

All birds seek spots to nest and hide from predators. Ornamental grasses—which come in all sizes, shapes and colors—serve as great shelter. Also try trees and shrubs like:
Spruce (Zones 2 to 9)
Pine (Zones 2 to 11)
Fir (Zones 3 to 9)
Hemlock (Zones 3 to 9)

BUTTERFLIES and HUMMINGBIRDS:

Color

Hummingbirds are drawn to brightly colored, trumpet-shaped flowers, such as:
Serbian bellflower (Zones 3 to 8)
Trumpet vine (Zones 4 to 9)
Fuchsia (Zones 9 to 11)

Host plants

Try this trick: offer host plants to feed the caterpillars that will eventually become the butterflies you desire. Here are a few:
Willow (Zones 2 to 9)
Elm (Zones 2 to 9)
Dill (Annual)
Parsley (Annual)

Nectar

The best bet to bring in all types of butterflies and hummingbirds is to fill your backyard with nectar-packed plants. Try shrubs, perennials and annuals, such as:
Delphinium (Zones 3 to 7)
Aster (Zones 3 to 9)
Bee balm (Zones 3 to 10)
Weigela (Zones 4 to 9)
Butterfly bush (Zones 5 to 9)
Salvia (Annual)
Snapdragon (Annual)

BEST ALL-AROUND BLOOM:

Honeysuckle vine (Zones 4 to 9). The nectar of this pretty plant attracts hummingbirds and butterflies, birds relish its summer fruits, and its leaves grow into a tangle of foliage that's suitable for nesting.

GETTING INTO THE ZONES

By Melinda Myers
Contributing Editor

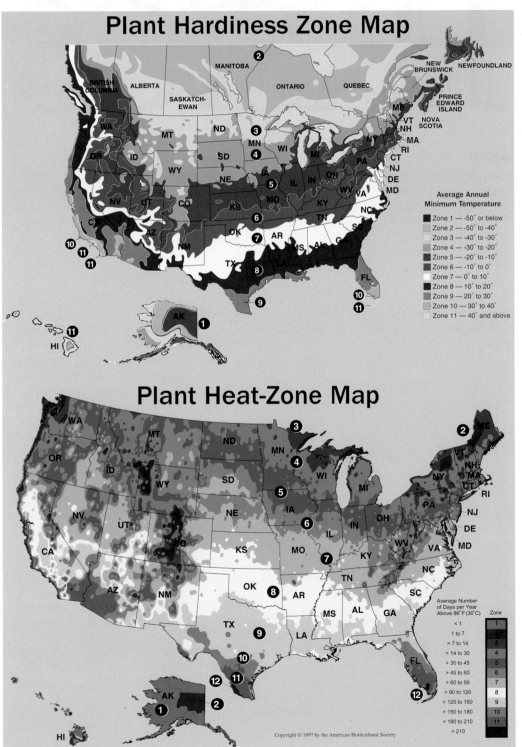

Plant Hardiness Zone Map

Average Annual Minimum Temperature

- Zone 1 — -50° or below
- Zone 2 — -50° to -40°
- Zone 3 — -40° to -30°
- Zone 4 — -30° to -20°
- Zone 5 — -20° to -10°
- Zone 6 — -10° to 0°
- Zone 7 — 0° to 10°
- Zone 8 — 10° to 20°
- Zone 9 — 20° to 30°
- Zone 10 — 30° to 40°
- Zone 11 — 40° and above

Plant Heat-Zone Map

Average Number of Days per Year Above 86°F (30°C) — Zone

Days	Zone
< 1	1
1 to 7	2
> 7 to 14	3
> 14 to 30	4
> 30 to 45	5
> 45 to 60	6
> 60 to 90	7
> 90 to 120	8
> 120 to 150	9
> 150 to 180	10
> 180 to 210	11
> 210	

Copyright © 1997 by the American Horticultural Society

Since my garden is in Wisconsin, I always look at a plant's hardiness to cold first. Likewise, my Southern gardening friends are particularly concerned with heat hardiness. Fortunately, there's help for all of us—heat and cold hardiness maps to help with making plant selections.

Cold hardiness ratings are based on the average minimum winter temperature in an area. The USDA Cold Hardiness Map is the most commonly accepted.

The American Horticultural Society more recently developed the Plant Heat-Zone Map. This rating reflects the duration and extremes of heat in each region. It's based on the average number of 86° or hotter days per year from 1974 to 1995. The 86° mark is where heat starts damaging plants.

On both maps, you'll notice small islands of warmer or colder areas surrounded by other zones. This is typically where elevation differences, bodies of water or urban areas create different growing conditions in a particular zone.

Your own landscape may have such islands, too. Fencing, stonework, construction materials and existing plants may block cold winds, reflect heat, cast cooling shade or create sheltered beds. These areas can be one whole growing zone warmer than the rest of your yard! Luckily for you, these microclimates can stretch your planting palette beyond what's recommended for your area.

To get a better idea of the microclimates in your backyard, conduct a hardiness rating of your own. Just monitor temperatures in different areas and record your planting successes and failures. Soon you'll have a personalized hardiness map customized to your yard.

BIRD TALES

Amazing bird encounters from the past year.

What a Hoot

MY HUSBAND, Chris, and I noticed a pair of osprey trying as best they could to build a nest on a utility pole (above right). For 3 days, we watched them unsuccessfully attempt to intertwine branches, only to have them fall into the river below.

Finally, they moved to a better location. They found a utility pole with double supports at the top, giving more stability for their nest of branches. Even the plastic owl that the power company installed on the same pole didn't discourage their nesting.

Employees from the local power company, N.B. Power, removed the nest twice before finally giving in. To help appease the osprey and keep them away from the live wires, they installed a second pole with the same supports adjacent to the one the birds selected.

Mr. and Mrs. Osprey gladly accepted the new pole and built a beautiful nest. Often, while one bird was sitting on the nest, its mate perched on the plastic owl's head. So much for intimidating owls!

—*Martine Cochrane*
Dalhousie, New Brunswick

Using Its Head

ONE NIGHT, about 1-1/2 inches of snow had fallen, covering the bird feeder on our porch banister.

The next morning, my daughter stopped by to visit before work, and she called me over to the window.

A blue jay was sitting on the banister about a foot from the bird feeder, sweeping its head rapidly from side to side, clearing off the snow with its bill.

When the jay had removed all the snow, it calmly walked to the feeder and started eating seeds. —*Irene Houck*
Branson, Missouri

Cure for Cold Feet

FOR ANYONE who doubts birds are intelligent, I have proof that they are!

"Lonesome George," the mourning dove that frequents our backyard, discovered a unique way to stay warm in winter.

I have a heater in my birdbath, and George realized the tube that holds the heater over the bath's edge is quite warm.

So every winter morning, George perches there to heat his cold feet. Seems pretty smart to me! —*Helen Willbond*
Oberlin, Ohio

Decorating Drama

WHEN WE LIVED in Vermont, we watched a household drama unfold at our bluebird nest box.

The female eastern bluebird was inside arranging the "furniture," while her mate was busy gathering nesting materials.

When the male arrived with grasses, he'd poke it through the hole and leave for more. As soon as he was gone, the female would appear at the opening and toss the grass out!

My husband concluded that it's not only humans who have trouble pleasing their mates when it comes to home decorating projects! —*Cicely Perrotte, Catskill, New York*

Tough Love

ONE AFTERNOON, I watched a mother American robin feeding her baby on the stone wall in our backyard. When the mother left to look for food, the young bird remained on the wall and looked around as if enjoying the view. Each time its mother returned, the young bird immediately acknowledged her and devoured the food she offered.

Then on one return trip with food, the adult robin landed on the wall behind the juvenile. The young bird apparently didn't hear her arrival, because it kept gazing in the opposite direction.

This lack of alertness seemed to upset the parent, who walked up behind the baby, grabbed its tail in her bill and gave it a good yank. I could just imagine her scolding, "Pay attention! I could've been a cat, you know."

I guess human parents aren't the only ones who sometimes use "tough love." —*Nancy Bruck*
Mt. Pleasant, Pennsylvania

Nice Assist!

DURING RECESS, one of my students dashed back inside and urged me to come to the playground…fast. A bird was trapped in the pipe that supports the basketball hoop. Apparently, it tried to perch on the edge of the pipe and toppled in.

When I put my ear to the pipe, I heard a frantic flapping and chirping—and something else. There was standing water in the pipe.

What could we do? We couldn't uproot the backboard; it was anchored in cement. But eventually, the bird would tire and drown.

I ran inside, found a ball of yarn and made several loops in one end. A boy shinnied up the pole and dropped the loop into the opening. I struck the side of the pipe to get the bird's attention. When we could hear the bird flapping its wings, the boy started pulling the yarn up.

A second later, the bird emerged with the loops of yarn. The boy gently untangled it, and the bird streaked into the woods.

It was an exciting rescue, but we plan to cap the pole so we don't have to go "fishing" again.   —*Shed Douglas Jr.*
Barnwell, South Carolina

Not-so-Clean Sweep

IT WAS LATE SPRING, and my husband was cleaning the pipes of our antique stove while I prepared a lunch of sandwiches and a pitcher of black tea. That's when my 4-year-old son, Nathan, burst into the room, yelling, "Mom, there's a bird in the house!"

I looked up, and, sure enough, a chimney swift was circling our kitchen.

I told Nathan to open the door to the room where my husband was so the bird could find an exit. But the bird had already located the perfect round hole for its getaway. It flew to the ceiling, gathered its wings to its body and plunged headlong into the pitcher of tea!

We were all surprised—the bird was, too, I imagine. We carefully pulled the bird out of the pitcher, ran warm water over it and set it free. Shortly afterward, we saw the swift in our birdbath. It must have needed more than a quick rinse to get that tea out of its feathers!

—*Joanie Young, Joelton, Tennessee*

Poolside Home

WE LIVE a block away from a park with a lake, so we weren't surprised to see a duck behind a fan palm tree in our backyard. She came and went every day and finally built a nest, which she gently covered with foliage whenever she left.

When she started incubating, we prepared for the new arrivals by setting up a kiddie pool, building steps up to it and buying duck feed.

The mom hatched nine healthy babies, eight multicolored and one yellow. We changed the water in the pool daily and watched the babies follow their mom around the yard.

After meals, the mother would gather the ducklings on the stepping-stones and take them for a swim. Then she'd fly over to the park. A drake followed her back a couple times, but she always ran him off.

When the ducklings feathered out, they made their way to the park. They eventually flew away, but we hope the mom will return to our yard to nest again someday.

—*Kathy McEntire, Mesa, Arizona*

Angel in Disguise

DO WE REALLY know what angels look like? After my experience with a unique bird, I began to wonder if we had our own angel quietly watching over our house.

Since I live in the city, I was surprised to find a helmeted guineafowl in my backyard one fall evening. The next morning,

I started offering it birdseed, and 2 weeks later, it was still here.

My son suggested we name the bird "Macy," and it is now a permanent fixture in our neighborhood. It ventures all around the block, but mostly stays near my house. And it certainly finds some interesting perches, as you can see (above left).

Maybe this is our angel…in an interesting disguise.
—*Mary Grimes, Asheville, North Carolina*

Pelican Campout

MY SISTER lives along a river near Manteca, California. One morning when she let her dogs out, they acted strange, running in different directions and barking.

Soon she knew why as she heard a large group of pelicans approaching. She looked up and saw a flock so enormous that it actually blocked out the sun.

The American white pelican flock (that's it below) stayed in the area for about 2 weeks, providing many opportunities

for some interesting pelican watching.

The pelicans' feeding habits were fascinating. The flock would gather together, then split into quarters and move out. Then they'd swim back toward each other, apparently pushing fish in front of them. When the gap was closed, all would dive underwater in unison and catch their meals.

After the pelicans moved on to another part of the river, my sister was left with many memories of these lovely creatures.
—*Marge Feldman, Highland, California*

Second Helpings

ONE SUMMER, hummingbirds nested in a fir tree in our yard. As I was sitting at our nearby picnic table, I noticed the young birds had recently left the nest.

One of them was sitting close to me in a shrub. Every half hour, its mother came to feed it. The fledgling always acted like it was starving, but as soon as the female hummingbird flew away, the young bird made a beeline to a nearby flower bed to feed. Then it returned to the shrub before the mother arrived.

No wonder that hummer was such a fat little one. It had fooled its mother into doling out rations…and it was feeding itself, too!　　—*Maren Griessel, Orting, Washington*

Winging It

WE WERE on the St. Johns River near our home when we spotted this great blue heron walking across a log. We shut off our pontoon boat and started taking pictures of it, admiring its grace and beauty.

To our surprise, the heron looked right at us and turned its wings inside out, as if to say, "How's this for a picture?" (See photo above.)

We've seen lots of birds in our trips up and down the river, but we've never seen one display itself like this. We think it may have been sunning the underside of its wings.

We stayed and watched this unusual fellow for 20 minutes. It was still posing like this when we left.
—*Carol Frendo, DeBary, Florida*

Wake-Up Call

IT WAS a pleasant summer night, so we left our screened windows open. At 3 a.m., I heard our cuckoo clock chime three times. After a pause, we heard three more "cuckoos"— but these seemed to be coming from outside.

The next night, when our clock cuckooed at 4 a.m., four answering "cuckoos" drifted in from the direction of the choke cherry tree, where a northern mockingbird had its home.

I called the Cornell Lab of Ornithology in Ithaca, New York to ask about this behavior. Experts there said it's not unusual for mockingbirds to sing at an early hour. They're capable of mimicking a cuckoo clock—as well as many other noises—loud enough to rouse people from a sound sleep.
—*Anne Fauvell, Rapid City, South Dakota*

Hitching a Ride

I'D OFTEN seen a greater roadrunner around our house and sometimes in our carport, but I never dreamed it was looking for a private chauffeur!

That's just what happened when I took my husband, John, to a medical appointment 55 miles away—with the roadrunner as a stowaway. I didn't discover it until I took John into the building, then returned to the car to retrieve some of his things. And there was the roadrunner, sitting on my dashboard!

The bird must've hopped in the car when I was loading it. But now what?

I rolled down the front window, and the roadrunner flew out and landed on the car next to ours. I rolled the window back up, assuming the bird would fly away. It didn't. I rolled my car window down again, and back in it flew. So I left the window open and went back inside.

When we were ready to go home, the roadrunner was waiting for us. It jumped onto the rear headrest, ruffled its feathers and sat quietly for the entire trip. It even appeared to be looking out the window at the passing sights.

At home, I opened the car door and the roadrunner quickly hopped out and walked off. Later that evening, we saw it with a small lizard in its mouth. I guess it was pleased to be home.　　　　　—*Marjorie Farr, Seymour, Texas*

Picture-Perfect

I'VE ALWAYS had an appreciation for woodpeckers. To me, the morning call of the pileated species or a woodpecker drumming on a tree are some of the most beautiful sounds found in nature.

During my 20-year career in the United States Air Force, I certainly missed those sounds. After my retirement, I took up photography as a hobby and vowed to capture a picture of a woodpecker. Every time I heard that familiar drum, I rushed outside with my camera, but the woodpeckers were always just out of reach of my camera lens.

After years without a picture, I decided to try packing suet in the weathered cracks of an old light pole where I often spotted the birds. I hoped it would entice them to come down within camera range.

Two days later, a pair of downy woodpeckers visited the suet, and I finally got my close-up (above, a female). And it only took me 11 years!
—*Terry F. Sweatman*
Colorado Springs, Colorado

Answering a Call

MY DOG and I walk in the woods behind our home every morning. In her enthusiasm, "Pearl" usually gets ahead of me, and I have to call out to her, "Wait for me." One morning, to my surprise, my call was returned—"Wait for me." I couldn't tell where the sound was coming from.

I thought someone entered the woods behind me, but I didn't see anyone. Again I called out to Pearl, and again I heard the echo. This time I could tell it was coming from the tree above me.

When I looked up, I saw a gray catbird watching us. What an amazing mimic!

For the rest of the summer, that catbird practiced the new phrase daily. Now, each year I listen for the catbirds, hoping to hear the one that knows our special call.

—*Dolores Kneeland, Thompson, Connecticut*

True-Blue Pet

WE LOVE having Asian peafowl as pets. They get along well with our cats and laying hens, eat harmful pests like grasshoppers and earwigs, and keep the herons and Canada geese away from our water garden. Our peacock "Flash" has even chased a fox out of our yard.

Last summer, though, Flash started exhibiting some strange behavior. On the day of trash and recycling collection, he would patrol the neighborhood, displaying his tail to the mail carrier, the garbage collectors and any other passersby.

I finally figured out what he was up to when I saw him walk up the road to display his tail at my neighbor's blue recycling boxes (above). He thought those big blue bins were a threat, and he was out to prove he was more blue and beautiful than they were! —*Sharon Bognar, Uxbridge, Ontario*

After-School Special

WHEN MY SON Brandon started kindergarten, he was afraid of taking the bus home from school. As I waited for him that afternoon at the end of our driveway, I noticed a beautiful white dove nearby. I gave it some seed, and it stayed until Brandon arrived.

The bird returned every day for the next week and gave Brandon something to look forward to after his bus ride. Then one day, it was gone. When Brandon got off the bus, he happily announced, "I'm not afraid to take the bus anymore!" Later on, he realized the dove was gone, but he didn't seem to mind.

We decided it must have flown to the driveway of another boy or girl who was afraid of taking the bus. We were confident it would stay with them until they weren't frightened anymore, either. —*Liz Fesczenko, New Braunfels, Texas*

Dog's Best Friend

ONE SUMMER, a fledgling American robin adopted our family and took a special liking to our dog, which happily returned the affection.

The bird followed us around the backyard and would even perch on our hands and shoulders. But its favorite companion was our pooch (see photo at right). It would jump on him and ride along wherever he went!

We called our feathered friend "Robbie" and enjoyed the laughs and attention the little bird gave us that summer. Who knew a dog's best friend was really a bird?

—*Donna Jaeger, Battle Creek, Michigan*

Unlikely Abode

WE'D SEEN eastern bluebirds in our area, but rarely near our house. My husband did some research and learned bluebirds like houses of a particular shape, with a specific size opening, about 4 feet off the ground and in a clearing.

But that sounded too technical for me. I just wanted a birdhouse I could easily see. I convinced my husband to hang a plain old birdhouse on a tree near the house, about 9 feet off the ground.

He thought I was crazy. Bluebirds are very particular, he said, and I was ignoring all he'd learned.

But I had the last laugh. A pair of bluebirds moved in a few days later. We watched from our gazebo as the female built a nest and incubated eggs, then the pair raised four hungry chicks!

We were grateful these bluebirds moved into the house we provided…even though it was the wrong type, in the wrong location and mounted at the wrong height! —*Glenda Walsh, Imperial, Missouri*

Who's the Boss?

ONE NIGHT after dinner, I tossed some leftover rolls outside for my backyard friends. After I went back into the house, I glanced out the window and saw a squirrel holding a dinner roll in its front paws and eating it.

While I watched it munch away, an American crow landed nearby and tried to grab the roll. The squirrel ran a short distance and then settled in again to enjoy the roll. The crow approached the squirrel a second time and tried to grab the roll, but the squirrel scurried away.

The crow slowly walked toward the furry critter, circling it and eyeing the roll. Then the crow leaped in and yanked the squirrel's bushy tail. The squirrel jumped, but didn't drop its precious roll.

This bullying went on for at least 10 more minutes, but neither one of them would give in. Unfortunately, I had to leave, so I don't know who ended up with that roll. However, I'd like to think the squirrel got to keep its meal.

—*Sharon DeBruin, Gowrie, Iowa*

Riverside Perch

DURING A TRIP to Minnesota for a soccer tournament, our whole family decided to take a break between games. On our way through town, my dad, Richard Hendrikson, wanted to stop to admire the Mississippi River.

As he looked out over the water, a northern rough-winged swallow scooted in from the river and landed right on my dad's head (right).

It sat there for a few quiet moments and then took flight again. Luckily, I had my camera ready. This is now one of my favorite pictures of my dad.

—*Audrey Szymanski*
Merrill, Wisconsin

Gobbler Had to Go

ONE JULY, I was fishing in our pasture pond when I heard a soft "keck, keck" sound behind me. When I turned, I met the stare of a male wild turkey about 20 yards away. I'd never been able to get anywhere near one of these birds before!

We watched each other for a moment, then I threw him some of my catfish food pellets. Within 30 minutes, he was circling me and eating every pellet.

When I left to check on the birdhouses on my bluebird trail, the turkey followed me through the pasture and back home. He walked up the driveway with me and flew into the woods behind our house.

He was waiting on the porch the next morning, so I fed

him—much to my wife's dismay. Within days, the turkey had taken over the porch and deck, and circled me whenever I sat on the patio.

It was a happy relationship...until I tried to stroke his back. He pecked me and fanned out his tail (see photo above). Plus, we discovered that he'd ventured into our garage and scratched up the roof of my wife's car. I definitely was in the "doghouse."

So, I released the turkey in the woods about 10 miles away. I learned that being adopted by a wild turkey isn't easy. I'm still trying to live it down! —*Robert Walshaw*
Field Editor, Coweta, Oklahoma

Fly-in Dining

EACH MORNING, a blue jay wakes us up with a *b-r-r-r* sound and shrill, high-pitched call as it perches just outside our bedroom window. We love listening to the wake-up serenade, and usually put peanuts out for our visitor.

One morning we forgot the peanuts and left our window open. When the jay arrived, it must have spotted the box of peanuts on the windowsill inside, so it boldly flew in to help itself.

The jay picked at the nuts for a few seconds, chose one and flew back outside to enjoy breakfast! —*Gilda Smith*
Pompano Beach, Florida

Hey, Good-Lookin'!

A BROWN-HEADED cowbird came to the feeding station on our deck every morning. One day it sat down on the back of a lawn chair and looked into the nearby window. Immediately, the bird seemed transfixed by what it saw there—a shiny black bird with a chocolate-brown hood.

The cowbird turned its head from side to side. So did the other bird. It flapped its wings up and down. So did the other bird. For the rest of the day, the cowbird remained on the chair, admiring its new "friend."

Early the next morning, the cowbird returned to the same chair, watching its twin. It came day after day, week after week, all summer long. The cowbird became such a regular that when visitors stopped by, their first question was, "Is the bird back?"

The cowbird returned the following season, but we didn't see it the next year, and summer just wasn't the same without it. After all, who could resist a bird that finds happiness admiring its own reflection? —*Klara Cook*
Huntington, West Virginia

Gallant Gull

DURING HER WALKS on the beach, my mother spotted a

ring-billed gull with an amputated leg (left). She tried to feed it, but the other gulls chased it away. The gull just retreated silently. Mom began calling it "Renard the Brave."

In time, Mom and Renard became friends. Each summer, she worried whether he'd survived the winter. He always showed up in August, and Mom fed him until the other birds chased him off.

Eventually, Mom fed Renard by throwing food into the water. Renard caught it on the fly, coming within a couple feet of her. The other gulls squawked overhead, but kept their distance.

The next summer, Mom feared she'd finally seen the last of Renard. The local sardine factory had closed, taking much of the gull population with it. But Renard showed up in August, as always...and when she approached him with a piece of bread, he ate it from her outstretched hand.

—*Jane Woodruff, Pittsfield, Maine*

Winged "Intruder"

EVERY MORNING for several years, a male eastern towhee has perched at the transom window over our front door and tapped on the glass. Since we could not stop him, we just got used to the added noise.

Then one day when we were out, the tapping set off the motion sensor on our security system, triggering an alarm—and a police response!

We told the police we already knew the perpetrator's identity and supplied them with a "mug shot" of the towhee. Oddly enough, the camera flash seemed to put a stop to his tapping. He hasn't rapped on the window since!

—*Ramona Parris, Marietta, Georgia*

Winter Blues

I'VE BEEN TRYING to attract bluebirds to my backyard, but we live in a subdivision, so it's almost impossible, since these birds prefer wide-open spaces.

Then one winter day, I was surprised to see a whole flock of beautiful eastern bluebirds outside my window at work. They seemed to be enjoying the berries left on a crabapple tree (below).

My best friend said I should take some photos because

everyone would think I was seeing blue jays—not bluebirds—in northern Indiana in winter.

I waited almost a week before I was rewarded by another visit, and I was ready with my camera.

After capturing photo proof, no one can doubt my story. —*Mimi Swartout*
Elkhart, Indiana

Bird Camp

AFTER retirement, my husband and I bought a 30-foot trailer to take camping. We frequent a campground in Indiana from April through October, but we don't let our traveling hobby interfere with our love of birds.

Behind our trailer, we create a large area for seven feeders, including a sugar-water feeder for hummingbirds and a tube feeder for finches. After we add a birdbath, we sit back and wait for our winged visitors. We spotted more than 19 different birds at our campsite buffet last year, as well as chipmunks, squirrels, raccoons and a pair of wood ducks.

We enjoy this addition to the campground and have inspired many other campers to do the same. —*Carol Lee*
Kalamazoo, Michigan

Sound of Trouble

"PECK, PECK, PECK!" This was the sound of our early morning greeting, thanks to a resident woodpecker. Only this bird didn't peck at a tree; he pecked everything else—gutters, roofing, windows, siding, garbage cans. Nothing was safe.

We love birds and try to make a safe environment for them, but the pecking was driving us crazy—not to mention all the dents it created. The neighbors thought it was funny, but the woodpecker wasn't visiting them.

I called a forest ranger and told him our problem: A woodpecker that wouldn't peck wood. After he stopped laughing, he suggested hanging a metal pie plate in a tree. Unfortunately, the woodpecker loved it and made more noise than ever.

Then one day, we noticed the woodpecker flew away whenever the ice cream truck came by. Music was the answer! We hung wind chimes in a tree near the house, and the woodpecker promptly flew off to bestow his charms elsewhere— perhaps at the neighbor's house. —*M.J. King*
Corinth, New York

Relentless Robin

UPON RETURNING from Florida in mid-April, I found a nest over the light outside my back door. I knew birds would be unhappy with the amount of activity there, so I took the nest down.

The next time I went out, I found more nesting material placed on the light. I removed it.

When I went out again, I found a seemingly disgusted male American robin glaring at me. In my attempt to communicate, I pointed out the more appropriate nesting platforms under the eaves of the nearby workshop.

The robin took off, and I saw no more of him until 2 days later, when I found they'd built a nest over the light next to my front door! It already had a blue egg in it, so I didn't take it down.

The robins eventually hatched three babies…and I used other entrances to avoid disturbing them.

—*Ernestine Sproul, Windsor, Maine*

Babies' Day Out

ONE JULY day, we drove with my mother in her vehicle from her home in Suffolk, Virginia to Nags Head, North Carolina to pack up her belongings from her cottage.

We stopped for lunch, and my wife, Yvonne, heard a noise that sounded like a bird under the hood. When I looked, sure enough, there was a nest in the grille with three baby wrens, mouths wide open!

There was nothing we could do about the babies at that point, so I checked them before we headed back to Suffolk. Unfortunately, we ran into a terrible thunderstorm on the way. We had to pull over until it passed. I feared the babies had been washed away.

All told, we were gone for 10 hours. When I pulled back into my mom's carport, the mother wren was there, waiting for her babies. I checked the nest, and all the little wrens were alive and well.

The mother spent the rest of the night feeding a "welcome home" meal to her hungry brood. —*Charles Darden*
Chesapeake, Virginia

Room at the Inn

WHEN MY HUSBAND, Paul, and I visited Los Cabos, Mex-

ico, we noticed this beautiful hummingbird nesting at the hotel entrance (at left). The plant was in a busy hallway, but she didn't seem to mind. The tiny bird sat quietly in the nest, observing everything around her.

The staff put up a sign asking people not to disturb the mother bird, which they had named "Melia."

What a joy to finally see a hummer's nest. It was a highlight of our trip! —*Alice Ensogna, Winchester, Virginia*

INDEX

host plants for, 113
Comma, eastern, host plants for, 113
Compost, 202
Coneflower, purple, 244
Containers, 235-236
Coreopsis, 239
Cowbird, 250
Crescent, pearl, host plants for, 113
Cuttings, starting plants from, 51, 208
Crabapple, 240
Cranes, whooping, 30-33
Creeper, Virginia, 149
Crow, American, 249

D

Dahlia, 152-154
Daylily, 142-143
Deadheading, 176
Deer, deterring, 183-184
Delphinium, 244
Dill, 244
Dogwood, 207-208
    flowering, 212-213
    gray, 244
    red twig, 226-228
    yellow twig, 227-228
Dove, 177, 246, 249
    food for, 88, 225
Drought-tolerant plants, 129, 136, 207, 236-240, 243
Duck, nesting of, 247

E

Eagle, bald, 14-15
    attracting, 15
    food for, 15
Elderberry, 224-225
Elm, 244

F

Fan flower, 239
Feathers, color changes in, 241
Fecal sac, 90
Fertilizer, 221, 236, 238
Finch, food for, 69, 88
Fir, 244
Flicker, northern, food for, 225
Forsythia, 243
Fragrance, plants for, 125, 132-133, 138, 140, 146, 150, 157, 228,

239
Fritillaries, 108
    host plants for, 112-113
Fuchsia, 244

G

Garden profiles
    California, 194-196
    Colorado, 183-185
    Indiana, 197-199
    Kansas, 74-75
    Michigan, 180-182
    Minnesota, 42-44
    Missouri, 46-47, 203-205
    Nebraska, 61
    New York, 130-131
    North Carolina, 66-68
    Pennsylvania, 45, 58-60
    Saskatchewan, 48-50
    Tennessee, 52-53
    Texas, 54-56, 142-143
    Virginia, 186-188
Gardening
    basic guidelines for, 200-202
    in poor soil, 180-184, 195
    in small spaces, 57
    on slopes, 203-205
Gardens
    container, 234-236
    easy-care, 57
    high-altitude, 183-185
    hummingbird, 174-176
    new, 53
    preparing for winter, 202
Geranium, overwintering, 191
Gilia, globe, 243
"Glad You Asked!", 90-93, 108-109, 177, 206-209, 240-243
Goldenrod, 155-157
Goldfinch, food for
    American, 91-93, 241, 244
    European, 92
    lesser, 93
Goshawk, northern, 241
Gourds, 73, 76, 79-83
Grackle, 88
    common, food for, 225
Grass-free landscapes, 42-44
Grosbeak
    food for, 71, 88, 225
    pine, 90
    rose-breasted, 71, 92, 225

Grouse, ruffed, food for, 225
Guineafowl, 249
Gull, ring-billed, 250

H

Hairstreak, banded, 118-119
    host plants for, 119
Hardiness zones, 245
Harrison, George
    American robin, 8-10
    attracting hummingbirds, 164-165
    bird feeding, 87-89
    black-capped chickadee, 36-39
    blue jay, 24-26
    bluebird, 18-21
    bully birds, 69
    "Glad You Asked!", 90-93, 177, 240-243
    northern saw-whet owl, 34-35
    pileated woodpecker, 11-13
    whip-poor-will, 22-23
    yellow warbler, 27-29
Hawk, red-tailed, 93
Heat zones, 245
Heliotrope, 132-133
Hemlock, 244
Herbicide, applying, 207
Heron, great blue, 248
Holly, Meserve, 227-228
Honeysuckle, 208, 244
Horsechestnut, 214-215
Host plants, butterfly, 109
    American lady, 109
    Aphrodite fritillary, 113
    Atlantis fritillary, 113
    banded hairstreak, 119
    black swallowtail, 112-113
    Callipe fritillary, 113
    clouded sulphur, 110
    common buckeye, 112-113
    eastern comma, 113
    great spangled fritillary, 113
    gulf fritillary, 112-113
    monarch, 102-103, 113
    Mormon fritillary, 113
    mourning cloak, 113
    painted lady, 121
    pearl crescent, 113
    pipevine swallowtail, 106
    queen, 116
    red admiral, 113
    red-spotted purple, 97, 113